THE JEWS OF PLYMOUTH

AN ILLUSTRATED HISTORY

HELEN FRY

HALSGROVE

First published in Great Britain in 2015

Copyright © 2014 Helen Fry

All rights reserved. No part of this publication may be reproduced, stored in a retrieval system, or transmitted in any form or by any means without the prior permission of the copyright holder.

British Library Cataloguing-in-Publication Data
A CIP record for this title is available from the British Library

ISBN 978 0 85704 253 8

HALSGROVE
Halsgrove House, Ryelands Business Park,
Bagley Road, Wellington, Somerset TA21 9PZ
Tel: 01823 653777   Fax: 01823 216796
email: sales@halsgrove.com

Part of the Halsgrove group of companies
Information on all Halsgrove titles is available at: www.halsgrove.com

Printed in China by Everbest Printing Co Ltd

CONTENTS

	Acknowledgements	5
	Introduction	7
Chapter 1	Foundation of the Community: 1720s–1800	9
Chapter 2	The Synagogue	19
Chapter 3	Dock Minyan & Devonport Hebrew Congregation	35
Chapter 4	Rabbis, Ministers and Cantors	42
Chapter 5	The Burial Grounds	52
Chapter 6	The Community: 1800–1880	58
Chapter 7	Twentieth Century	71
Chapter 8	Two World Wars	85
Chapter 9	Post-War Community to Present day	100
Appendix 1	List of Rabbis and Ministers	114
Appendix 2	Officers of the Synagogue	115
Appendix 3	Roll of Honour for WW1 and WW2	118
Appendix 4	Plymouth Jewish Marriages	120
Appendix 5	List of burials in the two Jewish cemeteries	131
Appendix 6	List of Ceremonial Silver Sold in 2009	153
	Bibliography	157
	Index	159

The publication of this book has been made possible by the generous sponsorship of:

Hilda Marks with fond memories of her childhood and life in Plymouth and dedicating this book to her family's contribution to the Plymouth community.

The Goldberg family in memory of Arthur Goldberg, the first Jewish Lord Mayor of Plymouth.

The Black family in memory of Israel Bertie Black whose devotion to the Plymouth Hebrew Congregation was a central part of his life

ACKNOWLEDGEMENTS

THIS BOOK IS the first fully illustrated history of the Jews of Plymouth, building on the work of historians before me. One of those historians is Doris Black who was the first person to work on the history of the Plymouth synagogue and Jewish community. Her early research and work culminated in the publication of *The Plymouth Synagogue 1761-1961*, which provided me with an invaluable foundation from which to write this one. In recent years, I have very much enjoyed, too, the trips down memory lane and my discussions with Doris of those Plymouth days. Doris, who has had a long interest and great knowledge of the history of Anglo-Jewry, has a love for the Plymouth community which continues to this day.

At the start, I naively thought that I could cover all the families and their genealogies. The history of Plymouth Jews over 250 years is a huge one, and therefore it has not been possible to mention every family or member in this long history. The author wishes to cause no disappointment to those families not included, but hopes that the book will provide an interesting backdrop to their own family's experiences in Plymouth. Neither have I covered much about the recent history of the Plymouth Hebrew Congregation – that it is the prerogative of future historians. It is important to be mindful that the Jews of Plymouth did not live in isolation from their non-Jewish neighbours. They were not ghettoized, as in other parts of Europe, but lived an incredibly well-integrated life, and one that saw an incredibly close partnership with the civic side of the city. They were able to contribute hugely to the city's commerce, as well as political and cultural life. Theirs is important because of the Naval connections and their extraordinary contribution to local politics which appears to be unparalleled in other provincial Jewish communities of this period.

It is an honour to write this book because my own family on my paternal side lived in Plymouth for several generations. The ancestors of my paternal grandmother, Phyllis Doney (née Ellis) played a crucial part in civic life alongside the Jews of the city. Her maternal grandfather, Woon Lucas, was a property developer who built up much of the Lanhydrock Road area and served on the Town Council and various committees. He was a member of the Borough Committee for Parks and Cemeteries on the Hoe and that included oversight of the old Jewish cemetery on the Hoe. I grew up not realizing other links with the Jewish community on my paternal grandfather's side. In the 1910s one particular relative, J.H. Doney, was caretaker of the new Jewish cemetery in Gifford Place.

A large network of people have generously helped with material for the book. I wish to sincerely thank members of Plymouth Hebrew Congregation and its committee for their support, especially to Dr Peter Lee, John Hirshman, John Mitchell, Pat Goodman, Anna Kelley and Brian Aloof. The congregation generously provided a grant for my travel in connection with the research. Thanks to BBC radio broadcaster, Judi Spiers, who has supported my books over the years, but this particular history which touches on her own. Huge thanks to Simon Butler and his professional team at Halsgrove for publishing this history, and for supporting the recording of such provincial history.

My heartfelt thanks to Jerry Sibley, caretaker of the synagogue, who has spent so much time helping with information, giving up time to show myself and my son Jonathan around the synagogue and two cemeteries, and always ready to answer questions by email and telephone. Thanks also to the following people with Plymouth Jewish connections for help with their own personal histories: Doris Black and family, Dr Anthony Joseph, Eric Smith, Mrs Hilda Marks, Rochelle Selby, Harvey Harrison, Anne Muir, Baba Clarfelt, Estelle Levy, Maxanne Ezer, Brian Aloof, Marcus Aloof, Valerie Mellor, Sylvia [Biddy] Goldberg, David Goldberg QC, David Lang, Gareth Abel, Lisa Rosen, Eve Richardson, Rachel Miller, Betty Mottram, Giles Croft and Joy Gerzi.

For biographical details about Plymouth's ministers, my thanks to Stuart Goodman and Dr Rob Ginsburg of London, and Roy Susman of Israel for information on their respective fathers, and to Dr Michael Jolles of London for information on Emanuel Goodman. Also to Ron Arons in America for providing material on Revd Abraham Spier, his great-great grandfather.

Thanks also to John Gould for material on Revd. Michael Solomon Alexander. For Cornish genealogical information and links to Plymouth, huge thanks to Keith Pearce of Penzance for providing material from his substantial research with Godfrey Simmons from his recent book, *The Jews of Cornwall*.

I wish to pay tribute to the late Rabbi Dr Bernard Susser whose research on the Plymouth community, of which he was twice its rabbi, was the basis of his Ph.D thesis and book, *The Jews of South-West England*. I knew Rabbi Susser very well and, after I moved to London, he would often meet up to discuss his new research discoveries. Tribute must also be paid to local historian, the late Bert Emdon of Plymouth. My thanks to Rabbi David Katanka for translating Hebrew inscriptions in documents, on ceremonial silver, and headstones in the old cemetery. I am indebted to Elizabeth Selby at The Jewish Museum for help with material for the book. Thanks to Bonhams of Bond Street for the use of photographs of the synagogue silver. Also to Evelyn Friedlander for photographs from her own archive.

Special thanks, too, to my 16-year old son, Jonathan, for providing a substantial number of photographs for the book and for accompanying me on trips to Plymouth to photograph the synagogue and headstones in the two cemeteries. And to Brian Aloof who spent hours working through the marriage registers, double-checking material in the West Devon & Plymouth Archives, and headstones in the Gifford Place cemetery and checking factual details in the synagogue itself. To my circle of friends and family who enable me to carry out this work: my husband, our three sons, my mother Sandra Doney, and my father-in-law David Fry. Thanks too go to staff at the London Jewish Cultural Centre, most especially Carolyn Black, for unswerving support of this book.

Further information about my books can be found on the official author website: www.helen-fry.com

Are there people beyond the hill?
Do children play, does the sun shine still?
Do lovers stroll along a leafy glade?
Do the old folk sit and dream in the shade?
Is there happiness in the hearts of men?
When will it be mine, tell me when?
Will my son be grown and tall
At last when I walk from behind this wall?
Will I see my home, the woman I love?
I pray I do, my God in heaven above.

Jewish prisoner, Dartmoor Prison, 1980

INTRODUCTION

WITH ONE OF the largest natural ports in Europe, Plymouth has a long and fascinating naval and military history. It was from here in 1620 that the Pilgrim Fathers left for the New World on the historic Mayflower. Like other ports of the South-West, notably Exeter, Falmouth and Penzance, Jews were attracted to Plymouth because of the trading and business opportunities. Plymouth Synagogue is historically significant as the oldest Ashkenazi synagogue still in use in the English-speaking world. Jewish naval links to the city actually pre-date the foundation of a settled worshipping community of the 1730s/1740s. There was no known medieval Jewish community in the city, as there had been in Exeter and Bristol. From 1290, Jews were not legally allowed to live in England after Edward I's Edict expelling them from the land.

There was no official Jewish presence in England for three hundred years until Oliver Cromwell readmitted them in 1656. However, by Tudor Times, individual Jews had settled in Devon and Cornwall, in places far flung from the centre of power and government. Naval ports were obvious places to reside. From 1492, the Spanish Inquisition was another dark period for the Jews of Europe who were forced to flee to other lands. Some settled in the South-West of England. Marranos – Jews who had 'converted' to Catholicism but still secretly practiced Judaism – came from Spain to Plymouth, where they acted as agents for the London Marranos operating quietly from London. The Marranos in Plymouth promoted trade in the region for the London Marranos. They also advised those fleeing Spain and Portugal if, and when, it was safe to practice their faith again and where. One famous Marrano figure who landed in Plymouth was the wealthy widow, Gracia Mendes (aka Dona Gracia) who, in 1536, was en route to Antwerp, but diverted because of the Inquisition in Antwerp.

During the Golden Age of Elizabeth I, one figure stands out in Plymouth's history and has become legendry not only in the city's history but in our national consciousness. Sir Francis Drake became an iconic hero against the threat of the Spanish Armada in 1588. From the historic Hoe, he is said to have played bowls at low tide when Captain Thomas Fleming brought him news of Spanish ships near the Isles of Scilly. Drake reputedly told Fleming: 'We have time enough to finish the game and beat the Spaniards.' There is a surprising Jewish link to Francis Drake. When Drake circumnavigated the globe, his quartermaster was none other than 'Moses the Jew' from

Photograph of the synagogue interior.

the Barbican, Plymouth. In 1577, Drake recorded an entry 'Moses the Jew' in his log of the *Golden Hind*.

Around 1617, a Jew by the name of Antonio DaCosta Doliveira was living in Plymouth and conducting commercial business on behalf of the Spanish ambassador in London. Fragmentary evidence exists for other Jews in the city before Cromwell officially readmitted them in 1656. In 1634, there was Jewish scholar, Lawrenson, who originated from Germany and taught languages. The Jews who settled around 1720s/1740s found a very different city from today. Plymouth consisted then of approximately 1,600 houses, all clustered around Sutton Harbour. Millbay had not yet been developed and Devonport dockyard was in its infancy. The northern extremity of the town was located at the present day Royal Parade. Old Town Street led into open countryside. Although relatively small, the city became a key centre for international trading. The Stage Coach which ran from London to Falmouth carried goods bound to and from the West Indies, en route making Plymouth a key port in the development of this trade. Importantly in the 1880s, the Union Steamship Company operated a line for passengers and goods once a fortnight on a Friday from Plymouth to the ports of Cape Town, Mossel

Bay, Port Elizabeth, Port Alfred, East London and Natal, and St Helena. The Royal Mail Service operated to the Cape of Good Hope, Natal and East Africa. It was against this strong naval background that many local Jews prospered and gained an exceptional track record for fairness.

The links of Jews and the Navy in Plymouth continued for several generations. From the port of Plymouth sailed Sir Alexander Schomberg (1720-1804), son of Meyer Schomberg, physician to the Great Synagogue in London. Schomberg commanded the frigate *Diana* at the capture of Quebec in 1759/60. Midshipman Benjamin Da Costa fought aboard *HMS Temeraire* at the Battle of Trafalgar in 1805; and Abraham Barrett served aboard HMS Vanguard at the Battle of the Nile in 1798. One of the first names on the Naval Memorial on the Hoe is that of Midshipman V. Schreiber who went down with the crew of *HMS Monmouth* at the Battle of Coronel in November 1914. Also Jack Silverstone of Devonport who was lost at sea during WW1. Plymouth became a thriving, vibrant city in which its Jewish community settled with no fear of discrimination or religious intolerance. It is an incredibly rich history, and one which this books seeks to shed light on.

CHAPTER 1
FOUNDATION OF THE COMMUNITY 1720s–1800

IN THE EARLY 1700s, economic and trading opportunities brought Jews to Plymouth from Alsace, Rhineland and Bohemia. Others who settled in the city were Ashkenazi Jews who had fled the pogroms of Europe and the War of the Austrian Succession of 1740 in which Empress Marie Theresa threatened to expel all Jews from Moravia and Bohemia. Central Europe at that time was a pretty uncompromising place for Jews to live. Split into kingdoms and dukedoms, the Jews in these lands were at the mercy of change of the Monarchs and leaders and their changing racial and religious bigotry. The European Renaissance had essentially confined the Jew to the Ghetto, with every kind of repression heaped upon them. The tenacity and realism of Jewish philosophy and identity kept them alive and ironically, Jews emerged from these areas as virtually the only body of people possessed of a general education, able to read, write and do accounting. They found themselves in key places of influence, often as advisors to a ruler or government. Some looked to the New World beyond the seas where they could begin a new life, sometimes as far afield as the West Indies. Many did not make the full journey and disembarked halfway at the English ports. The colonial trade, which places like Plymouth offered, enticed many to stay. In Plymouth, they found a haven and were courteously and fairly received by the townsfolk. Most of these Jewish settlers lived in and around Southside Street. They found a city of tolerance that had once welcomed the religious rebels, the Puritans. Other Christian denominations found a fruitful preaching ground in Plymouth; for example, Whitfield the Calvanist, and Methodist preachers John and Charles Wesley. Into this milieu of religious tolerance, the Jews established a new life which marked an end to their persecution.

The first written record of Jews in the city occurs in *A Picture of Plymouth*, published in 1812, which mentions nine Jewish silversmiths in Plymouth, Dock and Stonehouse. A later printed source says that "about the year 1740, several Hebrew families settled in the town, and formed a congregation in Broad Hoe Lane."[1] Amongst the first settlers were Joseph Jacob Sherrenbeck and his wife Sarah who came to the city around 1744, originally from Sherrenbeck in Germany. Joseph Jacob Sherrenbeck is first heard of in 1734 at the Assizes at Taunton where he was found guilty of criminal conversation with the wife of Lazarus Chadwick, for which he was fined £20 and imprisoned for 2 years. A silver pointer in the Plymouth synagogue bearing an inscription about Joseph was given to the nascent Hebrew Congregation and read: *'this pointer belongs to Joseph ben Judah Jacob from Sherrenbeck, PH Plymouth in the year 5505 {1745}'*. The initials PH probably stand for 'Parnas Hakahel' i.e. President of the Congregation.[2] Joseph Sherrenbeck was a prominent business man and generous benefactor to the synagogue who died sometime between 1779

Moses Solomon

Tombstone of Joseph Jacob Sherrenbeck, the old cemetery

---

[1] R.N. Worth, *A History of Plymouth*, 1890.
[2] Susser, p.31.

and 1782.[3] He is buried in the Jewish cemetery on the Hoe, which he had founded forty years earlier. His brother Gershon Sherrenbeck died in December 1781 and is also buried there. Other founding fathers of the community were the brothers Asher, Samuel and Hayil Hart and their cousin Asher Hart, also brothers David Cohen and Horah Cohen (sons of Shimshon Cohen), and brothers Alexander Abrahams and Joseph Abrahams, and Jacob (son of Mordecai). Their names are known because of the discovery of a silver pointer in 1967 bearing an inscription with their names. Another founding member was Gompert Michael Emdin, a goldsmith and jeweller, who advertised in the *Western Flying Post* in March 1761: 'where a great variety of all sorts of silver plate, jewels, trinkets, and all sorts of watches and haberdashery wares, may be had as cheap as in London.'[4]

Also arriving in the city around the same time as the Sherrenbecks and Emdins was Benjamin Nap, a box-maker, originally from Ilbersheim, near Mannheim in Germany. He arrived in England in 1745. Within five years, Joseph Cohen settled in the city.[5] By 1759, the community had fifty-two male members. Between 1757 and 1760, forty more families joined the community, having fled persecution in Europe. They arrived via the Post Boats which were free of charge until 1771. In 1771, a London Jewish gang decided to carry out robbery in Chelsea. It went disastrously wrong for them and turned into murder, sparking a wave of anti-Semitic mobs. The government's response was to stop the North Sea free passage from Northern Germany to Kent. This measure may have slowed the rate of immigration from Europe. However, those young Jews who left Germany in search of a new life in England usually knew their final destination. Once they had settled in ports like Plymouth, "nice" Jewish girls were sent over from their original homeland to marry them. If a suitable Jewish girl could not be found, Jewish settlers in the South-West tended to convert the local milkmaid.[6] Milkmaids were chosen because they had had cowpox and, as such, were immune from the deadly smallpox. Also, the cowpox gave them a fair, healthy complexion.

Many of the Jews who arrived in Plymouth were itinerant pedlars, selling secondhand clothes and other wares in one of Britain's busiest naval ports. One of the most popular trades for these Jews was as seamen's outfitter in which they sold goods to seamen and Naval officers. From humble beginnings, these Jews built up a substantial trade, such that by the end of the 18th century when the wooden warships anchored just off Mutton Cove and North Corner (two landing stages at the southern end of the River Tamar), they found a ready audience amongst the sailors. The Royal Navy had placed restrictions on crew coming ashore for fear of desertion. Jewish pedlars were granted

Trade Card, Abraham Joseph.
COURTESY OF THE JEWISH MUSEUM

permission to board the ships docked in the port. They sold all kinds of goods, from trinkets, old watches and rings to fancy goods, silk handkerchiefs, clay pipes and fresh food. They peddled their wares at certain times of the day. The ship's deck looked just like a marketplace and was quite a bustling site. Although the pedlars sold all kinds of goods, their main trade was in sailors' clothes or 'slops'. This gave rise to the term 'slopman', ie the name given to Jews who traded in 'slops'. The trade developed further, as the late Dr Mark Gordon once commented: 'the special "tiddly suits" of those days, which seamen wanted as their alternative to regulation dress, were often grand affairs involving finest quality broadcloths and trimmings.' The role of the slopman developed in an unexpected direction, and many found themselves bank-rolling the sailors and acting as Navy Agents:

'Until 1792 those who were paid off [sailors] received a wage ticket which was only encashable at the Navy Pay Office in London. This was an enormous inconvenience. The traders performed a dual function. They provided the seamen with cash by buying up the wage tickets at a discount, and at the same time they supplied the goods which the seamen wanted.'[7]

This led to accusations of inflated prices, faulty goods or wage tickets cashed in at highly discounted rates. There is no doubt that it was a profitable enterprise for some of the Jewish Navy agents. Historian Geoffrey Green noted: 'Just one London Prize Agent between 1806 and 1814 paid £4,225 to six Plymouth-based Jewish Navy Agents.'[8] That amounted to a considerable sum of money in the early 19th century. However, in due course, Plymouth's Jewish Naval agents became known for their exceptional fairness.

---

[3] His exact date of death is not known because his tombstone is illegible.
[4] The surname Emdin came to be spelt Emdon or Emden.
[5] *London Gazette*, October 1749.
[6] Cecil Roth, *History of the Jews in England*.
[7] Susser, p. 100.
[8] Green, *The Royal Navy and Anglo-Jewry 1740-1820*, p.107.

FOUNDATION OF THE COMMUNITY 1720s - 1800

Interior of the synagogue.

Some Jews took up apprentices locally. In 1762, for example, Moses Moses was apprenticed to jeweller Jason Halt of Plymouth. As early as 1710, predating the established Jewish community, there is mention of Pickas (Pinchas) Isaac of Plymouth being apprenticed to Edward Tookey of the city (an Apothecary). Abraham Abrahams was apprenticed to watchmaker Richard Temple in 1764, and Isaac Abrahams (probably brother Abraham Abrahams) was apprenticed to tailor John Bone in 1768. Solomon Nathan, who had registered as a Master jeweller in 1762, took on apprentice Judah Lyon in 1772. Other Jews in the city by 1799, included Moses David Angel from Poland and Joel Levy, a member of the Plymouth Meshivat Nefesh Society [burial society] in 1795, who was insured as a silversmith on premises in Market Street in 1800. In 1816, Levy was listed as a Navy agent near the Parade, and by 1822 as a silversmith in Market Street.[9] There was also Solomon Ze'ev ben Meir, an embroiderer in gold, and Abraham ben Solomon, a carpenter. Another helpful source for Jews in the late 1700s is the Plymouth Aliens List which lists 59 Jewish immigrants to the city.[10] It provides details of their date and place of birth, occupation and port of landing in England. Amongst those mentioned are Joseph Levy of Lissa and Moses Isaac of Mesteryz (formerly of Frankfurt) who landed in Harwich in 1748; both of whom are entered as "Clerk of the Jews'

Synagogue". Also mentioned are Joseph's brother, Mordecai Levy, and Joseph Cohen, originally of Brod in Poland. The years from 1798 to 1803 saw the arrival of brothers David Abrahams, Levy Abrahams and Mordecai Abrahams, Emanuel Cohen, David Jacob Coppel, Eleazer Emdin (in 1798), Moses Emdin and Solomon Emdin, Simon and Solomon Nathan, Aaron Jacobs, Levi Jacobs, Israel Jacobs and Nathan Jacobs (of Dartmouth), and Abraham and Jacob Simon.

Names of Jews in the community in the late 18th century are also known from the Plymouth Town Rental Books which show who utilized the Plymouth Conduit System. On the list are Joseph Jacob Sherrenbeck, Jacob Myer Sherrenbeck, Solomon Abrahams, Hart Abraham, Lyon Homberg, Abraham Symons, Mr Mordecai, Abraham Alexander, Mr Nathan, Mr Mayer and Mr Hart. By the turn of the 1800s, the conduit system was in use by more of the city's Jews, with the names of women amongst them: Abraham Aaron, Sander Alexander, David Cohen, Benjamin Hart, Samuel Hart, Henry Hart, Solomon Isaac, Jacob Jacobs, Sarah Jacobs, Joseph Joseph, Nathan Joseph, Rosey Joseph and Sarah Moss.[11]

In Plymouth was silversmith Benjamin Nathan who registered his mark at the Exeter Assay Office. His name ceases to appear in records after 1773. Also Lazarus Solomon, Rachel Karbman who hailed from Prussia, and

---

[9] He was married to Rachel bat Joseph who died on 14 February 1822.
[10] A copy survives in the Jewish Museum, London.
[11] Susser, p.52-3.

Tombstone of Jacob Nathan.

Ze'ev ben Judah from Shatwinitz who died of cholera in 1832 and is buried in the cemetery on the Hoe. Others from Poland were pedlar Isaac Neuman (born Souack) and Samuel Levy, a secondhand clothes dealer and outfitter. Mordecai Jacobs (b. 1727, Prague), who landed at Harwich in 1750, spent 3 years in London and then moved to Cornwall from 1753 until 1773. He came to Plymouth in 1773, where he traded as an umbrella maker. In 1805, he was living at 85 Market Place. He remained in the city for the rest of his life and died on 4 October 1806. There was Phineas Levy of Devonport who arrived in the city from Portsmouth by 1812, one of the first Jews to hold elected civic office in England. He is recorded as a pawnbroker of North Corner Street. Later, he is listed in various trade directories as a clothes dealer and naval slopseller. His progress is marked by the change of business addresses. From the waterside shack of his first address in North Corner Street, he moved to Cornwall Street, then Queen Street before finally trading in Fore Street (Devonport).

The Plymouth community maintained close ties with other Jewish communities, most especially Exeter, Falmouth, Penzance and Portsmouth. A number of Jews moved from Portsmouth to Plymouth during this period: Michael Barnett Levy in 1776, Moses ben Joseph Gosport who married Zirrele (daughter of Benjamin Jonas of Plymouth) and, by 1805, Barrow Moss who married Sarah Isaac, daughter of Solomon Isaac.[12] Barnet and Esther Levy moved from Portsmouth in 1775. They had eight children, most of whom married into Plymouth Jewish families. One child died in 1791. The other seven were Elizabeth (1757-1832) who married Solomon (son of Israel Solomon), Joel who married Rachel Joseph (daughter of Joseph Joseph), Sheba (1766-1850) who married Elias [Mark] Elias, Hannah (1770-1851) who married Abraham Joseph (son of Joseph Joseph); Sarah, and Abraham who wedded Zipporah (daughter of M. Benjamin) circa 1810. Abraham Levy and Zipporah went on to have six children, one of whom, Caroline, married Henry Nathan (son of Jacob Nathan).[13]

Abraham Joseph I (1731-1794)

Exactly when Abraham Joseph I first arrived in the city is unknown, but he quickly established himself as a man of some financial substance. One of his descendants, Wilfred Jessop (né Joseph), had two small paintings of Abraham Joseph in his possession and wrote that they showed "a man correctly dressed in the height of current fashion." In one of them, Joseph is wearing a periwig, and in the other, a tricorn hat worn above a wig without a tail. His eyes were described as "piercing blue in a well-proportioned face not

Tombstone of Abraham Joseph I, the old cemetery

Section C, the old cemetery

---

[12] Barrow Moss's daughter Caroline married George David Jackson of Liverpool in Portsea synagogue on 27 August 1845.
[13] Abraham Levy died in 1834 and is buried in the old cemetery.

without its humour and kindliness." Abraham Joseph became an important figurehead in the local Jewish community. His name appears on a 1786 lease for the synagogue in Catherine Street. He was the son Joseph Joseph, but not to be confused with his own son Joseph Joseph. Abraham Joseph I was soon seen as a leading Jew in the South-West and referred locally as 'the King of the Jews.'[14] He married Rose Abrahams whose grandfather was resident of Cree Church Lane, London, the site of the first synagogue opened in the capital after the readmission of Jews in 1656.[15] Abraham and Rose had eight children: Samuel, Phoebe, Esther, Joseph, Brina, Aaron, Gella and Henel. It was in Plymouth that Abraham Joseph could practice as a merchant slopman and Naval agent for the Royal Navy. His trade card, which survives in the Jewish Museum, confirms that he was appointed slopman to HRH Prince William Henry, third son of George III. In 1780, then in the rank of Midshipman, the prince landed in Plymouth with his brother and heir Prince George (Prince of Wales) with news of Rodney's victory and the relief of Gibraltar. Six years later, Prince William Henry was once again in Plymouth on his appointment as Captain of the frigate *Pegasus*, just before his twenty-first birthday. Two years later, in 1788, he found himself in disgrace with his father, the King, and was compelled to spend a period of disgrace in Plymouth, during which he frequently called upon the help of Abraham Joseph.

Abraham Joseph had several properties: two on the Barbican, two other leasehold houses and three dwellings on the quay in East Stonehouse, freehold dwellings in Castle Street and Stillman Street, a house in Pyke Street and one in Great George Street. On his death in November 1794, the Gentleman's Magazine noted that: 'he amassed a considerable fortune by very fair and honest means… He was one of the people called Jews, but the actions of his whole life would have done honour to any persuasion. As an agent for seamen his practice was well worth the imitation of every person in that business as several orphans and indigent widows can testify.'[16] It was not the only accolade. *Trewman's Flying Post* of 27 November 1794 noted: 'As an agent for seamen, his practice was well worthy the imitation of every person in that business, as several orphans and indigent widows can testify.' Abraham Joseph I is buried in Section C of the old Jewish cemetery in a special section reserved for members of the Joseph family. In his will, which was witnessed by the local Rabbi Moses Ephraim and Charles Yonge (a member of the famous Plymouth family), he bequeathed his real estate to his seven children. Joseph Joseph and Samuel Joseph received the two leasehold dwellings on the Barbican. Two other leasehold houses in the possession of Thomas Rowland and John Elliot and three dwellings on the quay in East Stonehouse were held on trust for Joseph Joseph and siblings Gella, Henel, Samuel, Phoebe and Brina. His wife Rosa and their sons received the freehold dwellings in Castle Street, Stillman Street and Seven Star Lane, which were also held in trust for Esther Joseph. A house in Pyke Street, used by his son-in-law Abraham Aaron, was held in trust for Phoebe Aaron (née Joseph).[17] Of the residue, £500 went to Abraham Joseph's wife and each child (except Joseph and Phoebe who already had their share). The remainder was divided into eight parts to Rosa Joseph and the following children: Joseph, Samuel (provided it did not exceed £500) 'to set up or continue as a pawnbroker', Phoebe, Gella, Brina, Henel and Esther. His scrolls of the Torah in the synagogue were bequeathed: one to his son Joseph, another to Samuel, and the oldest to the "Synagogue and the Jew people frequenting same". Of the ceremonial silver, the will stated: "the pair of Aaron silver bells and the plate thereto belonging shall never be sold or alienated from my family." Joseph Joseph's son Henry, Abraham Joseph's grandson, received a gold watch, silver shoe and stone knee buckles. To Moses Ephraim, schoolmaster, he bequeathed £12. 12s. 0d on condition that "within twelve months to say certain prayers for me daily." The interest of £100 in the Okehampton Turnpike was to be paid to the Beth Hamidrash in London. 'The interest on £100 for the Synagogue in Plymouth upon condition and in confidence that proper prayers are said for me in the synagogue every Jewish Sabbath Day, and every holiday, and if the people attending at such times shall refuse, neglect, or omit to say such prayers for me, then the executors are to pay the interest to the Institution in London'.

On his death, Abraham Joseph I was living in a highly desirable property at 6 George Street. When it was finally sold the advertisement read: 'two good parlours, a drawing room, several lodging rooms and all convenient offices, together with a garden adjoining. The rooms are furnished with neat grates, and all necessary fixtures are on the premises. And the whole is fit for the immediate reception of a genteel family.'[18]

Samuel Joseph

Born in Plymouth in 1759, Samuel Joseph was the eldest son of Abraham Joseph I. Sometime before 1805 he married Rebecca Myers and they had one child, Jane, born in November 1806. Samuel practiced as a Navy Agent and was active in the Plymouth Hebrew Congregation and a Vestry Member until he and his family emigrated to America around 1817. By the mid-1820s he had established a business as a beer and cordial purveyor in Cincinnati, then

---

[14] Cecil Roth, *The Rise of Provincial Jewry*, p.92.
[15] According to Bert Emdon, Rose Abrahams was related to Moses Samuel, secretary to the infant Plymouth Jewish congregation, resident in the city with his unmarried sister, Bilah.
[16] Gentleman's Magazine 1794, p. 1156.
[17] Phoebe Joseph and Abraham Aaron had a large family, Many descendants emigrated.
[18] *Trew. Flying Post*, 29 December 1794.

the second largest Jewish community in America after New York. This trade he may well have learned from Lemon Hart of Penzance before leaving England for America. There is a tenuous link to the American Declaration of Independence. Samuel Joseph's third grandchild Julia married David Johnson whose brother Phineas Johnson had married Clarissa Clark, daughter of the signer of the Declaration. The Johnson brothers had emigrated to America from Portsmouth in 1786, and their descendants went on to live in Cincinnati and St Louis.[19]

Joseph Joseph (1766-1846)

Joseph Joseph, son of Abraham Joseph I, was probably named after his deceased grandfather as is the custom in Jewish tradition. He traded as a silversmith, slop merchant and Navy Agent.[20] He married Edal (born in Liskeard in 1771), daughter of Abraham Levy.[21] Amongst their children were Abraham Joseph II and Ruth whose death and burial in Penzance he recorded:

> "My daughter Ruth went to [her] eternal rest the weekday Friday on the eve of the Holy Sabbath 16 MarHeshvan '593 at KK [Holy community] Penzance and was buried there on Monday. My dearly Beloved Daughter Ruth Ob. on (Thursday Night that is) Friday 9 Novr 5593 (1832) at Penzance & Buried there this day."[22]

Continuing in his father's footsteps, Joseph Joseph was a generous benefactor of the synagogue. In 1796, he gave £157 to enable the community to compete the purchase of the burial ground on the Hoe. In 1798, he donated an Ark curtain, two golden breastplates and a small cover. He acted as *mohel* for the Plymouth community from 1784 to 1834, performing his first circumcision when he was 18 years old. His circumcision register survives. The Jewish Museum has two silver goblets once belonging to him; one to be used for wine, the other for whisky during the circumcision ceremony.

After his father's death, Joseph Joseph acquired a number of properties in Plymouth. The leased properties from the Corporation of Plymouth included cellars in Castle Street, a dwelling house on Southside Quay, a plot near Dung Hill, a shop with chambers in Whimple Street, and a cellar and loft in Middle Lane. Later, he became a publican. Amongst the inns and taverns he owned was the Mayflower on the Barbican. It was probably from here that he traded as a Navy agent and received £2,258 on behalf of seamen over a period of nine years from just one London Prize Agent. Of the Mayflower Inn, a family memoir written by descendant Bert Emdon records:

> 'There is a family tradition that it was in this Inn [Mayflower], a hostelry of some repute, that he extended hospitality to a royal party of HM King George III, who at the time was holding court at Saltram House. The sudden descent of a sea mist had made it impossible to return to the Laira (the estuary of the river Plym) by royal barge, the mode of transport then used between Saltram and Plymouth. The royal party therefore sought shelter at the hostelry of the Navy Agent, conveniently situated immediately opposite the Mayflower Steps, the usual point of embarkation. Family tradition has it that the party included the King and his three sons: the Prince of Wales,[23] the Duke of Clarence (later William IV) and Prince William Henry. It also included the future wife of the Prince of Wales, Princess Caroline of Brunswick. It is said that during the course of the evening Joseph Joseph danced with the Princess, and renamed the inn the Brunswick in her honour. The family story also insists that Joseph also burnt the royal I.O.Us, but there is no way of establishing whether this was true or not.'

Rose, wife of Abraham Joseph II

The inn remained as the Brunswick except for the period of WW1 and WW2 when, because of its German associations, the name was dropped in favour of the Mayflower again.

Joseph Joseph was deemed to be extremely honest and carried a letter of recommendation from none other than William, Admiral of the Fleet, dated 1812, and sent from St James's Palace:

> 'I do hereby certify that Joseph Joseph of Plymouth has at different times supplied the Crews of His Majestys Ships when under my Command with Cloathing [sic] to my entire satisfaction, and I do hereby recommend him to the Admirals, Captains, and Officers of His Majestys Navy, to be permitted to transact any Business that may be done on board the respective Ships under their Command.'

The Royal connections continued. Joseph Joseph moved in high society and was a friend of King William IV when the latter was at Dartmouth in his youth. But prosperity did not last for Joseph. In spite of having a

---

[19] Samuel A Johnson of Cincinnati was President of the American Legal Bar Association and deputy mayor of Cincinnati in 1912.
[20] He is not the same man as Joseph Joseph from Alsace. Keith Pearce has shown that the two Joseph families of Cornwall and Plymouth are not related.
[21] Abraham Levy's sister Minnele married Henry Hart. Information taken from the Plymouth Pinkas (Death Register).
[22] Joseph Joseph's Circumcision Register, p.13 of a photocopy of the register.
[23] Also Prince Regent and later George IV.

number of properties in the city, his income was insufficient and he was forced to declare bankrupt. This led to the revoking of his licence as a Navy agent in July 1817. He did, however, continue his association with the Navy as a slopman. Two years later, on 11 June 1819, Joseph decided to try his luck abroad and sailed for Gibraltar. His exploits did not last and he returned to Plymouth in 1824. By the 1830s, he once again enjoyed a good name doing what he knew best as a Navy agent. In 1833, Admiral Thomas William Hargood, Flag Captain commanding Plymouth station, gave him a letter of recommendation. As did the Admiral of the Blue – the Royal Duke of Clarence, the "Sailor King".

By the 1841 census, Joseph Joseph was registered as living in Frankfort Street with wife Edal and of independent means. He died on 6 September 1846; his wife Edal on 21 February 1861. Both are buried in the old cemetery. Of their children (covered in more detail below), their eldest son Henry continued the royal links. On the recommendation of William IV, he received a legal post in Gibraltar, which he filled with great aplomb. He rose to become Recorder of Gibraltar and lay Reader of the Gibraltar Hebrew Congregation.

Nathan [Altmann] Joseph

Brina Joseph (b. 1781), daughter of Abraham Joseph I, married Nathan Altmann whose Hebrew name was Nathan Nota ben Joseph K"Z. He and his sons were *Cohenim* (priests). Nathan Altmann was born in Ransporke, Bohemia in 1766. In 1784, at the age of eighteen, he landed at Gravesend and that same year settled in Dartmouth. From there he moved to Plymouth where he traded as a jeweller in Broad Street. Just over a decade later, in 1816, he was listed at 72 Fore Street (Plymouth Dock) as a Navy agent and property owner. He anglicized his name and thereafter became known as Nathan Joseph, probably because he was Nathan son of Joseph rather than taking his wife's maiden name which was also Joseph. He had decided to settle permanently in England as demonstrated by a document which he signed in 1801:

> '13 August 1801 ... I forever renounce and disclaim of all the possessions of my father Joseph Altmann Inhabiter of the Herrshaft of Ronsperg in the town of Ronsberg Co. Klattauer Kingdom of Bohemia, to which possessions being the first born son I might be entitled to, as well local as Familiae Numerum, and that I transfer them to my second brother Joachim Altmann who in consideration thereof is to be married to Miss Theresa Mosses. As I am now near 18 years in the Kingdom of England, in the town of Plymouth established and settled and having no children ... Nathan Joseph Altmann.'[24]

Nathan and Brina had twelve children: Abraham (b.1801), Gertrude, Rachel, Samson (b. 1804), Michael, Joseph (b. 1813), Julia (1816-78), Sarah, Simeon, Rosa, Annie (b. 1823) and Henry (b.1827). When their firstborn son Abraham was born in December 1801, a *mappa* (binder for a Torah scroll) was presented to the Plymouth Synagogue to mark his birth. It may have been embroidered by Brina herself. Such binders were a custom from German-speaking land, and Evelyn Friedlander describes this binder as 'one of the only English-made binders known in this country.'[25] The inscription reads:

> 'Abraham ben Nathan Nota KZ born for good luck on Thursday 28 Kislev '562 [= 3 December 1801]. May the Lord rear him to the Torah, to the Chuppa, and to good deeds. Amen. Selah.'

Tombstone of Nathan Joseph (Altman)

In the 1960s, an exquisite hand-embroidered cover for a Torah scroll was discovered in the synagogue by Bernard Susser. It had been given by Nathan and Brina, and is now only known by a photograph.[26] Embroidered on it were priestly hands, covered in fine lace gloves and giving a blessing, with a crown of the Torah at the top. The inscription read:

> 'This belongs to the honourable Nathan son of the late Joseph of blessed memory and his spouse Mistress Breinelah daughter of the honourable the

---

[24] It survives in Plymouth's records.
[25] Evelyn Friedlander, *The Jews of Devon and Cornwall*, p.33.
[26] Evelyn Friedlander, op.cit, p.32.

late Abraham Isaac of blessed memory in the year, 'and may He give you the blessing by Abraham' (Genesis 28:4) = 1815.[27]

By the 1841 census, three Joseph children (Julia, Annie and Henry) were still living at home in Queen Street. Eldest child, Abraham, married a daughter of Judah Cohen of Plymouth and had eight children: Henry, Albert, Lewis, Esther, Alice, Sarah, Eva and Edward. Of Nathan and Brina's other children, Gertrude married Samuel (son of Alexander Lyons of Plymouth), Rachel married Godchalk Asher of Montreal, Samson wedded Hannah (daughter of Alexander Lyons), Simeon married Rosa (daughter of Solomon Blanckensee), and Annie married Jessie Lawrence in December 1862.

A glimpse of the family's lifestyle can be found in the synagogue archives. In 1819, Nathan Joseph was paying 5 guineas per annum for his seat in the synagogue. His household must have eaten well because his bill in that year was reduced by 2 guineas Meat Tax. As Susser notes: 'The butcher paid over to the Congregation one farthing for every pound weight of meat purchased by a customer, and this amount was credited to the customer's synagogue account. Two guineas was 2016 farthings, so the Joseph household in 1819 was consuming just under 40 lbs. of meat every week'.[28] Nathan Joseph had done well for himself. Between 1801 and 1805, he was the owner of a house in Great George Street, known because he paid 12s. a year to be attached to the water conduit system.[29] On 24 November 1815, he signed a lease for water on a house in Union Street, by Mr Little. By 1822, Nathan Joseph is described as a mercer and draper. The following year, he is listed as a linen and wool draper at 9 Higher Broad Street.[30] Significantly, in 1825, he was one of 116 prominent Plymouth business men who declared that they had confidence in the Plymouth Naval Bank.

On his death in October 1851, Nathan Joseph left property to his sons Sampson and Michael, both then surgeons of Kingston, Jamaica. Although he had lived in England for 65 years, he signed his will in Hebrew. On the 1851 census, his wife Brina is described at an annuitant and proprietress of houses. Living with her were four daughters, all teachers or governesses. In 1861, she was still at 21 Queen Street, described as a 'gentlewoman'. Brina died in August 1865 and is also buried in the old cemetery.

Abraham Joseph II (1799-1868)

Like his forebears, Abraham Joseph II was a leading figure in the Plymouth Jewish community and a wealthy benefactor. Born in Plymouth in 1799, the son of Joseph, he became slopman to Prince William Henry. He left Plymouth for Penzance and, a deeply religious man, he became a kind of lay minister, reader and general factotum to the Penzance Synagogue. On 31 January 1828, he married into a well-known Cornish Jewish family when he wedded Telza (Eliza) Woolf, born in 1808, the eldest daughter of Asher Woolf (Lemon Woolf) of Penzance. She was a granddaughter of Moses Jacob of Redruth and great-granddaughter of Zender Falmouth and known locally as the Belle of Penzance.[31] Abraham and Eliza had nine children: Rose (1829-1887), Hyman (b.1830), Henry (1832-1888), Solomon (1834-1900),[32] Sarah (1836-1911), David (1838-1841), Ruth (b.1840), Hannah (1843-1919) and Eliza (1850-1924). Abraham's fortunes flourished and they left Penzance and lived for a time in London. They returned to Plymouth and took up residence in style in Lockyer Street. He was by now a figure of some standing in the Jewish community locally and nationally. He became president of the synagogue on a number of occasions and a member of the National Board of Jewish Deputies where he exercised considerable influence. In 1841, the family was living at Southside of Frankfort Street. Abraham's first wife Eliza died in childbirth on 17 January 1850 at the age of 42 and is buried in the old cemetery. The surviving child was named Eliza after her. In adulthood, she married Eleazar Emdon in Plymouth on 6 February 1878.

By the 1851 census, Abraham Joseph II was registered as a bill broker at 6 Mulgrave Place. He married again, this time his first cousin Rosa Joseph of Plymouth and they had one daughter, Floretta. He was a friend of Chief Rabbi Nathan Adler, who happened to be his second cousin, to whom he bequeathed his library on his death in 1868. Abraham Joseph II is buried in the old cemetery. His tombstone describes him as 'Parnas and Manhig to his congregation'. His descendant David Lang has inherited a Hebrew Prayer Book inscribed in gold on the cover:
REV DR SOLOMON HIRSCHELL
TO ABRAHAM JOSEPH
AS A TOKEN OF HIS ESTEEM
AM 5593

Daughter Rose Joseph went on to marry Leon Solomon of Dawlish. Their eldest son emigrated to America and changed his name to Simpson. It was his son Ernest Simpson (grandson of Leon Solomon) who married Wallis Warfield. (Wallis Simpson), the woman for whom Edward VIII gave up his throne in 1936.

Abraham Joseph II's son Hyman emigrated to New Zealand. His second son, Henry Joseph, emigrated to Australia in 1853 during the period of the Gold Rush where he used his specialist knowledge of minerals to become an assayer. His brother Solomon emigrated to Australia six years

---
[27] Evelyn Friedlander, op. cit.
[28] Plymouth Hebrew Congregation Vestry Book, p. 159.
[29] Plymouth Town Rental Books.
[30] Plymouth Directory 1823.
[31] *The Lost Jews of Cornwall* (ed. Keith Pearce & Helen Fry).
[32] Solomon Joseph was the grandfather of Wilfred Jessop.

FOUNDATION OF THE COMMUNITY 1720s - 1800

Tombstone of Abraham Joseph II, old cemetery

(1799-1872) who married Rachel (daughter of Mordecai Benjamin), Hannah (b. 1801), and Woolf (b.1805) who married Rebecca.[34] Eleazer Emdon died on 6 February 1844 at the age of 80 and is buried in the old cemetery. In his will, he specified that a light should be burnt in the synagogue for a year as a memorial.

In 1803, Eleazer Emdon's youngest brother Solomon (Selig) was listed as a hatter of 9 Cat Street, Plymouth. His wife Freda bat Judah died in 1843 and is buried in the old cemetery.[35] Solomon acted as beadle to the synagogue and was permitted to live in the congregation's first house next to the synagogue. He died on 24 July 1850.

An Emdon

later in 1859 and went into journalism to become a pioneer of the Australian provincial press. Abraham Joseph II's daughter Sarah married Rev Raphael Harris of Bayswater Synagogue, a noted cleric for his charitable work with the blind and rabbi there for 47 years from 1864 to 1911. Hannah Joseph married Henry Nathan.

Emdon Family

The first Emdons to come from Amsterdam to Plymouth were brothers, Gompert Michael Emdon and Abraham Emdon. They were said to be related to Rabbi Emdon of Amsterdam, a powerful opponent of Shabbatai Zvi who himself was probably descended from the famous scholar Rabbi Jacob Emdon of Prague. There seem to be various spellings of the surname, but within a generation of arriving in Plymouth it was spelt Emdon. Gompert Emdon's name appears in the *Pinkas* and also the deeds for the synagogue in 1762; the latter showing that he was a 'shopkeeper of the Parish of Stoke Dameral'. Abraham Emdon's three sons, Eleazer (b. 1764), Hiam (b.1767) and Solomon (b. 1774) eventually came over from Amsterdam to join their father and uncle. They are listed on the 1798 Napoleonic Aliens Register.[33] In 1786, Eleazer came first to London where he remained until 1794, then moved to Portsmouth and finally to Plymouth in 1798 where he traded as a dealer in old clothes. By 1844, he had achieved some financial stability as a pawnbroker in Cornwall Street, Devonport. He and his wife Kitty were known to have had three children: Abraham

Samuel Hart

Samuel Hart, who married Henna bas Haim Dov, was one of the founders of the Plymouth Jewish community. The son of merchant Henry Hart, he served as its treasurer in 1779, and President of the Machinath Nefesh Society (Burial Society) in 1797 and 1808. He also served as president of the synagogue in 1827, 1828 and 1832. Samuel's brother Menachem never married and died a bachelor in 1809. Samuel himself strived to be an artist but never achieved his dream. He took up an apprenticeship with miniaturist and engraver Abraham Daniel of Plymouth (see below), but throughout his life was always short of money and owed the synagogue for unpaid seat rental which he eventually managed to pay off. He joined his son, Solomon Hart, in London and was painted by B. R. Haydon in his famous work "The Mock Election". Samuel Hart died in 1838 and, although during his lifetime he never succeeded as a painter, he lived just long enough to see his son become one of the most distinguished society artists and a Fellow of the Royal Academy. More about Solomon Hart later.

Abraham Daniel

A notable local artist was Abraham Daniel, one of three brothers, all miniaturists, who worked in the South-West. Abraham, Joseph and Phineas Daniel were the sons of Nechaniah Daniel of Bridgwater, Somerset. By the 1770s, Abraham Daniel was living in Plymouth and working as a painter, engraver and miniaturist. In 1779, he took on an

---

[33] Hiam married Hannah, daughter of Lazarus Jacobs.
[34] Surname unknown.
[35] Plot B35.

Miniature by Abraham Daniel, 1785 *Tombstone of artist Abraham Daniel, 1806*

apprentice Samuel Hart (above), but Hart did not do as well as he had hoped. Abraham Daniel's only signed work was a portrait of Moses Ephraim, the first rabbi of Plymouth. Unusually for an artist, Daniel did not die in poverty. After his death on 10 March 1806, he left £50 in his will to his mistress Elizabeth Codbury, £50 to his son Edward Elliot Daniel, £100 to his son William Daniel, and £20 to Plymouth Synagogue. The total value of his estate was £1,500 – a large sum in those days, especially for an artist. The residue of his estate was bequeathed to his two sisters, Rachel Nathan who had married Solomon Nathan, and Rebecca Alman who had married Isaac Alman of Bristol. Executors were local Jews, Joseph Joseph and Samuel Hart, although when Daniel came to sign the codicil appointing them as his executors, he was on the point of death and unable to sign it. Testimony to this fact was given by surgeon Thomas Williams, and silversmiths Solomon Isaac, Samuel Hart and Manley Hart. Abraham Daniel is buried in the old cemetery.[36]

Joseph Hart

Joseph Hart was only fourteen when he arrived in England in 1770 from Mannheim, Germany. It did not take long for him to establish himself as a silversmith and earn a decent living from 35 Market Street, Plymouth. In 1779, he was able to contribute one guinea to the War Levy. He appears to have briefly left the city from 1798 to 1803, but returned again and remained until his death at his lodgings in June 1822. His landlord William Pyne found a considerable amount of wealth in his room: four banknotes of £100 each, gold and silver coins, as well as gold and silver to a total value of between £700 and £800. After Pyne refused to hand it over to the heirs, the Plymouth Hebrew Congregation set up a committee to recover the property and successfully recovered the money.

Minor Jewish Settlement in the Region

During the 18th century, there were other minor settlements of Jews in towns not far from Plymouth. In Tavistock, there was Jacob Jukel Tavistock, and in Yealmpton, Esther daughter of Agnes and Jacob Moses who had been born in the town in 1829. Samuel Hart (brother of Moses Hart of London), who married out of the faith, lived in Yarnscombe where he drew up his will in 1744. In Dartmouth, there were several Jews: Nathan Dartmouth, silversmith Moses Mordecai from 1764, Nathan Joseph from 1784, and members of the Bellem family. Matathias Hyman ben Elijah Bellem was living in Dartmouth around 1786 and registered as a member of Plymouth Hebrew Congregation. His son Aaron Bellem (b. circa 1870) married Rachel (b.1783, Plymouth, surname not known). They had six children: Harriet, Hannah, Jacob, Abraham, Esther and an unnamed child who died. When Aaron died on 23 October 1833, his body was brought to Plymouth for burial. By 1841, Rachel Bellem and her children moved into Plymouth and lived at Morley Place. By the 1851 census, her son Jacob was living in the same household. When Rachel died in 1863, the Plymouth Congregation financially supported her deaf/mute child Harriet. Rachel is buried in the old cemetery, as is her son Abraham after his death at the age of 44 in 1866. Harriet Bellem died in October 1890 at the age of eighty and is buried in the Gifford Place Jewish cemetery.

Close links existed between the Plymouth Jewish community and others in the South-West, with some intermarriages between Jewish families of Penzance, Falmouth and Exeter. In the latter half of the 18th century, for example, Anne Ezekiel of Exeter married Benjamin Jonas of Plymouth Dock. She was the sister of eminent engraver, silversmith and optician, Ezekiel Abraham Ezekiel of Exeter. Another example can be found with the descendants of Alexander Moses of Falmouth who married into Plymouth Jewish families. As the Plymouth Jewish community expanded and thrived from the 1760s, so too its members became involved in the civic life of the city. Over the next 250 years, Plymouth's Jews would play active roles in the Corporation, serving on various Municipal committees. By the end of the 18th century, the community was strong and confident in it surroundings. Jews had found in Plymouth a city where they could be happy, live in peace with their Christian neighbours, and raise their families in the Jewish faith. It could move into the 19th century with confidence.

---

[36] The plot has now been identified by the author as B41a.

CHAPTER 2
THE SYNAGOGUE

THE FIRST JEWS in Plymouth worshipped in makeshift premises in Hoor Street, Woolsten Street or Lion Street.[37] This was probably in a private house before they acquired a rented room in Broad Hoe Lane. In the early days, there were apparently three small worshipping Jewish communities at the then separate towns of Devonport, Stonehouse and Plymouth. Sometime between 1741 and 1745, these small prayer groups, or *minyans*, amalgamated.

Exterior of Plymouth Synagogue

By 1742, they began to look for land to construct a purpose-built place of worship and acquired land in 'St Katherin's Lane', now Catherine Street. The synagogue is located in the heart of Plymouth, just a stone's throw from the historic Hoe. Its whitewashed exterior and arched windows could easily be mistaken for an 18th century non-Conformist chapel. This Grade II Listed building with its Cornish slate roof and plain exterior, belies an historic gem which is not only the oldest synagogue outside London, but the oldest Ashkenazi place of worship in the English-speaking world. The entrance is located around the back of the building, accessible via a side alley. Ahead, is Synagogue House, or Vestry, which once housed the rabbi's flat and the community's religion school. The alley opens into a small, but exquisite, courtyard with the entrance to the synagogue on the left. Here is another world – a time capsule that transports the visitor back to the mid-18th century. The entrance, like Exeter synagogue, is hidden and discreet, built in a period when Jews feared to be prominently noticed because of anti-Jewish feeling in society. Anglo-Jewish architectural historian, Sharman Kadish, suggests that "the stuccoed front, with prominent cornices, scrolled brackets and segmental-headed openings" date from 100 years after the building of the synagogue, i.e. probably an addition in 1863 or 1864.[38] She also advocates that the stone lintel over the entrance is probably not part of the original build either. A marble plaque over the entrance gives the date the synagogue was built and reads in translation from the Hebrew: Holy to the Lord, this sanctified and honoured house, was founded in the year [Psalm 100], "we will bow, prostrate ourselves, then bend our knee before the Lord our maker" [1762].

---

[37] Cecil Roth, *The Rise of Provincial Jewry*, p. 91.
[38] Sharman Kadish, *Jewish Heritage in England*, p.90.

were dedicated in a special service which took place in 1929, attended by many Civic dignitaries in which the procession from the Council Chamber was headed by the Mayor, the Chief Constable, and the Mace Bearers. The officiating clergy were Revd. Wykansky (Chazan) and Revd. Woolfson (minister). Miraculously, the windows survived the blasts of heavy bombing in WW2.

The synagogue was originally built with a seating capacity of 142 to allow for future growth. The interior woodwork is all made from pine, as are the handmade benches which have been lightly varnished to give a softer look. During the restoration of the 1960s, the craftsman noted that none of the benches are screwed or nailed, but plugged together with pieces of dowel, the method typically used by shipwrights in the 18th century. This led him to suggest that they were made by carpenters from Plymouth dock.[39] On the east wall, forming the centrepiece of the sanctuary, is the ornate gold, white and blue Ark. It is the original Ark from 1762, probably imported from Germany, the cost of which was borne by Mordecai ben Yehiel who gave £33 for its purchase. It has undergone some restoration over the centuries. When restored in 1965, the architect wrote:

> 'The great Ark which closely resembles the one in the old Synagogue in Venice, with its pediment cartouche at the top, its beautiful cornice and carved decorations in the Roman Corinthian order, was completely covered with silver and gold leaf. The columns, capitals, cornices, flowers and mouldings were all in gold leaf, while the plain surfaces which are now painted dull red, were in silver leaf.'[40]

From the secluded courtyard, stone steps lead into the synagogue lobby where a number of plaques on the walls commemorate key markers in the community's history and the generous contributions of particular members of the community to synagogue funds. There are also two framed Rolls of Honour for members of the congregation who fought in the First World War and Second World War. The synagogue has several stained-glassed windows, which were not part of the original build of 1762, and dedicated to the memory of former members. The two great arched windows on either side of the Ark were installed by an old firm of Plymouth glaziers *Osborne & Co* of York Street and donated in memory of Israel and Rachel Roseman and Myer and Rebecca Fredman. After their installation, the windows

Prayer for the Royal Family inside the synagogue

---

[39] Sharman Kadish, *Jewish Heritage in England*, p. 90.
[40] Susser, p.132.

Ladies gallery

The central *bimah* (or dias), also of pine, is topped with eight electric candlesticks, replicas of those of Bevis Marks Synagogue in London. The Prayer for the Royal Family which hangs on the back wall is unique in England. Although it names King George V and Queen Mary, its date is deceptive. Over the centuries it has been over-painted and in fact dates to the foundation of the synagogue in 1762. The first monarchs named were William IV and Adelaide, and as such, it is one of the oldest extant Prayers for the Royal Family in any synagogue in the United Kingdom. It was purchased with a donation of 8 guineas from Mordecai ben Yehiel. Upstairs is the ladies gallery, originally built only across the west wall. In 1807, iron pillars were added below to support it. The gallery was enlarged along the north and south walls in 1863, thanks to the generosity of Leon Solomon. Although the community is small today, it is still used by the ladies during worship. Also upstairs is the communal *succah* which is decorated with greenery and fruit during the Festival of Succot, or Tabernacles. This temporary shelter is a reminder of the Israelites' time in the wilderness. A communal *succah* in Plymouth is first mentioned in 1884. It too has stained glass windows.

Deeds and Leases

A number of Deeds and Legal Documents relating to the Hebrew Congregation have survived and are now in the Plymouth & West Devon Record Office. The earliest lease is dated 1st and 2nd February 1721 and related to the garden plot on the Hoe, leased from Benouad to Jones. The next is dated 20 and 21 September 1725, a lease from Jones & Anor to Goulding. The third is dated 6 and 7 May 1726, leased from Benouad to Daggat. Another lease exists for 6 and 7 October 1732, released from Goulding to Cearn. A lease dated 30 August 1742, relates to a plot of land for the building of a synagogue. The land was leased by the Mayor and Commonality of Plymouth to George Marshall:

> 'A plot or piece of ground formerly a messuage or tenement and garden in ... St. Catherine's Lane ... bounded on the east by the lane; on the west by lands of the Mayor and Commonality; on the north by land of the Hospital of Poor's portion; on the south by lands of High Cornish, with liberty to convert the premises into a garden for 99 years, in the lives of George Marshall, Elizabeth, his wife, and John Marshall, their son. Rent five shillings per annum.'[41]

Nothing appears to have been built for twenty years between the lease of 1742 and a Deed of Trust of 1762. However, the fact that the Jews were acquiring land for a permanent place of worship back in 1742 suggests that they were well-established in the city earlier than this and had sufficient numbers to warrant it. Traditionally, historians have argued that the community began in the 1740s. A case can be made for much earlier, possibly as early as 1720s when Jews settled also in other parts of Devon and Cornwall. A growth in numbers by 1759, brought an urgency to the quest to construct a permanent place of worship in Plymouth. On 27 April 1762, a Deed

---
[41] Doris Black, *The Plymouth Synagogue 1761-1961*.

of Trust was granted on a piece of land in St Katherin's Lane by the Mayor and City to a non-Jew, Samuel Chapman, who was acting on behalf of Joseph Sherrenbeck and Gompert Michael Emden, described as 'the elders of the Synagogue of the Jews'. The lease stated that the land was to 'erect or build any houses or edifices thereon'. It was granted for 99 years on the deaths of George and John Marshall and Joseph Jacob Sherrenbeck for an annual rent of £2 12s. 0d. The sum of £300 was raised on a mortgage from Mrs Elizabeth Aven of Plympton to 'complete the buildings and edifices and erections now building and erecting thereon and which is designed for a Jewish Synagogue or place of worship for those persons professing Judaism'. It was now the mid-1700s and as yet there was no Devonport Dockyard as such. The town centre as known today did not exist and the synagogue was built on marshy land in a salubrious area at the back of the town. There was no decent view or beautiful surroundings, yet the Jews were grateful to acquire any plot to build a place of worship. Ironically, today the synagogue stands on prime real-estate just a stone's throw from the main city centre and the historic Hoe and Barbican. According to communal records the synagogue was completed in 1762. The name of the original architect is unknown, although it was likely to have been a local master-builder and possibly one who had erected non-Conformist chapels. Two years before its completion, Joseph Sherrenbeck had donated £52 in 1760 and a further £30 on Passover and Festival of Tabernacles. He also contributed £10. 10s. 3d. for the cost of the platform in front of the Ark.

By 1770, the congregation was unable to pay even the interest due on the original mortgage of £300 from Mrs Aven. She had passed away and a non-Jew, Mr Christopher Harris, had taken over the debt owed. On 26 January 1770, a mortgage on the land was transferred to Harris, acting on behalf of local Jews Jacob Sherrenbeck (gentleman) of East Stonehouse, Lyon Homberg (Merchant) of Plymouth, Hyam Lazarus (shopkeeper) of Stoke Damerel, Joseph Joseph (shopkeeper) and Samuel Hart (silversmith). The mortgage was finally paid off thirteen years later on 19 April 1783. Doubts still simmered over the legality of Jews owning land in the 1780s, even for a place of worship. In 1786, the lease was surrendered and a new one was taken out in the name of five Protestants, held in trust for Abraham Joseph 'of the Hebrew Congregation'. In 1797, another 99-year lease was granted to Henry Hart (silversmith), Joseph Joseph (shopkeeper) and Samuel Hart (silversmith) on payment of £30, granted on the lives of Robert Fuge, Levi Nathan and Henry Joseph at an annual rent of £2 12s. 0d.

At a meeting on 8 November 1812, the Vestry committee decided that the deeds of the synagogue should be held in trust for the Vestry members. The Vestry members were Michael Hart [Yehiel ben Zvi], Sander Alexander, Abraham ben Menahem, Judah Ralph, David

Indenture on the synagogue, 1834. NATIONAL ARCHIVES

Abraham, Abraham Levy, Lion Levi, Zenvel ben Abraham Isaac, Benjamin ben Samuel and Phineas ben Judah. It was decided that five trustees should be appointed to act for the whole congregation, and they were Michael Hart, Alexander ben Abraham, Abraham ben Menahem, Simhah ben Isaac and Benjamin ben Samuel. The Minute Book entry noted: 'so that the property of the synagogue shall belong to the whole congregation for all generations so that no other person can claim or have any rights in the synagogue but the property of the synagogue belongs to all the congregation everybody equally.'[42] The original and new deeds for the synagogue were held for safe-keeping by Michael Hart during his time as president. Difficulty arose when he was no longer president. The Vestry asked him to return the deeds, but he replied that he no longer had them. The Vestry committee gave him one week's notice to deliver the deeds or face court action. The outcome must have been favourable because no court action appears to have ensued. In August 1834, the Mayor and Corporation of Plymouth transferred the freehold of the land to the Jewish community for the sum of £100 in the name of seven trustees of the synagogue. They were Joseph Joseph, Samuel Hart, Phineas Levi, Charles Marks, J. Lyon, Lewis Jacobs and Samuel Mordecai Levi. At a Vestry meeting a couple of months later, a select committee was elected to alter and amend the rules of the Congregation. That committee consisted of Phineas Levi (President), L. Solomon (Treasurer), A. Joseph (Hon. Secretary), Solomon Lyons, Abraham Levi, Charles Marks, J. Mandovsky and Samuel Levi.

The final surviving indenture is dated 16 July 1873, for a piece of land amounting to 656 square feet situated on the eastern side of the synagogue that had been the site of

---

[42] Vestry meeting, 22 November 1812.

the public workhouse. For a sum of £300, the Mayor and Corporation of Plymouth conveyed this extension to the synagogue trustees: Hyman Hyman, Eliezer Emden, Edwin Wolf, Abraham Levy, Moses Rosenberg and Aaron Wolf. During the 1890s, the Borough Authorities cut a new sewer through the lane adjoining the synagogue. The work caused subsidence to the foundations of the synagogue and cracking in its walls. Legal action ensued. On 28 March 1893, an Arbitrators' Award was granted in favour of the Jewish community for damage to the synagogue and Vestry House. A formal Deed of the Settlement was drawn up between the Mayor and Burgesses of the City of Plymouth and the Hebrew Congregation, represented by Asher Levy, Eleazar Orgel and Myer Fredman. The community was awarded £350 to carry out the necessary repairs and for the diversion and laying of new drains to the Vestry House.

Renovation and Restoration

One of the earliest known repairs to the synagogue took place in 1795, just thirty-three years after its construction. No details have survived about the work undertaken. In 1805, further repairs were carried out which brought pledges of £141 from eighty-seven people. The largest donations came from Joseph Joseph who gave £40 6s. and Abraham Emanuel who gave £20. 4s. Interestingly, amongst the donors were seven widows and an unmarried woman. By 1806, the congregation appeared to have been £120 short to pay the repair bill to the builders. It was therefore agreed by the Vestry committee to take out a loan in their names for a year. This was necessary because one member, Judah ben Moses, had refused to give his signature to release funds from stocks held by the congregation. The following year, the synagogue was repainted after Pentecost and four iron pillars added to the main sanctuary. In 1811, additional seating for children was added along the west wall. Repairs to the synagogue in 1813 brought in pledges of £160. 1s. from twenty-six donors.

The first major restoration of the synagogue took place in 1863 when Leon Solomon paid for its redecoration out of his own pocket. As mentioned above, he also extended the ladies gallery. Repairs were carried out again in 1894 at a cost of around £400, the cost of which was largely borne by the Corporation of Plymouth from the Arbitrator's Award. A re-consecration service was held, led by Chief Rabbi Adler, who came from London for a few days to lead services. They stayed at the Grand Hotel in Plymouth and, that evening, were guests at dinner at the home of Eleazer Orgel, president of the congregation. The consecration ceremony was assisted by Revd. E. Jaffe and J. Posner, attended by the Mayors of Devonport and Plymouth. Chief Rabbi Adler also inspected the Jacob Nathan School and complimented the master, Mr. J. Goldston, on the results. On Monday, the Chief Rabbi and his wife were taken on a private tour of the mansion and grounds of the Earl of Edgecumbe's estate. After lunch at the Orgel's, they were escorted to North Road Station, where quite a crowd turned out to see them off. It included Revd. Jaffe, J. Posner, Mr. J. Goldston and the pupils of the Jacob Nathan School, Mr and Mrs Lewis, Mr. Conick, and Mr and Mrs Asher Levy. Miss Freda Levy presented Mrs Adler with a large basket of flowers. The visit had done much to gain the respect of the local Christian population.[43]

In 1870, Katherin's Lane was widened and became known as Catherine Street. There were changes as a result. Synagogue House/Vestry was built (see below), and the caretaker's residence was moved from the eastern wall to Synagogue House. During 1909/1910, further repairs were overseen by the president Tobias Brand, Secretary Mr Hershell Orgel, and Myer Fredman (Burial Warden). These renovations included the installation of electric lighting and new ventilating shafts. On Sunday 27 February 1910, the synagogue was reconsecrated. The *Western Morning News* reported:

> 'With solemn and picturesque ceremonial, the synagogue in Catherine Street was yesterday reconsecrated after extensive renovation. Internally a scheme of decoration in white has been introduced, brightened by the adornment of its ark in more striking colours – gold and red... While the synagogue was in the builders' hands, the Scrolls of the Law were removed to a place of safety, and the chief feature of the re-consecration service was the restoration of the treasured writings to their original place in the Ark. The scrolls were brought to the door of the synagogue by elders of the congregation – fourteen elders each carried a scroll and to the Hebrew chanting of Revd. A. K. Slavinsky and the choir under Mr. Ellis – they were carried to the ark. The procession walked round the synagogue seven times, singing Psalms, and the ark then being opened, the scrolls were deposited within.'

A sermon calling for a deepening of religious fervour was given by Revd. D Jacobs who served the congregation from 1903 to 1912. Afterwards a reception was held at the home of the President and Mrs Brand.

The communal succah

Synagogue House and Jacob Nathan School

Opposite the entrance to the synagogue is the Victorian Synagogue House or Vestry. Constructed in 1874, it was used to house the rabbi/minister on the first floor, the caretaker flat on the second, and religion school on the ground floor. The original Vestry House had been built in 1808 and located on the eastern side of the synagogue in Catherine Street itself.[44] When Catherine Street was widened in 1870, the house and site of 1808 were exchanged with the Corporation of Plymouth for the current site of the Vestry House. Over the years, the current Vestry has needed substantial repairs that have matched those undertaken on the synagogue. In 1963, a surveyor's report from *W. Roseveare & Son* of Tavistock Road confirmed

---

[43] Jewish Chronicle, 23 March 1894.
[44] The decision to build a new Vestry House was made at a meeting on 23 October 1808.

structural work was necessary to the outside of the Vestry that would amount to between £1,400 and £1,600. The cost included repairs to the slate roof, loose brickwork on the north gable which had several bricks missing, some roof timbers had been attacked by woodworm, and joints of the gutters needed tightening to make watertight. Rotten window sills needed attention, as did the lintel to second floor window which was cracked and displaced. Most of the external walls needed render work and the external paintwork was generally in a bad condition.

Founded 1869, the Jacob Nathan School moved into the Vestry/ Synagogue House from its original address at 69 Well Street.[45] The school provided a Jewish education in Hebrew and scripture for local Jewish children over the age of five. A charity attached to the school gave aid to poor Jewish children from a fund of £200, including provision for clothing. In the will, Jacob Nathan bequeathed a house in Hoe Street as a residence for the school master, who at the time was Mr. Congdon. Nathan's cousin, Abraham Ralph, was named overseer of the property. The bequest provided a sum of £600, free of duty, for the establishment of the Jacob Nathan School and a further £3,000 for its maintenance and support of teachers. In an indenture dated 8 September 1868, the trustees purchased a piece of land of 1,180 square feet in Well Street 'with the dwelling-house thereon' for the sum of £420, conveyed to Abraham Ralph and two others (and their heirs). The residue of money was invested in £300 of National War Loan Stock, overseen by trustee Asher Levy. The house in Hoe Street was later sold. The school master moved into Synagogue House. By the 1891 census, the school master was listed as Joseph Goldston (b. 1862), unmarried. He married Ida Levisohn in the Bayswater Synagogue and, on 22 March 1895, Ida gave birth to a daughter.

The Jacob Nathan School had its own set of rules, a copy of which survives in the synagogue archives. The school committee consisted of five trustees and five elected representatives from the congregation. Each member was required to visit the school at least once a year to see that it was being properly attended. It was ruled that children of non-members could not be admitted unless approved by the congregation. In terms of the curriculum: 'the teacher shall submit to the Chairman, seven days before the beginning of each term, a written curriculum for the ensuing term, based on the syllabus recommended by the Jewish Board of Education.' In 1895, the school regulatory committee consisted of the following members: Abraham Cohen of 45 Frankfort Street, Abraham Conick of Tavistock Road, Abraham Titlebaum (photographer) of 6 Exeter Street, Mr. J. Jacobs of 38 High Street, Elias Ellis of Russell Street, Mr. J. Maunchester of 17 Lisson Grove, Tobias Brand of Union Street, Mr. I. Lazarus of 65 Union Street and Myer Isaac Roseman of 44 Marlborough Street. Everything was not necessarily running smoothly because after the prize-giving in 1889, distributed by president Mr

Plaque on outside of Vestry House

Pupils of Plymouth Synagogue Hebrew classes visited by Herbert Adler, with Revd Zeffert, Maurice Sanger and Mr. Solomon

J. Cohen, Mr S. Friedlander gave a vote of thanks in which he 'emphatically condemned the apathy with which the school was regarded, and announced that unless more help was forthcoming the Hebrew and religious education of the Jewish children in Plymouth would have to be discontinued.'[46] The school continued, and a list survives of the children attending in 1897. They were Annie Fredman, Annie Cohen, Isaac Roseman, Mordecai Weinberg, A. Brand, Huish Orgel, Israel Fredman, Bertie Roseman, Montie Cohen, Joseph Roseman, Colman Orgel, Shiel Orgel, Montie Jacobs, Morrice Cohen, Rosie Fredman, Jacob Posener, Herman Cohen, Jacob Lewis, Leah Lewis, Miriam Orgel, John Lichterman, J. Conick, Beatie Roseman, Bertie Woolf, Minnie Teitelbaum (sic), Lewis Fredman, Nathaniel Feather, Pol Feather, Lilly Cohen, Tilly Orgel and Solly Orgel.

---

[45] Susser, p. 135.
[46] Jewish Chronicle, 22 March 1889.

By 1918, it was necessary to draw up a legal agreement between the trustees because of ongoing difficulties over the school. The trustees were Asher Levy, Herschell Orgel, Charles Brock (all of London) and Arthur Brand and Abraham Robins of Plymouth. The new agreement allowed for the formation of a committee consisting of the trustees and five members of the Hebrew Congregation to ensure the school remained open every day except Shabbat and holidays. The committee was responsible for appointing a Head Teacher who might also be the minister of the congregation. Clause 7 of the Agreement stated: 'The name of Jacob Nathan shall be incorporated in, or connected with, the name of the School, and the anniversary of his death shall be commemorated by the scholars attending a Special Service at the Plymouth synagogue.' Clause 8 stated that: 'in view of the many benefits conferred by the late Jacob Nathan, not only on the Jewish Community, but on many other local and other charities, the Vestry shall keep in good order and repair the grave and tombstone of the late Jacob Nathan at the Old Jewish Cemetery Plymouth.' Today, there is no functioning school. The Vestry House has the caretaker's flat, plus another flat for a visiting rabbi and his family. The ground floor is used for meetings and Kiddush after the Shabbat service.

Mikveh

The earliest reference to a mikveh, or ritual bath, in Plymouth is 1821. Known as 'mikveh house', it is referenced in the Plymouth Minute Book II and the Chief Rabbi's archives for 1833 and 1854. It was originally located under the current Guildhall, but had to close. From 1910, the Corporation of Plymouth agreed to the congregation paying £50 to build a mikveh at the Public Baths, for which the community paid £25 per annum for its use. This mikveh fell into disuse and was abandoned. A mikveh was then built at the back of the Vestry. It used running water from an underground spring rather than rainwater (as is traditional). It was renovated by Revd. Alec Ginsburg during his ministry, but again, later, fell into disuse. For decades afterwards, it was a dumping ground for all kinds of rubbish and remained boarded over. In the last few years, it has been fully restored and, although it is not in use for ritual purposes, can now be viewed by visitors.

Artefacts and Ritual Silver

The synagogue once possessed some of the finest pieces of ceremonial silver. In recent years, much has been auctioned to raise funds, and the other pieces remain in a bank vault. According to a roughly compiled list, the congregation once had a silver bowl and jug donated in 1808 by Libra, widow of Joshua Levi Hacohen (priest), as a mark of appreciation to the congregation for burying her son after his body was brought back from Maderia;[47] 1 set of rimmonim (bells) with plush crowns (1808) and another set of rimmonim, hallmarked 1783-4 with maker's mark 'I.R', described as: 'in English style with alternately concave and convex fluting in its layers, surmounted by crowns with a red velvet cushion in the style of secular beadles' and sheriffs' staves of the City of London.'[48] A set of silver rimmonim were given by Abraham Joseph I with the inscription: 'a pair of Aaron silver bells and plate thereto belonging shall never be sold or alienated from my family.' There was a silver Kiddush cup, hallmarked London 1755-6, and given by Joseph Joseph in 1775 when he was only nine years old, now in the possession of Elkan Levy. In 1798, Joseph Joseph donated a curtain for the Ark, a small cover and two golden Meils.[49] Another Kiddush cup (undated) was given by Joseph the son of Abrali Yziav in 1835, and a set of filigree bells from Edward Basch in 1902. A silver shield, 7 inches by 5 inches, dated 4 Sivan 5544 [May 1784], contains the names of nine Vestry members and is thought to commemorate the completion of works. The names are:[50]

Yechiel son of Zvi,
David son of Solomon
Asher son of Zvi
Alexander son of Abraham
Samuel son of Zvi
Yosef son of Abraham
Judah son of Samson

Mikveh

---

[47] Hallmarked SH = Simon Harris.
[48] Evelyn Friedlander, p.73.
[49] Minute Book entry, 23 October 1808.
[50] Translation by Rabbi David Katanka.

Above left: *Silver Kiddush cup, hallmarked 1755/6, now in the possession of Elkan Levy*

Above right: *Silver plaque with names of nine vestry members, 1784*

Left: *Silver rimmonim, 1783,* COURTESY OF EVELYN FRIEDLANDER

Asher son of Abraham Zvi
(on right hand side) work was finished Sivan 4th 5524
(left hand side) Samuel son of Zvi and Jacob son of Mordecai.

The same names appeared on a silver pointer, also dated 1784. Amongst other early ritual silver was an elegant pointer from 1765, belonging to Abraham Joseph I; also another pointer 11 inches long with an inscription which suggests that it was made in 1782 by Judah, the son of Abraham Ralph of Barnstaple, who eventually settled in Plymouth and was active in synagogue life. Another pointer of the same length, with a London Assay mark, was a gift from Samuel Hart in 1814.

In 1832, a silver *Cohenim* (priest) bowl was given by Phoebe Aaron, daughter of Abraham Joseph I, because her son had survived the cholera epidemic which had claimed the lives of other members of the community. In 1887, a breastplate was given to the congregation by Alexander Jacobs, son of Nathan Jacobs of Dartmouth. In 1892, Mr I. Goldman gave a breastplate with a musical motif. In 1914, Mrs E. Cohen donated a two-tier set of rimmonim with eagles. In 1924, an oil painting of the synagogue was presented to the community by Mr T. Abrahams of Devonport, but its whereabouts is now unknown. Another set of rimmonim and a breastplate were given by Mrs H. Cohen and Mr D. Fredman in 1925. A pair of silver bells were given by Myer Roseman in 1932. Other donations included: a pair of Venetian candlesticks given by Mrs King Field, a large Chanukia from the Roseman family in 1960, and a Megillah (Scroll of Esther) in a silver case from Bettie Gordon, Neville Peck and Henry Peck, donated in 1962 in memory of their parents Mr and Mrs Caple Peck. Mr & Mrs J. Sanger donated a silver salver in 1926, Mr D. Greenburgh gave a pointer and breastplate in 1937, and Mr and Mrs R. Robins gave a three-branch candlestick in 1966. A Kiddush cup was donated by the Aloof family in 1963. By the 1960s, the congregation had 12 ceremonial mantels for the Torah scrolls, not all of them in good condition, 3 sets of red/white/blue satin Ark curtains, two sets of red/white covers for the *bimah* (dias), two sets of matching desk covers, and one *chuppah* (canopy) for weddings.

In 1998, a survey of the silver and textiles was carried out by Evelyn Friedlander and the author, and a list

Mappah, 1842, COURTESY OF EVELYN FRIEDLANDER

Old Pinkas

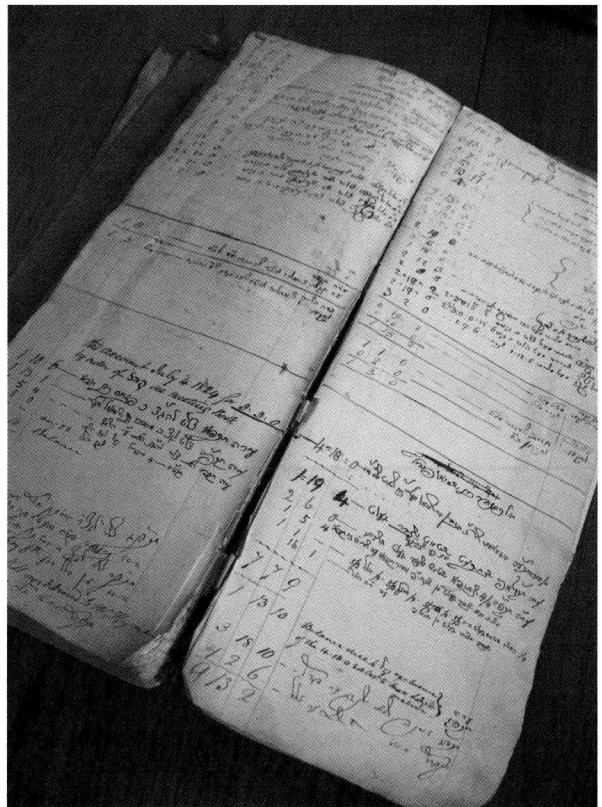

Page from the old Pinkas

Silver pointer, no maker, 1783

compiled. The community possessed a Torah mantle dating to 1902, given by the women of the synagogue, another mantle dating to 1939, and another with no date, inscribed with the words: 'Shimshon ben Schmuel and his wife Sheina of blessed memory with love from their sons and daughters'. There was a three-piece set with 1 blue *mappah* (cover), 1 blue mantle with Star of David and crown, and 1 blue Ark curtain with 2 lions and a crown, dating to 1923, and embroidered with the words: 'Given by the important women of Plymouth.' The set was made by R. Mazin & Co of Whitechapel Road, London. There were also two white Torah mantles, both given in 1954 [5714] in memory of Morris Richman by his family, plus 1 red mantle with bright yellow lions, a crown and Star of David which once belonged to the Torquay Hebrew Congregation.

The congregation possesses an old *Pinkas* (ledger) dating from 1760-1826, written in Judeo-German in Ashkenazi cursive script with occasional English. The first part is an alphabetical list of names of members of the congregation, many of whom are identified by the places where they lived. The next pages contain the names of those being called up to read from the Torah on High Holy Days and festivals, followed by a list of pledges to various charities for the years 1760 to 1826. The community also possesses a beautiful *siddur* (prayer book) dating to 1805 with an ornately inscribed frontispiece. In translation from the Hebrew it reads: 'Order of prayer and praise for Sabbath and Festivals, to give thanks to God, present of Joseph the ruler (chieftain) to the lovely city of Plymouth in the year 5565 [1805].' Underneath is another Hebrew inscription which reads in translation: 'This was done by Jacob Segal for the glory/honour of his friend, leader Joseph son of Abraham, Head and leader of Plymouth: "We will sing and praise His might". It was a gift to the community from Joseph Joseph. There are numerous different scripts and handwritings throughout.

In the 1970s, Bernard Susser carried out a survey of the Torah scrolls in the synagogue. He noted that there were then fifteen scrolls, all in differing conditions. Some were beyond repair, torn or faded and may well have since been buried. One scroll was described as a' beautifully written miniature Sefer, typically 18th century, with traces of a label of who had donated it'. Susser suggested that it had probably once belonged to either Joseph Jacob Sherrenbeck or Abraham Joseph I. When Abraham Joseph I died, he was known to have bequeathed the oldest of his scrolls to the synagogue. Another scroll, although faded and the ink not in good condition, had an interesting inscription on both Etz Hayyims (wooden rollers):

"וה' ברך את אברהם בכל" הוא הנדיב הספר התורה
הזאת לבנו הבחור החשוב יהודה לייב בן אברהם
לרשותו ולא לרשות אחרים בשנת "עץ חיים היא
למחזיקים בה ותמכיה מא·ש·ר· לפ"ק

It reads in translation: 'And the Lord blessed Abraham with everything. He it is that bestowed this Sefer Torah to his son, the bachelor, the worthy Judah Leib b. Abraham into his possession and not into the possession of others, in the year *It is a tree of life to those that take hold of it, and those that seize it are happy* [1780/1]'. This scroll appears to have belonged to Abraham Ralph I of Barnstaple and used for synagogue services which he held in a room in his house for over forty years until his death in 1805. His immediate descendants lived in Plymouth, were members of the synagogue and donated the scroll after his death. It is believed that Abraham Ralph I is buried in the old Jewish cemetery on the Hoe, although no tombstone or record of the burial survives today.[51] The congregation was given a pointer in memory of his son, Judah Ralph, with the inscription: 'A gift of the hand to the memory of Yehuda son of Abraham from Barnstaple in the year 5442.'[52]

The earliest mention of any scrolls was in a mortgage deed dated 26 January 1770 which lists three scrolls in the property of Joseph Jacob Sherrenbeck; two of which he left to the synagogue. These may not have been in usable condition because by 1782, Hirsch Nathan felt it necessary to lend his scroll to the community. Within a month, the congregation raised £18 by public subscription to purchase a new scroll. In 1819, Abraham and Menachem Cohen each presented the synagogue with a scroll, and later Abraham Emanuel also loaned a scroll. In 1892, the congregation possessed twelve large scrolls and three small ones.[53] One of these scrolls had been loaned to the Dock Minyan in 1814. Another scroll was given by Myer Fredman with an inscription on the silver bands of the wooden rollers: 'Presented to Plymouth Hebrew Congregation by Alderman Myer Fredman J. P. 25 Jan 1925, Teves 5685.'

One of the oldest scrolls held by the community, but not in a useable condition, was a family scroll given by Lord

Silver breastplate given in memory of Myer and Rebecca Fredman

Scroll of Esther once belonging to the Lopes family,
COURTESY VALERIE MELLOR

Roborough, descendant of Menasseh Massah Lopes. Lopes had abandoned his Judaism in 1802 to enter politics (Jews not then being permitted to become MPs). It is thought that the Roborough Scroll originated from Venice and dates to 1722. Only three fragments survive today from a tiny scroll written by Revd. Abraham Spier during his time as minister of the Plymouth Synagogue and used during services. First mention of it appeared in the Jewish Chronicle in 1892:

> 'The Torah is of an extraordinarily small size, and measures five and a half inches in height. The columns are three and a half inches long by one and

---

[51] It is likely that he is buried in Plymouth.
[52] It was sold in Bonham's auction along with other items of Plymouth synagogue silver in 2009.
[53] The synagogue also once had two Olive wood yadim [pointers] which have since been lost.

a quarter wide. Notwithstanding its diminutive size and the extreme smallness of the letters, it is so written that it can be read without the slightest difficulty. The weight of the Sepher is one pound six ounces. Mr Spiers is to be congratulated on his work, which must have entailed a large amount of trouble.'[54]

The rest of the scroll has disappeared, but the fragments have been returned to Plymouth synagogue.

Synagogue Life

Surviving Minute Books offer an insight into the life of the community. At a meeting on 15 October 1794, it was agreed that if a Vestry member does not live in the community he must pay 5 shillings a year to hold his membership. By 1797, the congregation had a religion school with a membership of 23 children. It ran from 9am till 12 noon, and 1pm until 4pm, except on Shabbat or Festivals. An entry for Sunday 10th Ellul 5539 [1779] shows that the community sent a significant sum of money to the war effort for Britain's part in the French Revolutionary Wars:

'All the vestry were gathered and it was agreed together with the President Joseph Sherrenbeck and three men that the vestry should give a donation of £50 to the Mayor at the Guildhall for the war. And everyone shall pay immediately what they have promised.'

To put this war contribution in perspective, Plymouth's Rabbi did not receive £50 in annual salary until 1816, so this amount given to the war effort seventeen years earlier in 1799 was more than the Rabbi's annual salary. The congregation upheld its responsibility towards the poor. A meeting in February 1816 agreed that 'when a poor man shall be in the workhouse, the Honorary Officers of the congregation must not allow him to remain there without the knowledge of a meeting of the Vestry.' The Minute Books record how the community made special provisions for Passover. It was the responsibility of the officers to ensured that there was enough flour and suitable utensils to make *matzot* (unleavened bread) locally. For the next twenty-two years, the community baked its *matzot* locally at 7½d. per pound, baked over two days. As Susser noted, everyone with a seat on the right hand side of the synagogue helped with the baking on the first day, and everyone with a seat on the left helped on the second day.

Rededication of the Synagogue, Chief Rabbi Brodie with Rabbi Bernard Susser and Revd. Alec Ginsburg, 1965

---

[54] Jewish Chronicle, 8 April 1892.

Above: *The Chief Rabbi meets the children of the religion school*

Right: *Visit of Chief Rabbi Brodie, 1965*

Anyone who needed *matzot* but had not helped bake it was fined 2s. 6d. per pound. It seemed to work until 1803 when the baking was not very successful and the community decided to bring *matzot* down from London. This did not last long because the brittle *matzot* broke during the long journey to Plymouth. In 1805, it was decided to allocate the baking to Abraham ben Isaac and brothers Eleazer and Phineas Emdon. The Emdon brothers successfully baked it for over thirty years.

Over the years, the synagogue has seen a number of disagreements between members. The 1779 regulations made provision for the settlement of such disputes: 'They shall not go to the Gentile courts but it shall be dealt with by our vestry here. If the matter is difficult then they should bring it to the Priest, the Head of the Beth Din, the Gaon of the Great Synagogue.' The first recorded disturbance in the synagogue was recorded in the Minute Book for 20 July 1800. Simha ben Isaac 'made a great disturbance at the time of the reading of the law and insulted the Parnas [President] and Gabbai Zedakah.' It was decided at a meeting of Vestry members to exclude Isaac for six months from being called up to read the Torah. In 1804, Vestry members ruled that if two men in the community had a disagreement that could not be resolved, they were to seek arbitration from one of the two presidents of the Great Synagogue (London), or the vestry of the Portsmouth or Exeter synagogue. It gives an insight into the closeness of these communities. The Minute Book records another disturbance on in May 1817 when Samuel ben Alexander insulted the president in the synagogue and street 'for which the Vestry has fined him and directed him to beg forgiveness of the president of the synagogue. He shall not be allowed to take part in any religious duty until he has done so.' In September 1856, another unfortunate fracas broke out during worship which resulted in certain members being called before the local magistrates.[55] It centred around treasurer Josiah Solomon and four other members: Joseph Joseph, Hyman Hyman, Wolf Emden and Abraham Ralph. The four men were asked to explain why they had broken the peace with Josiah Solomon. Explaining the circumstances, Josiah Solomon said that, as treasurer, he acted from time-to-time in place of the president when he was absent. During the Shabbat

---

[55] Jewish Chronicle, 12 September 1856.

morning service, he was officiating with Rabbi Myer Stadthagen because the president was absent. It fell to Josiah Solomon to select eight men to be called up to read a portion of the Torah. The last man to be called up was Joseph Roborichkey, at which point Hyman Hyman called out: 'Shame, iron-hearted fellow, tyrant.' Other cries were used against the treasurer. Hyman then called him, 'a dirty fellow and dirty tyrant. I'll kick you out. I'll drag you out. I suppose you didn't intend to call me!' A great noise and confusion followed, which resulted in Stadthagen suspending the service for twenty minutes. Josiah feared that he might be physically attacked so he removed himself from the building. The parties eventually settled out of court and harmonious relations were returned to the community by appointing Jacob Nathan as president.

Another dispute was reported in the Jewish Chronicle when, in March 1857, the newspaper printed a public apology from Edward [Ephraim] Basch of Whimple Street (Plymouth) to Hyman Hyman which read:

> 'Edward Basch do hereby express my sincere regret that I should at the election of officers in the Plymouth synagogue have used expressions reflecting on your character. I readily confess that I had no grounds whatever for the statement I then made, which was utterly untrue and unfounded.'

The outcome demonstrated a generous approach from Hyman Hyman who agreed to stay the legal proceedings brought against Basch, and paid his own costs which he had incurred as a result. Less than two years later, another incident occurred when Judah Solomon Lyon claimed that on 23 September 1858, the first day of Tabernacles, he was flung from his seat in the synagogue by William Woolf. Subsequently, when Woolf entered the vestry with his sister, Lyon squared his fists at him and shouted, "let me get at him" and seized a candlestick to strike Woolf. The incident was reported in the local press, but hereafter things went quiet again.

The newspapers provide an insight too into religious life and piety. The Jewish Chronicle, for example, noted in October 1884 that Plymouth Synagogue was decorated for the festival of Succoth 'with choice flowers and plants and looked very pretty.'[56] The special service was conducted by Revd. M. Lewis with the Mayors of Devonport and Plymouth in attendance. An address was given by Benjamin Woolf (master of the Jacob Nathan School), followed by tea for the boys. Of the Jewish communities of the South-West, Plymouth has had the closest relationship to the Chief Rabbi in London. In 1808, for example, the congregation sent ten pounds to the Chief Rabbinate and, in 1811, the sum of £15 for the period 1809-1811. Thereafter, they sent ten guineas a year in donation which afforded them the privilege of two votes in the election of a new Chief Rabbi in 1844. The community has also enjoyed a good relationship with its Gentile Christian

Arrival of Chief Rabbi Israel Brodie and Mrs Brodie at Plymouth station, c.1959. COURTESY OF STUART GOODMAN

neighbours who often attended special events at the synagogue. In May 1890, the congregation celebrated the *bar mitzvah* of two boys. The synagogue was reported to be "crowded with Christians".[57] The practice of a *bat mitzvah* (a parallel service for girls) came after WW2. The first *bat mitzvah* recorded by the community was that of Caroline Peck and Andrea Lewis, which took place on 21 June 1964. Another double *bat mitzvah* was held over a decade later on 3 December 1978 for Monique Hirshman and Sharon Aloof.

Until the Second World War, Vestry members wore silk top hats for Sabbath services and festivals. To this day, the Plymouth Hebrew Congregation preserves some beautiful traditions. For example, there is a classical German custom in its worship that, at the end of the service, when the mourners say Kaddish, they come out of their seats and line up between the Ark and the *bimah*, and recite the Mourners Prayer. This custom appears to have fallen into disuse in other Jewish communities. The congregation appears also to be the only one in the United Kingdom that follows the custom of reciting *The Hymn of Unity* from the old prayer book, something which stems from a medieval German custom.

Bequests

The synagogue has had a number of significant bequests in its long history, too numerous to list here. Amongst them, during the 19th century, was the Manley Hart's Gift for the benefit of the Jewish poor, overseen by Aron Wolf, Moses Rosenberg and Solomon Zeferett, and the Phoebe Levi's Gift of £100. Also the Barrow Moss Gift (originally for

---

[56] Jewish Chronicle, 31 October 1884.
[57] Jewish Chronicle, 16 May 1890.

Exhibition of silver from the synagogue, City Art Gallery, May 1961, in the presence of Rabbi Susser, Lord Mayor Arthur Goldberg and Lady Mayoress, and Bertie Black

£38. 17s. 6d) administered by Lewis Hyman, Joseph Joseph, Edward Basch and Samuel Samuels. The Michael Basch Gift of £100 was administered by Abraham Titleboam and Joseph Jacobs. In his will, artist Solomon Hart left the sum of £1,000, the dividends of which were to be paid into the synagogue's general account and managed by Eleazer Emdon, Aaron Lyons, Asher Levy and Herman London. Nathaniel Nathan's Charity directed that income from £100 should be distributed to the Jewish poor of Plymouth. One of the largest legacies ever received came from Jacob Nathan who left a large sum for the synagogue, numerous local non-Jewish charities and national Jewish charities. Two plaques in the lobby of the synagogue commemorate gifts of £500 given by two families in December 1951 towards the Synagogue Restoration Fund. The first was from Jacob Nathan Brock, in memory of his parents Louis and Henrietta Brock. The second was from Mrs Holcenberg in memory of her husband Ephraim Holcenberg.

Marking Royal Occasions

The congregation has always demonstrated a loyalty to the Crown, and celebrated Royal and national events. In 1886, Queen's Victoria's Golden Jubilee was celebrated with a special service in the synagogue, followed by a tea. In June 1897, Queen Victoria's Diamond Jubilee was again marked with a service, attended by the Mayor of Devonport and Stonehouse and many councillors and Aldermen. Half of the congregation that day were reported to be Gentiles. The minister, Revd. Dr Berlin, delivered a sermon in which he praised the virtues of the Queen in the emancipation of the Jews during her reign. It was reported that the sermon and the entire service made an excellent impression.[58] Revd. J. Posner led the choir which had been trained by the president, Mr M. Lewis. The children of the congregation received a commemorative medal and 'enjoyed a sumptuous tea' which had been prepared by Mrs A. Wineberg, Mrs Abrahamson, Mrs Joseph, Mrs Berlin, Miss Titleboam and Miss Shepherd. A congratulatory telegram was sent to Her Majesty. When the new King Edward VII and Queen visited Devonport on 7 and 8 March 1902, the Jewish community was again actively involved. The Corporation of Plymouth erected a grand stand at the entrance of the city to accommodate members of various Public bodies. Amongst the dignitaries were Myer and Israel Fredman, and Miss Fanny Fredman. Seats were given also to the children of the Jacob Nathan School

---

[58] Jewish Chronicle, 25 June 1897.

and their master Mr Goldston.[59]

On 22 June 1911, the congregation celebrated the Coronation of George V and Queen Mary. Other national occasions that were marked by special services were the Restoration of Peace after the Great War and the Armistice Day services. In 1929, prayers were held for the massacre of Jews by Arabs in Hebron and other places. On 11 May 1935, the synagogue marked the Silver Jubilee of George V and, the following year on 28 January 1936, mourned his death. In 1937, it celebrated the Coronation of George VI and Elizabeth. When George VI died in February 1952, a memorial service was held. The following year there was a service to mark the Coronation of Elizabeth II. In 1977, the congregation sent a telegram to Elizabeth II on her Silver Jubilee, which read: 'The Plymouth Hebrew Congregation, the oldest provincial Jewish Community in England, send their loyal greetings to her Majesty and wish her long life.' A reply was received from Buckingham Palace two weeks later and said: 'The Queen sincerely thanks the members of the Plymouth Hebrew Congregation for their kind and loyal message on the occasion of Her Majesty's Silver Jubilee.'

---

[59] Jewish Chronicle, 14 March 1902.

CHAPTER 3
DOCK MINYAN AND DEVONPORT HEBREW CONGREGATION

IN THE HISTORY of Plymouth Jewry, there have been two offshoot congregations in the Dockyard area of the city. The first, known as the 'Dock Minyan', functioned from 1805 until 1844. The second, established around 1890, was called the Devonport Hebrew Congregation. Both functioned as branches of the main synagogue in Catherine Street rather than as autonomous congregations. By 1805, there was a sufficient number of Jews in Devonport to warrant the establishment of a minyan for worship. It had its advantages too because setting up an offshoot place of worship prevented the three mile walk to the main synagogue on Shabbat. There may have been another reason for the formation of the Dock Minyan. Stonehouse is on a peninsula with a bridge known as Stonehouse Bridge, or Ha'penny Bridge (on account of the toll levied for pedestrians to cross it). It is thought that the Dock Minyan was formed to avoid Jews having to pay money to cross it on Shabbat. There is another tradition which says that some Jews paid the toll charge in advance of Shabbat.

For a period of five years, from 1805 to 1810, the main synagogue and Dock Minyan shared the cost of a shochet and Beadle, the cost of which was borne £36 a year by the synagogue and £10 by the Dock Minyan.[60] In 1810, the Dock Minyan appointed its own shochet to provide kosher meat to the Dock's Jewish residents. On 15 July 1810, the matter of the shochet and teacher was brought before a joint meeting of Vestry members of the Plymouth synagogue and members of the Dock Minyan. Mr. Jonas represented the Dock. A formal agreement was agreed by the two congregations, which stated in summary:

1. No misunderstanding would come between the Dock Minyan and the Plymouth Hebrew Congregation

2. The shochet must have a written agreement with the Plymouth Hebrew Congregation but was not officially employed by that congregation. He must reside in Dock area of the city and supply only people in that area with kosher meat

3. The shochet from the Dock must go and slaughter for the congregation of Plymouth one week in every quarter. Likewise the Plymouth

Thought to be the interior of the Dock/Devonport Synagogue

shochet must go and slaughter for the Dock Minyan one week in every quarter

4. The supervision of the shochet in the Dock must be supervised by a committee of five people: four men from the Dock Minyan and the fifth to be the president of the Plymouth Hebrew Congregation. The committee must meet only in the Plymouth Vestry

5. The expenses of the shochet and teacher must be paid by the Dock Minyan

6. If the shochet is qualified to lead prayers on the Days of Awe, he is to lead prayers for the Plymouth synagogue whenever requested and recompensed from the charity box

7. If either shochet of Plymouth or the Dock is unable to carry out his duties because of ill-health the other one is to cover both congregations

---

[60] Entry in the Minute Book, 14 July 1805.

8. The inhabitants of the Dock will carry out its duties regarding charity

9. The Dock Minyan will only conduct evening services, not morning services (with the exception of Yom Kippur)

The agreement was signed by Joseph Joseph on behalf of the Plymouth Hebrew Congregation and Benjamin ben Samuel on behalf of the Dock Minyan, witnessed by Cantor Lima and Chaim Issachar. On 16 September 1810, the men from the Dock Minyan came again to the Plymouth Synagogue to sign a longer version of the articles, sealed by a handshake with Joseph Joseph, the president of the synagogue.

At a joint meeting on 17 February 1811, it was decided that a third shochet should be appointed to serve the needs of both congregations for the slaughter of large and small beasts, and birds. The Dock Minyan agreed to pay the following expenses for the shochet's services: 5s. for a cow, 1s. for a lamb or sheep and 2s. for a calf. Isaac Falk Valentine was appointed as the third shochet, who also carried out financial business for the Joseph family. The following year, Valentine was caught up in a case of premeditated murder when he was enticed to bring £260 to Fowey by an innkeeper, Wyatt. Wyatt proceeded to murder him and dropped him into the water. Later, a roll of wet bank notes were found in the stables at Wyatt's inn.

Siddur, 1805

Plymouth Hebrew Congregation bore the legal costs of the long probate to get the money back, which cost the community over £250 in legal fees. Each member was asked to pay a year's seat money in three installments, thus raising £150. The community was still left with a deficit of around £125 which was raised by appealing to other congregations in England.[61] The Minute Book lists the names of the Vestry members who resolved the Valentine case. They were Joseph Joseph, Abraham Emanuel, Nathan Joseph, Samuel Hart, Sender Alexander, Judah Ralph, David ben Sampson Moses, Joseph ben Judah, Moses Ephraim from Zillig, Menahem Aryeh and Sampson ben Jacob. Wyatt was eventually hanged for the crime at Bodmin. On 30 November 1811, Valentine was buried in the old Jewish cemetery on the Hoe, plot Q24. He was replaced as shochet by Enoch [Zundel ben Zvi] whose condition of employment was a requirement to live in the Dock area and prepare meat for the community. In April 1814, the Vestry committee decided to appoint Enoch to duties of Reader of the Scriptures, at a wage of £40 per annum, exclusive of slaughtering fees.

Members of the Dock Minyan did not require its own separate burial ground. Its members were given the same rights of burial in the old Jewish cemetery on the Hoe as members of the main synagogue. Overseeing the cemetery was a shared responsibility of both congregations. In October 1812, Emanuel Hart [Manasseh ben Zvi] of the Dock Minyan was appointed by the Vestry committee to be one of two treasurers of the Cemetery Fund. The other treasurer was Judah Ralph. On 18 July 1815, supported by Chief Rabbi Hirschell, the two congregations drew up another formal agreement that would essentially ensure that they came together for High Holy Days:

At a meeting of Plymouth and Dock Committee held on Tuesday the 10th July 1815, the following Resolutions were entered into for the regulation of the Dock Minyan by the undersigned, Mr Henry Ralph Nathan:-

Resolved Firstly: That every member of the Dock Establishment shall for the benefit and mutual good of the Plymouth *shool* [synagogue] be obliged to hold a seat at the said *shool*, in default thereof he cannot have a seat in the said Dock Establishment.

Resolved Secondly: Should any resident of Dock now or hereafter have any manner or question of litigation with the Plymouth *shool*, such person cannot be considered a member until the question in point be amicably arranged, nor can he be allowed to receive the honours of the Dock Minyan Room.

Resolved Thirdly: All Mitzvahs and Snoddering [giving to charity], both public and private, contributed by the members of the both Institutions or by any other person or persons whatsoever shall absolutely and bone fide [be conducted on the same lines as those] of Plymouth and the same paid now to their Treasurer at the extension of every three months without any deduction whatsoever.

Resolved Fourthly: That the Dock place of worship be open for the purpose of performing Divine Services every day throughout the year, save

---

[61] Minute Book entry, 7 June 1812.

and except the days of the New Year and the Day of Atonement, when the members of the Dock Institution will cheerfully attend the *shool* at Plymouth.

Resolved Fifthly: That the offering money on High Holy Days be regulated on the same principal as those in the Plymouth *shool*.

Resolved Sixthly: That the "calling up" in the Dock Minyan Room be conducted in a similar plan to that of the Plymouth *shool*.

Resolved Seventhly: That the Treasurer of the Dock Establishment be elected by the general voice of the members of the Establishment, and that every member of the same be considered eligible to vote for the aforesaid.

Resolved Eighthly: That the Elders and Committee of Plymouth *shool* be solicited for the loan of two *Sifrei Torah* with the adornments appended thereto belonging, and that an understanding be given to Plymouth *shool* that in the event of the Dock Establishment ceasing to resolve the *Sifrei Torah* in question should again be returned to them in the like manner they are received.

Eleazar Orgel

A vote of thanks was subsequently offered to Henry Ralph of the Dock Minyan for chairing the meeting. The above resolutions were signed on behalf of the Plymouth Synagogue by Joseph Joseph, S. Alexander, B. Jonas, B. Levy and L. Zageh and on behalf of the Dock Minyan by Henry Ralph, Joseph Levy, Abraham Emanuel and M. Mordecai. It was agreed that these resolutions would be formally put to the whole Plymouth Synagogue on 23 July 1815. Before that happened, another meeting took place on 16 July 1815, at the house of Abraham Emanuel. A vote was taken on whether the main synagogue should loan a Torah scroll to the Dock Minyan. Fifteen men voted for the motion, five against.

The loan of a Torah scroll was formalised at another committee meeting on 23 July. A record exists of the men who attended. On behalf of the Plymouth Synagogue, they were Joseph Joseph, Sender Alexander, Benjamin SGL, Simhah ben Isaac and Judah Ralph. On behalf of the Dock Minyan, they were Joseph ben Judah, Abraham Emanuel, Mordecai ben Samuel SGL and Abraham Ralph I. It was decided that 'the men of the place Dock shall have permission to have a prayer meeting with scrolls according to the resolutions.' In the 1970s, Rabbi Dr Bernard Susser carried out a survey of the scrolls and noted a beautiful scroll that had not ever needed any serious repair. It had the following Hebrew inscription on its wooden rollers:

יום א שהוא יום ד' של חו"ה פסח תקע"ד
קהל פלימוט שלחו ס"ת זו לדאק מנין חדר
חיים שמש

In translation it reads: 'Sunday the 4th Intermediate day of Passover (5)574 the Congregation of Plymouth sent this Sefer to Dock Minyan Room, Hayyim, Shammas. The date of sending was the 10th April 1814.' Susser also discovered a piece of paper rolled around the wooden roller which had an inscription on it and appeared to refer to a second scroll lent to the Dock Minyan. He noted: 'The appearance [of the scroll] is not unlike the 1780/1 inscription. I have tried to read it under Ultra Violet light but with no result. An infra-red photograph may reveal something of interest.' He was never able to solve the inscription.

At the end of the Napoleonic War in 1815, the Plymouth Dock began to assume more importance as a centre of naval affairs. In 1824, the area became the municipality of Devonport, separate from Plymouth. Other Jews began to settle there, and within five years, local Jew Phineas Levi was appointed commissioner at a time when it was unusual for Jews to hold public office. In its heyday, the short length of William Street in Devonport was dominated by naval outfitters, most Jewish-owned. The Dock Minyan finally closed in the mid-19th century, although the reason for its closure is unknown. Did Jews move to a more fashionable part of the city? It is puzzling because the census returns from 1841 show that Jews still populated the dock area. It was formally dissolved in 1844. This is known because of an inscription on the base of a filigree silver spice box which was donated to the main synagogue by Mrs Baruch Moss, for use during *havdalah* at the end of Shabbat.

The Devonport Synagogue

By the 1890s, another minyan appears to have opened in Devonport, probably due to the influx of Jewish immigrants from Eastern Europe and Russia. Worship initially took place in a private house in St. Aubyn Street. The founding fathers were Jacob Greenburgh and son Harry Greenburgh, Hugh Ralph Emdon, Solomon Robins and Hyren Feodor. The Feodor family were amongst the new immigrants who arrived in Plymouth in the 1890s. Hyren Feodor led some of the services for the newly-formed congregation. By the 1901 census, the family had anglicised its surname to Feather. Grandson, Dr Robert Feather, recalls:

Hyren Feather

'Speaking only Russian my grandfather used to row out to Russian ships in the harbour of Plymouth and trade with them. He had only arrived with some gold coins hidden in his belt but it didn't take long before the family started doing quite well, and they acquired a horse and trap. He established a small synagogue and took services.'

The Feather family subsequently moved from Plymouth to the East End and, with tailoring expertise, went into the smutter (rag) trade. Robert's father and brothers (Nathaniel, Morris, Aubrey and Sydney) eventually developed a large chain of outfitters, Scott & Reid, across the UK and built up a multi-million pound business.

By the 1890s, the Devonport congregation had its own religions school which met at 65 George Street (Devonport). A list of children who attended has survived. They were Fannie Fredman, Sarah Robins, Phoebie Robins, Rosie Robins, Reggie Emdon, Bertie Emdon, Athie Abrahamson and Hyman Roseman. The new Devonport congregation had been around for at least a decade, as suggested in an entry in the Jewish Chronicle for 14 August 1903 which pays tribute to the minister who was leaving:

'A largely attended meeting of members of the Congregation was held at the Vestry Room to witness the presentation to the Revd. J Posner & Mrs Posner, prior to leaving after a ministry of ten years. At the request of Abraham Tittleboam (Chairman of the Committee), Mr E. Orgel made the presentation and spoke of the deep regret felt by the Congregation at their departure.'

The congregation generously presented Revd. Posner with a silver spice box, a Kiddush cup and set of inscribed silver fish-knives and forks.

In May 1907, the congregation moved from the makeshift synagogue in St. Aubyn Street to converted premises above a carpenters workshop at 66 Chapel Street, and it officially opened as the Devonport Synagogue.[62] A modest place of worship, it had with a *bimah* and separate area for the women. The late Bert Emdon remembered it:

'Up a rather narrow and steepish flight of stairs over a garage and taxi business [this was the business when he first saw it]. It was all on one level, the ladies section being divided from the gents by a lattice screen. It was a conversion from what had been two residential rooms in a large Victorian terraced house. It owed its existence largely to the Jewish Naval outfitting fraternity and was a very successful conversion. The main synagogue was of very pleasing proportions and was possessed of a very delightful little Ark that had been purpose constructed, and apparently, the Plymouth Ark had been used as a basic design. The same remarks could also apply to the Bimah, or reading desk. The size of the room used had not permitted the construction of a Warden's box. It was also possessed of a number of Torah scrolls, at least three of which were complete with vestments, breastplates and bells, and it also had all the other appurtenances, such as books, Kiddish cups and Megillot (scrolls of Esther) necessary for the functioning of a synagogue. It was also possessed of a number of curtains for the Holy Ark, the one that I best recall was a beautiful red satin velvet and a gift from the Greenburgh family.'[63]

---

[62] Jewish Chronicle, 10 May 1907.
[63] Digest, May 1980.

The first minister was Mr J. Goldston, one-time master of the Jacob Nathan School, who conducted the opening ceremony: 'The scrolls having been deposited in the Ark and the usual prayers said, the minister delivered a sermon in which he said that their firmness and perseverance had triumphed over every hindrance.' It gives the first and only hint that there were difficulties for the congregation in getting a formal, separate synagogue from the main one in Catherine Street. After the consecration, a meeting was held to elect members to the committee. Elected were Mr. J. Greenburgh (President), Mr J. Goldberg (Treasurer), Mr H. Emdon (Hon. Sec), and also Mr J. Abrahams, J. Goldston, S. Chaplain, S. Berg, M. Morris, L. Freeman, O. Bertwick, L. Luddon and Samuel Wolfson.[64] The following year, there was a change in committee. Mr M. Stein was elected President, Solomon Robins as Treasurer and Mr H. R. Emdon as Hon. Secretary. The following year, on 23 March 1908, committee member Samuel Woofson married Leah Cohen of London in the Bayswater Synagogue. Samuel and Leah decided to settle together in Plymouth, and he continued to be active in the life of the Devonport Synagogue.

The Silverstone family were known to be connected to the Devonport congregation. Myer Silverstone, a tailor, and his wife Esther, had a number of children: Ellen, Rebecca, Augusta, Sarah, Louis, Abraham, Harry and Arthur. Esther Silverstone died on 1 February 1922 and Myer on 9 July 1923 at the age of 78. Both are buried in the Gifford Place Jewish cemetery. Their daughter Rebecca married Nathan Charles, a tailor of 36 Cornwall Street (Devonport) on 21 August 1901. The following year, Augusta Silverstone married another tailor, Joel Levy (son of the late Myer Levy). In August 1906, Sarah Silverstone married Louis Michael Jacobs in Oddfellows Hall (Devonport). Sarah was widowed just over a year later on 30 November 1907, her husband aged only 29. Three years later, on 17 August 1910, she married Julius Astley, a tailor from Burton. Marriages of members of the Devonport Synagogue took place under the auspices of the main synagogue and were entered in the Marriage Register for the Plymouth Synagogue, even though the weddings may have taken place in Devonport. Generally, the relationship between the two synagogues was amicable and one of cooperation. This may have been due, in part, to figures like Levin Fredman who forged close links between them. When he died in October 1912, his obituary stated that he had performed the opening ceremony of the Devonport synagogue five years earlier.

In March 1911, the following men were elected to the committee of Devonport Synagogue: Solomon Robins (President), Lewis Joseph (Treasurer) and H. R Emdon (Hon. Secretary). At the AGM the following year, Mr Lewis Joseph was elected President and Samuel Woolfson as Treasurer. In 1913, Mr M. Stein was elected President, Samuel Woolfson as Treasurer and Mr H. Laurence as Honorary Secretary. In March 1916, Nathaniel Jacobs (son of Revd. D. Jacobs of Glasgow) was elected minister.

Ritual Objects

The Devonport Synagogue had a number of items in use for services. In the autumn of 1912, Mr and Mrs Lewis Joseph presented a handsome brocaded silk mantle for the Torah scroll. In September 1914, a consecration service took place for a scroll given by Mrs Ellen Cohen of London. She also donated a silver pointer and pair of rimmonim, with the inscription: 'presented to the Devonport Synagogue by Mrs E Cohen, 13 September 1914.' The service was conducted

Silver spice box from the Dock Minyan.
COURTESY OF BONHAMS

Inscription on the base of the spice box.
COURTESY OF BONHAMS

---

[64] On 23 March 1908, Wolfson of Devonport married Leah Cohen of London in the Bayswater Synagogue.

by Revd. S. A. Slavinsky and A. Sheinrock. Mr R. Triblich preached a sermon in English, and Mr. Ellison in Yiddish. A reception was held afterwards by the then president Solomon Robins.[65] That same autumn, Joseph Goldberg presented the synagogue with a handsome white satin mantle, embroidered with gold lace for use with the new scroll. In June 1919, Mrs G. Robins presented a silver breastplate in memory of her husband. In September 1923, the children of Mr and Mrs Silverstone gave the synagogue a Torah scroll during a service conducted by Revd. Wykansky and Revd. Zeffertt. Jacob E. Ellison, Mr F. Joseph and Mr Solomon also spoke during the service. It was an opportunity to give thanks to Simon Roseman, Joseph Greenburgh and Laurence Cainer for their services to the community thus far. The sum of £8 was collected for the purchase of silver rimmonim. Mrs J. Astley, a daughter of the Silverstones, gave a mantle for the scroll. Two years later, Mrs Astley's eldest son Harry celebrated his *bar mitzvah* in the synagogue. It was one of two known *bar mitzvahs* to take place in the Devonport Synagogue. The other was Reginald Lewis, the only son of Mr and Mrs Joseph Lewis.

At the end of the 1990s, when Evelyn Friedlander undertook a survey of ritual objects and textiles in Plymouth Synagogue, she discovered some of the ritual artefacts from the former Devonport Hebrew Congregation. This included an Ark curtain in cream damask silk and Mantle for Torah scroll, given by Mr and Mrs Myer I. Roseman in March 1915, and another Ark curtain in cream with gold edging presented in 1937 by Esther Bass in memory of her husband Charles.[66] According to the late Bert Emdon, the Devonport Synagogue had three Torah scrolls, one donated by the Greenburgh family, another by the Emdons, and the third belonged originally to the Lopez family (ancestors of Lord Roborough).

Devonport Synagogue in Wartime

During the First World War, the synagogue was conscious of its responsibility to Jewish service personnel in the area. In September 1916, its officers placed an advertisement in the Jewish Chronicle about religious services: 'The minister and the wardens of Devonport Congregation will be pleased to see all Jewish officers and men in the Army and Navy stationed in and around the area at services in the synagogue (66 Chapel Street, Devonport) during the High Festivals.'[67] Many Jewish servicemen participated regularly. For example, an entry in the Jewish Chronicle for 19 April 1918 noted that Sergeant D. Reuben of the Royal Fusiliers 'conducted the evening service at the Devonport Synagogue prior to his departure abroad'. During the war years, officers of the synagogue were Solomon Robins (President), Mr J. Greenberg (Treasurer), Mr S. Roseman (Hon. Secretary), and Mr J. Lewis and Mr S. Caplan as honorary auditors. By April 1919, the elected officers were Solomon Robins (President), Mr J. Greenberg (Treasurer), Simon Roseman (Hon. Secretary), and Mr A. Erlich and Mr M. Seskin as honorary auditors. The Devonport Synagogue was fortunate to have a benefactor in Lord Rothschild.[68] Occasionally the congregations of Plymouth and Devonport joined together for outings. Children from their religion schools were taken to Paignton for the day, accompanied by their parents and Revds. Wolfson and Wykansky.

During the inter-war years, the Devonport congregation thrived. Kosher meat was provided to members of the Devonport Synagogue by Alfords. Hyman Aloof, Beadle of Plymouth Synagogue, went there every Tuesday to act as *Shomer* (kosher supervisor) and Porge the meat. Chazan Wykansky acted as shochet. However, post-WW1 saw the passing of one of its founding members, Hugh Ralph Emdon, son of Alderman Eleazar Emdon. The Jewish Chronicle of 6 February 1920 noted that 'to perpetuate his memory, a number of radiators have been installed in the building by one of his personal friends, in appreciation of the useful work rendered by him to the synagogue and other institutions.'

In March 1922, new officers were chosen at the AGM. They were Mr J. Greenburgh, senior (President), Mr B. Joseph (Vice-President), Solomon Robins (Treasurer) and Mr L. Cainer (Hon. Secretary). Joseph Greenburgh and Simon Roseman were appointed honorary auditors. In February 1925, another stalwart of the community, Jacob Ellison, passed away. An obituary in the Jewish Chronicle noted: 'His extensive knowledge of all religious matters was a great help to many, and his loss will be keenly felt by all who knew and respected him. Laurence Cainer, Honorary Secretary of the Devonport Hebrew Congregation said of him that he passed his life in the service of God and Mankind.'[69] Two years later, a set of Parochet (ceremonial textiles) was presented to the synagogue in his memory by Mr and Mrs Greenburgh. In 1928, Solomon Robins was again elected president, Samuel Woolfson as treasurer, Mr E. H Caplan as Honorary Secretary, and Simon Roseman and Mr Abe Milner as honorary auditors. They served in their posts until 1933.

The Devonport Synagogue began to struggle to raise a *minyan* of ten men to recite the prayers, so one of the Emdons was known to go out to round up male members to make up the numbers. Services were usually conducted by three stalwarts of the community: Saul Lempert, Samuel Woolfson and Mr. Bence. By now, Solomon Robins was almost permanently the president. For High Holly days, a retired chazan, Mr. Marks, came down from London to

---

[65] Jewish Chronicle, 18 September 1914.
[66] Catalogue *The Jews of Devon and Cornwall*, p.17.
[67] Jewish Chronicle, 22 September 1916.
[68] Jewish Chronicle, 30 April 1915.
[69] Jewish Chronicle, 15 February 1925.

assist. Bert Emdon recalled of him: 'although an elderly gentleman, he [Mr Marks] was still possessed of a fine voice, and often on Yom Kippur people used to walk across from Plymouth synagogue especially to hear him dovan (recite prayers).'

The religion school was held in the ladies section of the synagogue, conducted by Revd. Wykansky who came from Plymouth every Monday and Wednesday evening, and Sunday mornings. Travelling on a Sunday caused a bit of a problem because there were no public buses or trams to Devonport, so Revd. Wykansky took the train from North Road to Devonport Station. Now, kosher meat was being supplied twice a week from Devonport's Meat Market at the bottom of Tavistock Street. Later, it was sold from Harris's butcher shop in Tavistock Street, and after that, again from Alford's in Marlborough Street. Bert Emdon once commented that there were enough Jewish traders at the top end of Marlborough Street to form their own minyan.

In August 1932, the death of the congregation's cantor Saul Lempert caused profound sadness in the community. He was the son of the late Rabbi Lempert of Jerusalem and had arrived in Plymouth over 40 years earlier. Lempert had identified himself with many charitable causes in the city, served as vice-President of the Zionist Society and was an active member of the Chevra Kadisha [Burial Society] and Bikkur Cholim Society. He and his wife are buried in the Gifford Place Jewish cemetery.

Services continued at the Devonport Synagogue on a daily basis until the premises was destroyed in the blitz on Plymouth in 1941. The army's Pioneer Corps was instructed to excavate the ruins of the building and it was then that the commanding officer, Israel Fredman, being Jewish, was able to identify a Torah scroll when it was pulled out of the rubble. Miraculously, most of the scrolls and appurtenances survived the bombing. There is a tradition too that the remainder of the scrolls were rescued from the rubble by F. Ashe Lincoln QC. A large bound prayer book, also rescued then, survives in the Plymouth Synagogue' archives. Inside is a typed notice:

This book was salvaged from the rubble of the Devonport Synagogue which was destroyed in the Blitz, March 1941. It was repaired and presented to the Plymouth Hebrew Congregation by H. Greenburgh, Esq. October 1957. In memory of his father, Jacob David Greenburgh who was a founder of the Devonport Synagogue (Minyan) 1907.

Thus far, no historian has reconstructed anything other than a few sentences about the Devonport Synagogue. This chapter has therefore been able to record much more about the Devonport Synagogue than was hitherto known.

CHAPTER 4
RABBIS, MINISTERS AND CANTORS

THE HISTORY OF the Rabbis and ministers of Plymouth is a chequered one with a number of gaps. The community had a full-time Rabbi or minister until 1981, yet very little biographical details are known about some of them. Between 1796 and 1816, the community appointed two cantors, both of whom were required to be present at all services, even if not taking part. From the mid-19th century until 1959, there was just one full-time cantor. The congregation is known to have had some particularly learned men in its history. One such example was Lazarus Solomon from Lublin, described on his tombstone in the old Jewish cemetery as *torani*. He led prayers in Plymouth on the Days of Awe for over 25 years.

Rabbi Moses Ephraim by Abraham Daniel

The first known rabbi of Plymouth was Moses Ephraim (b.1745) whose portrait was painted by Plymouth Jewish artist Abraham Daniel. Moses served the community for over thirty years until his death in 1815. After the death of Moses Ephraim, Joseph Joseph recorded in his register:

'In Memoriam: The scholar Moses Ephraim from Zelig went to his eternal rest on the weekday Friday on the night of the Holy Sabbath 16 Shevat '575 LF"K and was buried with a good name on the weekday Sunday 18 Shevat. He was the teacher in the house of my lord, my father, nine years, and also teacher in my house for 23 years. Died Friday night 27 January 1815.'

No record survives for Moses Ephraim's burial, but it is highly likely that he was laid to rest in the old Jewish cemetery. By the time Revds. Berlin and Susser carried out their surveys of the site, Ephraim's headstone (if it existed) was no longer legible. Between 1761 and 1763, Hirsch Mannheim, from Mannheim in Germany, was appointed by the Chief Rabbinate as a shochet to Plymouth on an irregular basis. From around 1769, Revd. Levi Benjamin served as cantor for over sixty year until his death in 1829. He also traded as an umbrella maker.[70] Joseph ben Joseph Meir served the community sometime before 1779 until 1784.

By the mid-eighteenth century, the leadership was drawn from its Polish immigrants. Around 1778, Moses Isaac was officially appointed Beadle, teacher and *mohel*. He was born in Mezeritz, Poland in 1728, moved to Frankfurt and came to England in 1748. He appears to have served the community until his death in 1790 and is buried in the old Jewish cemetery. After his death, his wife Dikah bat Jacob remained in the city and was supported by the congregation with an allowance of 2s. a week, plus free accommodation. When she died in 1815, there were insufficient funds to pay for her funeral, so her possessions were sold to raise funds. She is also buried in the old cemetery, but has no headstone and therefore her precise resting place is not known. The Minute Book for the 1800s refers to another cantor, Jacob Judah ben Benjamin, who had been in the post for over forty years.[71] He was appointed in the 1770s.

Joseph Levy arrived in Plymouth from Lissa (Poland) around 1795. At some point, he served as Beadle, shochet and teacher. This may have been in the period between Moses Isaac and Hayyim [Chaim] Issachar. The latter served as Beadle from around 1810 to 1830, at an annual salary of £50 a year. Issachar was required to supervise any matters relating to kosher food.[72] He also traded locally as a slop-seller. He became well-known for his piety and

---

[70] He had three known daughters: Rachel, Leah and E. Benjamin.
[71] Minute Book entry, 17 April 1814.
[72] Minute Book entry, 20 February 1814.

learning, and held a position locally for half a century. He died at the age of 80 on 7 August 1854. Then there was Cantor Lima. The first reference to him is in 1796 when he was appointed Reader at a salary of £25 per annum. In 1800, he was earning 3 guineas a month from the congregation. His salary went up to £42 per annum in 1802, and £50 in 1816. Cantor Lima's name appears in the Minute Books and also the *Pinkas* as 'Shimshon bar Lima, Chazan Rishon'. His wife Sheincha predeceased him in 1793 and is buried in the old cemetery.

Rabbi Phineas ben Rabbi Samuel was appointed from London in 1800 and served the congregation until 1803 on a salary of £45 a year, including coals and lighting.[73] In February 1801, the Vestry members voted for him to be allowed to undertake marriages in the community as long as he was a resident of Plymouth. The following year, they considered the case of Elimelech, son of Rabbi Moses, who wanted his wife's daughter by a previous marriage (Pessela, daughter of Nathaniel) to marry in the synagogue, Zelig, son of Asher. The Minute Book entry for 14 June 1802 notes: 'and he has asked us to send on his behalf for authorization of the wedding ceremony. However, these men have no portion or inheritance in our congregation, neither do we know anything at all about the bride or groom.' The congregation withheld its permission unless the Rabbi consented. That permission was granted by the Rabbi, and Pessela and Zelig appear to have married at some point in the Plymouth Synagogue. In 1800, Reb Joseph {Levy?} was appointed shochet, Beadle and teacher to the children for a year, for a sum of £15 per annum.

Michael Solomon Alexander

Michael Solomon Alexander (b. 1799) came from Schönlanke, a small town in the Prussian province of Posen.[74] He began his education in learning the Talmud at only 7 years old. From the age of 16 to 20, he taught Talmud and German in his home town. He had also trained as Shochet. In 1820, he came to England as a private tutor to a provincial Jewish family. It was during this period that he first came into contact with the Church Mission to the Jews (CMJ) which gave him his first interest in Evangelical Christianity. He was then employed for a short time by the Norwich Jewish community before moving to Plymouth where he became second chazan and shochet at an annual salary of £57. 15s. In 1824, he married Deborah Levy, the daughter of the warden of the synagogue.

In 1825, Alexander abruptly left the Jewish congregation and converted to Christianity on a Saturday in St Andrews Church, the church opposite the very synagogue where he had once ministered. The exact circumstances are hazy and it appears that he had caused some kind of problem in the Jewish community even before he converted. Descendant John Gould has noted:

Revd. Aharon Slavinsky

'In the biographical notes read out at his baptism service in 1825, Michael Solomon, though claiming to have been Rabbi at Norwich, made no claim to have been Rabbi at Plymouth. Contemporaneous Jewish sources merely state that Michael Solomon received a licence from the Chief Rabbi to practice as ritual slaughterer in Plymouth on 3rd August 1823. Frustratingly, the Plymouth Congregation's Minute Book entries for 1823-1825 make no mention at all of Michael Solomon Alexander or of his duties with the congregation. It has been suggested that perhaps the elders of the Plymouth Congregation were so appalled by Alexander's apostasy that they systematically removed all mention of him from their records.'

Six months later, Alexander's wife converted too and they left for London. Alexander's swift exit from Plymouth Hebrew Congregation was followed by the arrival of Revd. H. Harris who served in office for a short time from 1829 to 1831.

The saga of Michael Solomon Alexander does not end there. In 1827, he was ordained as an Anglican priest in Ireland. From 1827 to 1830, he was based in Danzig where he worked as a missionary for CMJ, converting Jews in his native Prussia. From 1830 to 1841, he was back in London

---

[73] Minute Book entry, 22 June 1800.
[74] Thanks to Elkan Levy and John Gould for providing information on Michael Solomon Alexander.

in charge of the CMJ's London mission at Palestine Place in Bethnal Green. A group of Jews, including Isaac Lyons Goldsmith, founded University College London (UCL) for Jews, Catholics and atheists. It became famously known as 'the godless institution on Gower Street.' As a countermeasure to UCL, King's College London was founded. Michael Solomon Alexander became the first professor of Hebrew and Rabbinic Literature there. On 7 December 1841, Alexander was appointed the first Bishop of Jerusalem, causing one churchman, John Henry Newman, so much outrage that he converted to Catholicism. Newman subsequently became a Cardinal. Alexander took his own chaplain with him to Jerusalem, also a converted Jew, by the name of Kauffman. Alexander died suddenly during a trip to Sinai and is buried on Mount Zion. His forty-year old widow Deborah was left with nine surviving children between the ages of 1 and 17.

Following his conversion, Alexander was ostracized by the Jewish community of England. In Plymouth Synagogue, the Gabbai Abraham Alexander, a wealthy merchant with premises in the Old Town, decided to change his surname because of the shame of Alexander's conversion.[75] Alexander's conversion always remained a controversial point for Plymouth's Jews who felt a sense of betrayal. Perhaps this, and a sense of embarrassment is why nothing has survived about Alexander in the community's records.

Revd. Myer Stadthagen

Born in Bischofwerder (Prussia) in 1804, Myer Stadthagen arrived in the West Country from London in October 1827. He settled first in Penzance where he was appointed to the Penzance Synagogue.[76] He married Arabella Joseph (1802-62), daughter of Moses Isaac Joseph and Judith Rebecca Joseph (née Jacob) of Falmouth. Judith was a daughter of Moses Jacob of Redruth, and granddaughter of Alexander Moses of Falmouth. Sometime after May 1829, Myer and Arabella moved from Penzance to Plymouth, where he served first as shochet, then undertook duties as minister to visit the sick and those in prison. His English was initially so poor that, for a number of years, the sermons were given by members of the congregation. He was aided from 1829 to 1831 by Revd. H Harris. Myer and Arabella Stadthagen lived at 21 Queen Street with their five children, Selina, Phoebe, Sarah, Ellen and Isaac; all born in Plymouth. Their only son Isaac died in Plymouth. The daughters all married. On 7 February 1855, Selina married Barnett Barnett, a wholesale jeweller in the city. On 16 August 1858, Phoebe married Abraham Isaac, a pawnbroker from Newport. Sarah married Edwin Woolf of Plymouth on 22 August 1860, and Ellen Stadthagen married Edwin Selig of Manchester in Birmingham in 1864.

By all accounts, Myer Stadthagen's ministry was an interesting one. In early November 1854, at 7am, the

Sarah Harris, wife of Revd. Raphael Harris

Phoebe Stadthagen

---

[75] Abraham Alexander was one of the few Jews who could afford the luxury of piped water to his home.
[76] Keith Pearce, *The Jews of Cornwall*.

Preussischer Adler steamer brought a second division of Russian prisoners-of-war from the Crimean War to Plymouth. Amongst the prisoners were 8 officers, 2 ladies, 333 soldiers, and 18 women and children.[77] They arrived under guard and landed at Millbay, from where they were marched to the military prisons. Their arrival swelled the number of POWs in Plymouth to 698.[78] Amongst the total prisoners were 60 Jewish males and 3 Jewish women, some of whom were originally from Poland. Revd. Stadthagen visited them regularly and provided them with meat, bread, fish, coffee, tea, sugar and milk to enjoy 'the feast of Tabernacles'. Supplies came from the Plymouth Hebrew Congregation to build a *succah* in prison. All this was possible because of money sent from Plymothian Abraham Joseph II, then living in London, and a donation of £6 from Sir Moses Montefiore. Another contingent of POWs arrived from the Crimean War the following April and were again, given assistance by the Jewish community.[79] After their release, some Russian prisoners settled in Plymouth and married local Jewish girls. Throughout his ministry, Revd. Stadthagen regularly visited Jewish inmates of Dartmoor Prison and attended to their religious needs.

Revd. Stadthagen's long period of office was not without its troubles. Finally in 1856, he tendered his resignation after he had sued Aaron Levy the previous year for libel. Chief Rabbi Adler, who intervened to have the case dropped, famously wrote to Plymouth Congregation: 'in former times your congregation was one of the most united and disciplined, now it has become a byword throughout the Empire.'[80] It appears that Revd. Stadthagen did not resign as such and carried on until his death at the age of 58 on 21 April 1862, 'after a long and suffering illness'. The Jewish Chronicle reported: 'He performed sacred duties of his office for the last 32 years with unswerving zeal and fidelity… He retained full possession of his faculties and was perfectly sensible to the last.' The Hebrew inscription on his tombstone in the old Jewish cemetery records that he was buried on the last day of Passover. The family was still plunged into deep mourning when, five days later, his wife Arabella died at their home on 26 April after 'a long and severe illness of great suffering, borne with exemplary patience and resignation.'[81] She is also buried in the old Jewish cemetery.

In his will, Revd. Stadthagen left under £1,500. He bequeathed £200 to Ellen 'when she should marry, which should not be without the consent of Barnett and Abraham, if it be against our religion'. The sum of £400 was bequeathed to his son-in-law Barnett, which Stadthagen had already lent him, and called on him 'to pay into the estate some £610, the value of railway shares which were in his possession'. His son-in-law Edwin Wolf owed him £20 and Mr J. Joseph owed £14, for which Stadthagen

Tombstone of Revd. Myer Stadthagen, old cemetery

had mortgaged his house. He left £3 to the synagogue 'as a memorial to be made every festival of freewill offerings and to pay some fit person to say a prayer for me during the year, and a light shall be burned…' He bequeathed a silver cup to each son-in-law, and stipulated that the circumcision boxes should be kept in the family. It may be this circumcision set which survives in the Jewish Museum today.

Isaac Stone and Leopold Stern

Polish-born Isaac Stone (b.1828) had arrived in the city already during Revd. Stadthagen's time. From 1846, he served as the Hebrew teacher. The following year, he married Anna Mordecai, and that same year left the city for Australia on health grounds. Also at this time in Plymouth was Revd. Leopold Stern, although details of his ministry are extremely sketchy. However, it is known that, like Revd. Stadthagen, he undertook the welfare of Russian prisoners-of-war:

> 'They [the POWs] were never so well lodged in their own barracks as in the building which is called the prison of Plymouth. Comparing the mouldy bread and the rotten vegetables which used to form

---
[77] Jewish Chronicle, 3 November 1854.
[78] Twenty five of whom were women, and twenty three were children.
[79] Jewish Chronicle, 20 April 1855.
[80] Chief Rabbinate Archives, and also quoted in Susser, p.158.
[81] Jewish Chronicle, 2 May 1862.

the staple of their fare when in garrison, with the wholesome and substantial food which they are provided with, this circumstance alone would make them disposed to congratulate themselves on the change in their position. But that which is more particularly makes them satisfied with their fate is the fact of having escaped from the cruel treatment to which they are subjected under the horrid military system of Russian despotism. The only fear which these unhappy men entertain is to be obliged to return to their former life.'[82]

Revd. Stern was followed by Revd. Joshua Levy who served from 1865 to 1867. Revd. Levy's ministry overlapped with Revd. L. Rosenbaum who served from 1863 to 1893. During their service in Plymouth, four Jewish prisoners-of-war arrived in the Plymouth Sound aboard the Prussian vessel *Confidentia*. There were allegations that these Jewish prisoners had been maltreated on the ship. Their case was heard before magistrates at Plymouth Guildhall. Mr L. Hyman, president of the synagogue, attended the court and spoke on their behalf. In April 1871, during Passover, Jewish convicts at Dartmoor Prison were visited by wardens and the minister of the synagogue and: 'amply supplied with matzos and Passover diet. A special room with cooking utensils was provided for them. The delegation from the synagogue was well-received by the prison governor.'

During Pentecost of 1875, the Plymouth Jewish community welcomed the Revd. N. Lipman of Falmouth Synagogue who gave lectures in Hebrew.[83] In 1884, Revd. Rosenbaum was joined by Revd. Moses Lewis who served for less than a full year.

Revd. Abraham N. Spier

After Revd. Lewis's short ministry, Revd. Abraham Spier arrived on the scene and served the congregation until 1896. A balance sheet for the congregation shows that in 1884, he was being paid 40s. a week as general factotum, although he may not have moved his family to the city until the following year. On the 1891 census, he and family are listed as living at Synagogue House at the back of Catherine Street. He and his wife Bessie, who both originated from Poland, had six children living with them at this time: Rebecca, Julia, Hyam, Eva, Sol and Edward. There was another son, Ezra, who died in 1918 in France during WW1. Services were sometimes led jointly by Revd. Spier and Revd. Greenbaum.[84] In February 1890, after the death of the Chief Rabbi, the Ark and reading desk in the synagogue were heavily draped in black and a special memorial service held. In his sermon, Revd. Spier

Revd. Abraham and Bessie Spier

said of the Chief Rabbi:

'His knowledge ranked him with the foremost of his predecessors, and he had been the most zealous in raising their feeble nation, whilst his fullness of mind and energy of soul were devoted to the object of filling them with the same love for God and love for mankind as he himself had, and that great object prompted his every thought. His exertions were always directed to one principle, that of improving their moral and religious life. It was not only in this country that the death of the Chief Rabbi would be mourned, but every Jew who was living, even in the remotest parts of the world, would keenly feel the loss. His counsel had been listened to with great interest by all men.'

Revd. Spier appears to have ceased his ministry in 1893 because, in April that year, the congregation advertised for a new Chazan, Minister and Teacher at a salary of £120 per annum and a house rent free. At the same time it, advertised for the post of shochet, second Reader and *mohel* for a salary of £60 per annum.[85] Revd. Spier did not leave Plymouth for another three years, but lived at 29 Oxford Place. On 23 August 1893, he officiated at his own daughter's wedding when Rebecca married Morris Hyman, a fur dealer of London (son of Israel Hyman, a rag merchant). On the marriage entry, her father is described as 'gentleman'. In 1896, Revd. Spier left Plymouth to become chazan, shochet and minister of the Sheffield Congregation in New Church Street, then Manchester where he also worked as secretary and investigative officer for the Manchester Shechita Board. He was succeeded at Plymouth by Revd. M Berlin who ministered until 1906. One of his daughters recalled how her father slaughtered the poultry two mornings a week in the back yard. There was Revd. Posner who mainly served the Devonport Minyan until 1903.

---

[82] Jewish Chronicle, 10 November 1864.
[83] Jewish Chronicle, 18 June 1875.
[84] Jewish Chronicle, 7 October 1887.
[85] Jewish Chronicle, 7 April 1893.

From 1903 to 1912, Revd. D. Jacobs became minister, overlapping with Revd. E Jaffe and Revd. A. K. Slavinsky, the latter serving the synagogue during the First World War. From 1918 to 1928, the community was served by Revd. M. Zeffert. In 1920, the congregation advertised for a chazan, shochet and *mohel* for £400 per annum,[86] and appointed Revd. Simon Wykansky for the years 1920 to 1932. After the departure of Revd. Zeffert in 1928, Revd. W. Wolfson arrived and remained with the congregation until 1944.

Revd. Emanuel Goodman

From 1933 until 1959, the congregation was served by Revd. Emanuel Goodman as the cantor and *mohel*. He had succeeded Revd. Simon Wykansky. Emanuel Goodman (Guttmann) originated from Oradea Mare/Nagyvarad (now in Romania) which had a Jewish population of 40,000. He had served in the Medical Corps of the Austro-Hungarian Army during the First World War. After a period as cantor at a Paris synagogue, he came to Britain. During his time in Plymouth, he was a devoted communal spiritual leader. He married Bessie Isenberg and together they had two children: Carmel and Stuart. During the Second World War, he was chaplain to the Jewish Forces in the South-West and, later, visiting chaplain to Jewish prisoners in Dartmoor Prison. By 1944, Goodman was chairman of

Revd. M. Goodman

Presentation to Revd. M. Goodman by the Lord Mayor for 25 years as Cantor & Mohel, May 1958

[86] Jewish Chronicle, 16 July 1920.

Plymouth's Zionist Society. He was described as 'a cantor of the old school and retained his melodious voice to the end.' Revd. Goodman died in office and is buried in the Jewish cemetery in Gifford Place. He was the last professional cantor at Plymouth synagogue. 'His fine baritone voice complemented the beautiful interior of the Plymouth Synagogue, the oldest Ashkenazi synagogue in Britain,' comments Anglo-Jewish biographer Dr Michael Jolles.

Revd. Simon Isaac Susman

From 1944, Revd. Goodman was joined by Revd. Simon Susman.[87] Born in Liverpool on 18 June 1911, Revd. Susman was the second surviving son of an immigrant family from Lithuania. The family had arrived in Liverpool by ship around the turn of the century and had been told that they had arrived in America – a common trick of unscrupulous ship owners and captains at that time. In his late teens, Susman was sent to Tels & Ponovich yeshivas in Lithuania. On Rosh Hashannah 1931, he suffered an appendicitis and was transported by ambulance to a hospital in Berlin, there not being a hospital in Lithuania at that time capable of dealing with the illness. While in hospital he caught paratyphoid fever and had to remain there for a year. As Hitler rose to power, Susman discharged himself from hospital to return to England. In December 1933, he married Sarah Swift, also from Liverpool, who came from a famous rabbinical family. Revd. Susman's first appointment was as minister to the Darlington Jewish Community. After a few months, he took up the post of minister to the Bristol Hebrew Congregation. A daughter, Doreen, was born in Bristol on 8 February 1935. Two years later, on 3 May 1937, a son Roy was born. Roy recalls: "in 1944 my father became ill with pneumonia (a potentially fatal illness at the time) and was treated with sulphonamide, a very new drug. He was advised to move to a better climate and coincidentally this coincided with a vacancy for position of senior minister at Plymouth." Revd. Susman became senior minister, *mohel* and shochet for the Plymouth Hebrew Congregation. He and his wife were known for their untiring work on various committees and the unstinting hospitality that they bestowed on every stranger who happened to turn up.

When King George VI and Queen Elizabeth visited Plymouth after WW2, as part of the victory parade, Revd. Susman as senior minister of the Plymouth Hebrew Congregation, had the honour of representing the Plymouth Jewish community, being presented to King George together with other local religious leaders and dignitaries.

Revd. Susman became unpaid chaplain to the Jewish prisoners in Dartmoor Prison, which he visited on the first Monday of every month. His son Roy remembers some of the anecdotes from this period:

'The first that Dad knew about Dartmoor Prison

Revd. Susman

was when he received a telephone call from the governor of the prison informing him that he had a Jewish prisoner who was demanding a spiritual visit from a Rabbi. My father wasn't too keen on the idea as Dartmoor Prison was very isolated, and apart from a lone road connection and a single line railway, there was no way of getting there. The governor suggested that if Dad could get himself to Yelverton by bus, the governor would send his car to pick him up and return him to Yelverton after the visit. A few weeks later, Dad found himself inside Dartmoor Prison visiting this lone Jewish prisoner. On his arrival, he was told that the governor wanted to meet with him afterwards. About an hour later, my father was ushered into the governor's office who told him that the prisoner was demanding regular prayer meetings. My father told the governor that he could not hold a prayer meeting without a quorum of 10 Jewish males over the age of 13. The governor was one step ahead and, to my father's amazement, told him that he would have another nine Jewish prisoners sent down from Pentonville to make up the Minyan. The Governor kept his word, and so my father made the journey to Dartmoor Prison on the first Monday of every month from then until we left Plymouth.'

---

[87] He was known as Simon Isaac Susman, but his birth certificate gives his name as Samuel Isaac Susman.

Revd. Susman insisted that the Jewish prisoners kept all the festivals. On Passover, he arranged for new crockery and matzo and wine so they could have two proper Seder nights. The Jewish prisoners were not allowed to work on shabbat or the religious holidays. The Governor informed Revd. Susman that after every festival he received a flood of requests from the non-Jewish prisoners to change their religion to Judaism. On one occasion, one of the Jewish prisoners wanted to petition King George VI to receive a pardon, but his request for writing materials was turned down – undeterred, he wrote his request on a piece of toilet paper. The "letter" was intercepted and not sent to the King, but the prisoner received seven days solitary confinement – for "misuse of His Majesty's property". Only when Revd. Susman announced his plans to leave Plymouth did he realise just how much his ministry had meant to the Jewish prisoners. In appreciation of all he had done for them, on his final visit they presented him with an inscribed volume of the complete works of George Bernard Shaw. Revd. Susman left Plymouth in 1952 to take up position as the Minister to the Leicester Hebrew Congregation. He died in February 1973 and is buried at Kibbutz Lavi in Israel where his sister was a founder member. From 1954 to 1956, the Plymouth congregation was served by Revd. D. Josovic, then Revd. I. Broder from 1958 until 1960.

Rabbi Bernard Susser

In 1961, Rabbi Bernard Susser was appointed rabbi. He had graduated from London University with a BA Hons degree and studied at Jews' College. During his time in Plymouth, and his subsequent term of office in the 1970s, he devoted himself to preserving and recording the community's heritage. His years of dedicated research also covered other Jewish communities of Devon and Cornwall, the results of which became his Ph.D thesis awarded by the University of Exeter. He founded the *Digest*, the congregation's monthly newsletter. In 1961, he was appointed Lord Mayor's Chaplain to Arthur Goldberg, the first Jewish Lord Mayor of Plymouth. On 3 June, Susser conducted a civic service of Prayer and Thanksgiving. The Plymouth Coroner, who attended the service, was heard to remark how impressed he was by the informality of the service. Rabbi Susser oversaw the Bicentenary Celebrations of the synagogue in 1964/5. His first term of office at Plymouth lasted until 1965.

Revd. Alec Ginsburg

Major Revd. Alec Ginsburg served as minister of the congregation for ten years from 1965 to 1975. He and his twin brother Sydney were born in Aberavon, South Wales in 1920, into a family of fourteen children. Both were sent to Gateshead Yeshiva (religious seminary) at the age of 13, shortly after their bar mitzvah, and were amongst its earliest students. Sydney was transferred to Manchester Yeshiva in 1935 and, after graduating, became cantor and junior minister at Westcliff-on-Sea Synagogue in the mid-1940s. After divorcing his wife in the early 1950s, Sydney resigned his post and moved to Plymouth to live with his older sister, Leah, who was married to a Plymothian, Roy Caplan. Roy helped Sydney set up a wholesale jewellery business. Sydney occasionally undertook cantorial and other duties in the synagogue, and stayed in Plymouth until he remarried in 1968. He was well-established in the town by the time his twin brother Alec arrived with his family to take up the post of minister in 1965.

Rabbi Bernard Susser

Revd. Alec Ginsburg

After leaving Gateshead Yeshiva in 1940, Alec Ginsburg took a number of teaching and junior rabbinical posts in NE England. He was recruited into the British Army in 1946 as Jewish Chaplain and was immediately posted to serve with MELF (Middle East Land Forces) in Egypt. Here he met and courted Rose Naim from Alexandria. They married in Ismailia in 1949, but following an attempt on his life in 1950, he was posted back to the UK at 24 hours notice, leaving Rose behind. She followed him to the UK six weeks later, only to find when she arrived, that he had already been re-posted to the British Army of the Rhine (BAOR) in Bad Oeynehausen, West Germany, where she subsequently joined him. Two children Robert and Michelle were born in Germany. They returned to the United Kingdom in 1955, living in London, where Benjamin was born in 1960. Alec Ginsburg remained in the army until 1962, when he was demobilised because compulsory conscription into the Armed Forces ended and was uniquely awarded the permanent rank of Major and Honorary Chaplain to the Forces (Hon CF) in recognition of his long service. He moved to Plymouth in September 1963 to join his twin brother Sydney and older sister Leah Caplan. After Rabbi Susser's departure in 1965, Alec Ginsburg was offered the post of minister of Plymouth Hebrew Congregation. He also lectured in Jewish Studies and Hebrew at the University of Exeter. Like ministers before him he was a regular visitor to Dartmoor and Exeter Prisons. He used his army skills to organise food for the prisoners over Passover. Like successive ministers before him, Revd. Ginsburg made regular hospital visits to Jewish patients. An entry in the *Digest* notes for 1971: 'Revd. Ginsburg and his elder son spent the Christmas weekend helping the depleted staff in a Plymouth hospital.'

On 28 January 1968, he officiated at the wedding of his twin brother Sydney to his second wife Anna Rotenberg, which took place in the synagogue. During his time as minister in Plymouth, Alec Ginsburg by virtue of his honorary rank of Major, took part in the many military and naval occasions in the city. His time in Plymouth proved to be an extraordinarily interesting one. His name appeared on all the VIP lists for special civic events, as well as military and naval commemorations in the city. This was the period when Sir Francis Chichester came home after his famous solo trip in which he sailed single-handedly around the world by clipper route. The city of Plymouth held huge celebrations in his honour. During this time, the Argyll and Sutherland Highlanders were stationed at Crownhill Barracks, and as an army chaplain Ginsburg officiated at a special anniversary. On 1 May 1968, he attended a dinner to mark the 50th anniversary of the Royal Air Force. The following year, on 13 May 1969, he was amongst the guests at a ceremony on the Hoe in the presence of the Queen and Duke of Edinburgh for the Ceremony of the Presentation of the Queen's and Regimental Colours to 45 Commando, Royal Marines. This was followed by a reception for the Royals at the Guildhall which Revd. Ginsburg attended.

On another occasion in the late 1960s/early 1970s, after the State of Israel purchased a submarine, a group of twelve Israeli Naval frogmen came to Plymouth to train in underwater techniques and diving at the submarine base. They spent up to twelve hours a day underwater. 'My father

looked after them very well,' recalls Dr Rob Ginsburg. 'The frogmen often came to our home for Friday night Shabbat supper.' Revd. Ginsburg was invited for cocktails aboard the de Ruyter, a Dutch vessel. On 22 February 1972, he was guest at the Lord Mayor's ball. In 1974, he became Patron of the RNLI on its 150th anniversary and exhibition. Ginsburg appeared on a Westward TV series with Revd. John Ashplant, and was often a guest on late night television chat shows. He had part share in a boat, formerly owned by the Marine Biological Association which had been used in the evacuation of Dunkirk in June 1940. He loved fishing on the sea and trout-fishing on the moor.

During his ministry, Ginsburg redesigned the Laws and Regulations of Plymouth Hebrew Congregation During a refurbishment of the Synagogue, he climbed up internal scaffolding to paint and restore freehand the Hebrew lettering of the 10 commandments above the Ark, and was instrumental in re-instituting the mikveh in the Vestry. One or two families used it in the 1960s. Ginsburg served as the community *mohel* and for most of Devon, Cornwall and Somerset and carried out circumcisions all over the West country as required. He was also a shochet, qualified to slaughter hens and ducks. He provided the poorer members of the community with kosher poultry at cost price – much cheaper than the cost of that transported from London / Reading. All other kosher meat came from Reading by train. For Passover, he made arrangements with a local farm and supervised the production of kosher pasteurized milk which had its own completely dedicated set of equipment. This was later delivered by a local milk firm. After that service ceased, a local delicatessen agreed to take the kosher milk and distribute it. One of the most challenging issues which faced Ginsburg during his ministry was inter-marriage. His son recalls: 'the corollary was that many members had family who were non-Jewish and there were frequent attempts to get these relatives buried in the Jewish Cemetery, something which was contrary to Halakhah (the code of Jewish Law). I remember there was a big debate over whether someone's mother-in-law could be buried in the Jewish cemetery. I can't remember how it was resolved.' Rob Ginburg grew up in Plymouth and has fond memories this period, and says: 'One of the annual highlights was the Chanukah prize-giving. Bert and Ernie Emdon had a wholesale toy business and warehouse and they provided the prizes every year. They gave out novelties to the children and the prize giving was often held in the Civic Centre.' Alec Ginsburg was succeeded in 1975 by Leeds-born Revd. Rockman who served for two years.

After Rockman left the post in 1977, Rabbi Bernard Susser returned for a second term in office. Susser was again involved in many civic occasions. On Remembrance Sunday 1979, he was present at the service at the Naval War Memorial on the Hoe, alongside the Mayor and representatives of the forces. He read the Second Lesson from the Book of Jonah and ended the service with the Priestly Blessing. He remained in Plymouth until 1981 and was the last official minister of Plymouth. Since the 1980s, the congregation has relied on visiting ministers, including Revd. Malcolm Weisman and, from 2004 until 2010, Elkan Levy. Elkan visited Plymouth often, which was one of his favourite communities alongside Exeter and Cornwall.

One of the services at which he officiated annually was the Purim Service when he read from the Scroll of Esther. On one occasion, he organised a pre-Rosh Hashanah seminar which attracted around a hundred people from all over the South-West. On another occasion he participated in the Hidden City Festival of Plymouth, of which he recalls: 'I ran a very successful introductory morning for local residents who had never been inside the synagogue building, even though some of them admitted that they walked past it almost every day.' From time to time, even though he now resides in Israel, Elkan receives enquiries from the congregation asking for advice. Visiting ministers to Plymouth who have conducted services since the 1980s have forged a remarkably close bond with the community. Plymouth, although small, continues to be a special congregation with a unique charm for those who are associated with it.

CHAPTER 5
THE BURIAL GROUNDS

LOCATED ON PLYMOUTH'S historic Hoe and within sight of the Citadel, is the old Jewish burial ground. Contained within high stone walls, the first burial took place in 1744, making it the oldest extant Jewish burial ground in the South-West. It was acquired twenty years earlier than the purpose-built synagogue, but within easy walking distance of the synagogue. When a member of the Jewish community died in 1744, they were buried in this private garden on the Hoe. The garden was owned, or leased, by a prominent congregation member, Joseph Jacob Sherrenbeck, who held it in trust for his wife Sarah. The Sherrenbeck 'garden cemetery' was soon formally acquired by the community, offering an alternative to transporting bodies the long distance to London for burial. Today it still has the feel of a garden cemetery. Indentures dating to 1721 and 1725 for the site survive in the synagogue's archives. There is no indication on them to say whether or not the land was leased to the Jewish community at this time. However, if the community did acquire use of the land in 1721, it means that the first formal Jewish settlement in Plymouth dates to at least the 1720s, and not the 1740s as previously argued by Cecil Roth and Bernard Susser. As the community increased in numbers, the ground was extended in June 1758 with the purchase of another quarter acre of adjacent ground, making the plot about 55ft by 35ft in size. This was leased for £40 in the names of three London merchants 'to permit and suffer all and every person as profess the Jewish ceremonies and religion and who now reside in or near the borough of Plymouth or at any time hereafter… to be used as a place of burial.'[88] The burial ground was formally acquired by the Plymouth Hebrew Congregation from Sarah Sherrenbeck in 1796. A large oval stone set into the wall commemorates the gift of £157 by Joseph Joseph in 1796 to complete the purchase of the ground. The inscription on the stone was recorded in the 1960s by Rabbi Dr Bernard Susser, but today is completely illegible.

The cemetery was extended further in 1811 with purchase of land on the south side of Gray Friars Street for the sum of £100 as 'a burying place for the Society of Jews in Plymouth'. The conveyance was in the names of three local Jewish men: Abraham Emanuel of Plymouth Dock (shopkeeper), Michael Nathan of Plymouth (shopkeeper)

Entrance of the old cemetery, The Hoe

and Benjamin Levy (optician) of Plymouth, and a prominent non-Jew, John Saunders (gentleman) of Plymouth. A chapel once stood in the cemetery, but has long since vanished. It was here that the last rites of washing the body were performed before burial. The chapel also provided shelter to members of the congregation who guarded a newly interred body from being 'snatched'. Body-snatching was a real concern. It was written into the Plymouth Synagogue Regulations in 1835:

> 'To guard against the robbery of graves, watch shall be kept on the ground for three nights after burial, by three Jews each night, to be decided by a ballot of every person in the congregation: in case of refusal to be fined Five Shillings.'

Today it is still possible to see a bricked-up area in the wall that was once the original entrance into the cemetery. At one time, the land on the other side of the wall was much lower. It was land-filled with earth to raise the ground level, such that the cemetery needed a new entrance. Once through the entrance, the cemetery is accessed down several steep stone steps. A little way along the wall is another, much smaller bricked-up area which suggests the presence of a window once, possibly part of the chapel. Today this crevice holds the large oval stone commemorating the gift by Joseph Joseph, mentioned above.

---

[88] Susser, p.128.

The old cemetery, The Hoe

The earliest tombstones from the 1760s may still survive, but if so, are completely illegible. Later ones have also deteriorated significantly, or have disappeared. In 1933, Revd. Dr Berlin made a transcript of 95 inscriptions of headstones, but these were by no means all of those which were then extant. Why he did not record all of them is not known, but for his foresight, even these headstones would not have been recorded before the weather eroded them. It was another forty years before another survey of the site was carried out, this time by Rabbi Dr Bernard Susser. In 1972, he deciphered a total of a hundred and forty-six inscriptions. Of the ninety-five inscriptions which Berlin had noted down four decades earlier, forty-five have totally disappeared, i.e. nearly half in a comparatively short space of time. The earliest headstone which Susser could still partially decipher was located along the north wall and dated to 1762. The earliest fully legible tombstone was for a child, Elijah son of Abraham, who died on 10 March 1767. Many of the headstones which Susser so carefully transcribed are now no longer legible. There are some very old tombstones along the back wall of Section B, but their inscriptions are too eroded to identify properly. It is thought that these could be the ones which Susser identified for the 1760s. For the first seventy years after acquiring the cemetery, the headstone inscriptions were

Stone plaque donating gift of Joseph Joseph

Original bricked-up entrance to the old cemetery

Plot 68, ewer and basin, now illegible, old cemetery

only in Hebrew. From 1825, English names began to appear on the reverse side, and from around 1840, English and Hebrew lettering appeared on the same side. In some cases, local stonemasons who were ignorant of Hebrew, made mistakes in the inscriptions. The proximity of stones here suggests that some burials took place on top of each other, something which is permitted in Jewish Law as long as six handbreadths of earth are between them. Susser noted that separate areas were reserved for Gentiles who married Jews, suicides, Jews who married Gentiles, and Jews who converted out of the faith. In 1867, for example, Abraham Joseph II wrote to the Chief Rabbi Dr Adler asking for advice on the case of Samuel Ralph. Ralph had married twice in church and the question was raised whether on his death in March 1867, he could be buried in the cemetery. Burial was granted and he is in plot A133, in the raised part of Section A. In some rare cases, the deceased did not have sufficient estate to pay for a headstone. This happened in the case of Samuel HaLevi who died in 1800, and also in 1815 when Dikah (wife of Moses Isaac, the Beadle of the synagogue) died. No headstone was erected but, as the Minute Book shows, the community gave them a burial with full respect.

The old cemetery is divided into three section: Section A, B and C. On the right hand side, within Section A, is a raised plot with a number of large flat headstones that once stood upright. The largest area is Section B which primarily contains burials from the 1800s. Section C, the smallest section, has just ten burials and was reserved for members of the Joseph family, one of the most prominent families and amongst the founding members of the community. On the edge of the Joseph plot is the tombstone for another founding member, Joseph Jacob Sherrenbeck. He died sometime between 1779 and 1782. His brother, Gershon Sherrenbeck and his wife, are also buried in this cemetery. Here too lies the famous miniaturist, Abraham Daniel, who died in March 1806; and Telza, wife of Abraham Joseph and great granddaughter of Alexander Moses, founder of the Falmouth Synagogue. Also buried here is David Lyons, son of the late Revd Solomon Lyons, whose headstone states 'formerly of Cambridge who died at Brixham on his voyage to Naples, 8 February 1819 aged 20 years.' And the community shochet, Isaac Falk Valentine, murdered at Fowey in 1811. The Hebrew on his tombstone reads in translation: 'he was slain by the uncircumcised and impure man Wyatt and drowned in the waters, 14 Kislev 5572 and buried on the 17th thereof [= 30 November 1811], aged 26 years.'

The old cemetery was the burial place for Jewish victims of the cholera epidemic of 1832, all of whom died in August. They were buried in Section B, not a separate section and not all together. They were Hannah Woolfson (wife of Jacob Woolfson of London), and Ze'ev ben Judah from Shotwinitz, Poland whose tombstone states that he died 'by decree of the plague on Thursday and was buried on 6 Av 5592 [= 2 August 1832].' Also Feigela bat Mordecai, wife of Isaac ben Avigdor, who 'died on account of the plague, Tuesday, 2nd day of Rosh Hodesh Elul 5592 [= 28 August 1832]'. She was Fanny, first wife of Solomon Lyon. The other victim was Meyer Jacob Cohen who died on 16 August 1832.

During the late 1700s and early 1800s, the congregation had two burial societies (*Masheefeth Nefesh*) – one for men, the other for women. It is known from the records that one was administered in the 1850s by Lewis Hyman, Myer Stadthagen, Barnet Mitchell and Abraham Ralph. The other was administered by Aron Wolf, Moseley Joel and Emmanuel Basch. It was usual for the congregation to elect a burial warden. In 1860, it was Barnet Mitchell. The old cemetery served the congregation until the 1860s when it became full.

Gifford Place Jewish Cemetery

By the end of the 1850s, the community looked to acquire a second burial ground. An appeal for funds was launched. Eighty-three donors pledged money which amounted to £1,035. Half of this was donated by one benefactor, the late Jacob Nathan. His bequest made possible the purchase of the land and the erection of buildings on site – a chapel and caretaker's lodge, known as Jews' Cemetery Lodge. The remainder of the money was raised from donations and a general fund. Rachel Benjamin, a feather maker, born in Plymouth and daughter of Levi Benjamin (cantor of the synagogue in 1813) donated £7.5s to the cemetery fund with her sister, Miss E. Benjamin. The congregation was able to purchase a plot of land in the Compton Gifford area, near Central Park.

The cemetery was opened in 1868, and the land conveyanced by John Winterbottom Babber and Alexander Hubbard for the sum of £650 to Lewis Hyman and ten others and their heirs. The indenture noted that, with the consent of the Vestry committee, they could 'permit the burial in the said piece of land of persons of the Jewish religions who should not have been living in Plymouth or its neighbourhood.' The first burial to take place was Councillor William Woolf on 3 December 1872. On 5 January 1958, a new extended area was consecrated by the minister, Revd. Goodman. A plaque in the ground marks the point where the cemetery was extended in 1958. It names the officers of the congregation at the time: Jack Smith (President), Reginald Lewis (Treasurer) and Percy Cohen (Hon. Secretary). That same year, the chapel was rebuilt and totally financed by money donated from Mrs Esther Black and her children, Israel Black and Hilda Marks.

Over a period of 140 years, there have been over 750 burials in the Gifford Place cemetery. Although there is no complete burial register, the congregation has two cemetery plans which record the names of those buried there. The Jews' Cemetery Lodge, which still exists, is one of the few caretaker's lodges in any Jewish cemetery outside London. Today, there is no caretaker and it is privately rented.

The new cemetery has a number of war graves from both world wars. From WW1, there is John Lithman who served with the Judeans, 38/40 Royal Fusiliers, and died

Gifford Place Jewish cemetery

Receipt from JH Doney

The chapel, Gifford Place cemetery

on 8 January 1919 aged 16 years and 9 months. The Hebrew inscription on his headstone uses the words *mitzeva ha-yehudit* (= from the Jewish Army). He falsified his age to serve in the Jewish Battalion and died in some kind of accident. Another casualty from the Jewish Battalion was Myer Nyman of Swansea, who served under the name Pte Michael Burns. He died on 2 February 1919, aged 18 years and 4 months. Also Stoker Harry Phillips of HMS *Vivid* who died on 2 April 1918, at the age of 29. There are two Commonwealth War Graves from the Second World War: Sgt Ralph Emdon of the Queen's Royal Regiment who died in 1944 of wounds received at Dunkirk, and Sgt Morris Solomon of the Royal Australian Air Force who died on 21 July 1942, aged 23. The cemetery also contains a double grave for Mary and Esther (Esta) Smith, the first civilian casualties of the blitz on Plymouth. They died on 10 July 1940 as a result of a heavy German bombing on the city.

Gifford Place cemetery is still in use as a burial ground today. It can be visited by prior arrangement with the synagogue caretaker. In terms of the headstones, these come from a local non-Jewish stonemason who carves the inscriptions, with guidance from Elkan Levy to ensure correct Hebrew on them.

For the future, both burial grounds suffer from the same ongoing challenge of maintenance. It is a massive job and one which the community manages well for the Gifford Place cemetery. However, the old burial ground proves much more difficult to keep up. The cost of ongoing maintenance is an issue. Because no more burials take place there, it does not have the same priority as the new cemetery. Periodically, the old cemetery is cleared with the help of local volunteers and it reveals an exquisite site that has a charm of its own. The effects last a few weeks before the process needs to start again. Over its long history, the headstones in the old cemetery have never been comprehensively photographed until the summer of 2013 when the author and her son, Jonathan, cleared the site and did so. Each headstone tells part of the story of this community. The history contained in this exquisite Georgian cemetery is part of Anglo-Jewish heritage and the rich tapestry of Jews in the South-West. It needs to be preserved in memory of those who are buried there and also as an important historical site.

Jews' Cemetery Lodge, Gifford Place cemetery

CHAPTER 6
THE COMMUNITY: 1800–1900

THE MAJORITY OF Jews who settled in Plymouth during the 19th century fled the pogroms of Russia and Poland. They joined a generation of Jews in Plymouth who had been born in the city. During this period, the Roseman and Fredman families settled. They would play prominent roles in the life of the community, both originating from Saki in Poland. This period saw the settlement of Nathan ben Reuben from Hungary, Michael ben Abraham, a scribe from Vilna, and Shemoel Hirsch from Poland. Also, Zvi ben Judah Lyons from Warsaw, Lazarus Solomon from Lublin and Joseph ben Samuel from Brisk. By 1822, there was merchant Jonas Mandovsky who, that same year, offered a large sum of money to aid the congregation. He married a Devon-born Jewess, Sophia, maiden unknown. There was Moses Solomon (Moses ben Jacob), born in London in 1775 who traded as a watchmaker in London before moving to Plymouth with his family, where he settled in Bedford Street. He died in Plymouth in 1838 and is buried in the old cemetery. Abraham Jonas and his two brothers, Baruch and Jonah, were members of the synagogue in 1815. Abraham Jonas later emigrated to Cincinnati, then Kentucky where he became a friend of Abraham Lincoln, 16th president of the United States of America. Miriam Jacobs (1771- 1850), born in Devon, was a silversmith in 1841 in Bedford Street. Her children were Alexander, Jacob, Angel, and Betsy who married B. L. Joseph of Liverpool; Martha who married Isaac Emanuel of Southampton and predeceased her mother; and Zipporah who married Hyman Hyman of Plymouth. Miriam Jacobs' nephews are said to have founded Crockfords. Aaron Levy, a jeweller in the city, traded by appointment of Queen Victoria from 1837-1840.

By the 1840s, the Plymouth community consisted largely of Ashkenazi members from British-born Jews of immigrant parents. The 1841 Census noted 18 foreign Jews resident in the city and 192 British-born Jews. This was a well-established community, at home in its surroundings, and making a major contribution to the life and commerce of the city. In March 1846, Charles Marks became the first Jew to be elected Assessor of the Borough of Plymouth. In 1855, William Woolf was elected Warden of the Poor, and nearly a decade later in 1864 Vice-Governor of the Poor Law Guardians. Also on the Town Guardians were Josiah Solomons and Joseph Solomons and, in the 1870s, Israel Roseman in Stonehouse. The late eighteenth century saw the arrival of a number of Sephardi Jews, in what was otherwise a predominantly Ashkenazi-led community. The most prominent settler was Menasseh Masseh Lopes, born in Jamaica in 1755 to a rich sugar plantation owner. In 1798, he came to Devon and purchased several manors: Maristow, Buckland Monachorum, Bickleigh, Shaugh Prior, Walkhampton and Meavy. Lopes became a Member of Parliament for New Romney in 1802, and later Barnstaple in North Devon. He converted to Christianity to progress in politics at a time when Jews could not hold office in Parliament, but he never forgot his Jewish roots. On his deathbed he is said to have asked for a Rabbi. One of his descendants, Lord Roborough, gave a Torah scroll to the Plymouth Synagogue, which became known as the Roborough Scroll. When one of Lord Roborough's houses was cleared in the 1970s, an exquisite *Megillah* dating to around the 18th century, and probably originating from Poland, found its way into a junk shop. It was spotted by local Jewish doctor Mark Gordon. He purchased it and it is now in the possession of his daughter, Valerie Mellor. In 1808, Solomon Sebag arrived in Plymouth, and by 1814, Mrs Pereira, a tea dealer in Little Church Lane. Other male Sephardi Jews are known because they were called up to read from the Torah. They were Moses ben Solomon Delavayo, Jacob ben Joseph Portuguese, Moses ben Hayyim Portuguese and Jacob ben Shalom Mogadore. They may have been in the city only temporarily as traders en route for the West Indies. In the Devonport area lived Joseph and Sara Montefiore (née

Rose Nelson

Mrs Isaacs

THE COMMUNITY: 1800 - 1900

Mocatta). By 1821, Abraham Franco lived in the city until his death in 1832. Although no tombstone survives for him today, it is likely that he was buried in the old cemetery. After his death, the Beth Din in London reminded the Plymouth congregation that his daughters, who had converted to Judaism, could not marry a Cohen, neither could Franco's converted sons say Kaddish (the Mourner's Prayer), a ruling that would not be advocated today.

Some Plymouth Jews decided to uproot and emigrate to America. These included Samuel ben Alexander Aryehin in 1819, Henry Hyman around 1830, and Abraham and Henrietta Cohen. In 1843, Issacher Hyman, son of Hyman Issacher (Beadle of Plymouth synagogue), left for Jamaica where he died ten weeks later of yellow fever. A branch of the Emdon family moved to South Africa, and so too descendants of Henry and Brayna Morris. In 1853, those who sailed for Australia included Simeon Cohen, Isaac Isaac, Mark Levy and Abraham Marks. By the 1870s, members of the Pearl family left for the United States. In the late 1920s that included Solomon Orgel, and Angel Emanuel, a nephew of Abraham Joseph I, who emigrated to the West Indies.

Naval Connections

The long Naval connection of the city's Jews with Plymouth reached its zenith in the nineteenth century. It was here in the busy Naval and military bases that many of Plymouth's Jews became slopmen and Naval agents. These were the days when press gangs roamed the streets and snatched men away and forced them to accept the King's Shilling and become members of His Majesty's Navy. Conditions and discipline in the Navy were harsh. All sailors, whether pressed or not and from all ranks, had to appoint a civilian agent to attend to his legal affairs. The agent became the main contact a man had with his family during his service. Jewish agents were popular because they had a reputation for fair and honest dealings. This was important because, when an enemy ship was captured, the bounty was sold off and the monies shared between all naval ranks – right down to the cabin boy. If, through death or injury, a sailor was unable to claim his share, his agent would act on his behalf and claim the money for his next of kin. The port of Plymouth became the most important centre in England for the sale of enemy prize ships. It was said that at one time one could walk all the way from Sutton Harbour to Turnchapel across the decks of these vessels awaiting sale.

On the scene in Southside Street by 1810 were Abraham Levy (pawnbroker and slopseller), Barrow Moss (silversmith), Elias Moss, Joseph Lyons, Moses Jacob, Benjamin Phineas Moses and Moses Moses (broker), A. Mordecai, Mark Mordecai, Isaac Isaac (slopseller) and Abraham Aaron (slopseller and watchmaker). In Plymouth

Dock, there was Morris Jacobs, Baruch Jonas (silversmith), Emanuel Hart (watchmaker) and son Samuel Hart (father of Solomon Hart, RA), David Israel, Philip Ezekiel (silversmith and watchmaker), Mark Cohen,[89] Saul Charles Aaron, Abraham Emanuel (jeweller and silversmith), Aaron Nathan, Michael Nathan, Asher Nathan, Henry Nathan (new and secondhand clothes dealer) and Lionel Nathan, Henry Ralph and Lewis Ralph, Joseph Sloman (silversmith) and Moses Solomon. Also the Joseph family, Nathan [Altmann] Joseph, Morris Freideberg, Aaron Levy and Joel Levy (silversmith), Lemon Abraham, Hyman Hyman (silversmith and goldsmith), Mark Levi and Jacob Levi, Charles Marks, Reuben Abrahams, Manly Emanuel, Elijah Levey, Marks Levy (pawnbroker, silversmith and clockmaker) and Sampson Levy. All had licences to trade as slopsellers or Navy agents. Mark Anthony Bozon, a Navy agent in Plymouth Dock circa 1743-1808, was brought to Bow Street Magistrate Court, London on alleged charges of forgery. The charges were dropped for lack of evidence.[90]

Another key figure on the Naval scene was Phineas Johnson who served as president of the synagogue in 1826 and 1833. As a supplier of Naval stores to Lord Nelson, he enjoyed the patronage of Jewish business magnate Abraham Goldsmid. Goldsmid organized a letter of introduction to be written for Johnson by Lord Nelson. The letter is dated 12 September 1805 and reads:

'The bearer Mr Phineas Johnson being recommended to me by Mr Abm Goldsmid as a very honest man for transacting business for seamen – You'll please allow him on board Ivy at Plymouth Dock. Lord Nelson will feel much obliged to any Captain who may be pleased to show attention to the recommendation of Lord Nelson's friend and neighbour Mr Goldsmid.'

Another Naval agent and silversmith, Jacob Jacob who died in 1811, left £100 to the synagogue. His will read: 'I bequeath to the Jewish Synagogue of Plymouth

---

[89] Esther Cohen was a pen and quill maker at the same address.
[90] Thanks to Jayne Hyslop, Canada for this information.

... £100 to be invested in five per cent annuities, the interest to be given to the poor Jews of Plymouth on every year in the month of Ellul... £10 towards 10 poor people for making competent meeting for prayers every Saturday and £5 for Mr Ephrim to say a certain portion of the Holy Scriptures, Torah, as a prayer for me on every Saturday, also £5 to my brother-in-law Rabbi Simon for saying Kaddish for me in the Synagogue every day.'[91]

Plymouth figures like Phineas Levi were not only active in naval affairs, but prominently involved in the civic life of the city. A Navy agent of 15 Catherine Street, Devonport, Phineas Levi was one of the first Jews elected to civic office in England as a member of Devonport Board of Commissioners. Born in Portsea in 1785, he later married Kitty Mordecai (Aschenberg), born 1788, of the same place. Their son Joseph was born in Portsea circa 1811. Their other children were born in Plymouth: David, Samuel, Henrietta, Rose, Sophia and Phoebe. Joseph Levi married Arabella Harris (1821-1904) of Truro, the great-granddaughter of Alexander Moses (1715-1791), founder of the Falmouth Jewish community. Subsequently, Joseph and Arabella settled in Exeter and raised their family there. On 24 July 1850, David Levi married Eve Hyman, the daughter of pawnbroker Samuel Hyman. Sophia Levi married Samuel Harris of Leadenhall Street, London, on 15 July 1851. Three years later, in February 1853, Henrietta Levi married Abraham Lemon Woolf, the son of Lemon Woolf. Within six months, Rose Levi married Simon Mordecai Levy of Plymouth. Phineas Levi served as the president of the synagogue in 1834, 1850 and 1851. His wife Kitty died on 15 July 1851 and is buried in the old cemetery, along with their daughter Traphina. Phineas died a decade later in 1861.

It is impossible to ignore the South-West's links to the rum trade and its import by Lemon Hart of Penzance. An advert was placed in the Jewish Chronicle in March 1879 by a supplier of rum, aimed at Plymouth's Jews. It read: 'Picker & Co, 24 Whimple Street, Plymouth will supply fine old Jamaica rum direct from Customs.' The following year, the company boasted in an advert that it had supplied fine old Jamaican rum 'by sanction of the Plymouth Hebrew Congregation' for over 80 years.[92]

The 1850s marked the heyday of the Plymouth Jewish community. Jewish families began to move away from the docks to more fashionable areas of the city. They also tried to keep within reasonable walking distance of the synagogue. Post-1850s, the area of Stonehouse became a busy commercial part of the city and attracted a Jewish presence. Plymouth's Jews found new creative ways to earn a living. Wolfram Ullman and Abraham Titleboam traded as marine photographers in what was essentially a new trade at that time. Titleboam organized the reception of Jews arriving by boat from the pogroms of Europe and arranged their onward rail journey to other parts of Britain. From 1870, trading as *Abraham & Sons*, Titleboam worked out of 39 Catherine Street, Devonport as both a marine photographer and picture frame manufacturer. The company kept in stock a supply of 'photographs of British and Foreign warships'. A branch was opened in Chatham in Kent. Joseph Jacobs of 23 Union Street advertised as an electro-gilder and tobacconist. Another electro-plater in the city by the 1880s was 17-year old Alfred Brock.

Solomon Hart, RA

Plymouth had its share of artistic talent. Native-born Solomon Hart became one of the most distinguished Jewish painters in English history and the first Jew ever to be admitted to the Royal Academy. Born in Plymouth in 1806, the son of Samuel Hart, Solomon Hart Solomon's early years were spent in Plymouth. He then attended a school in Exeter for a year, before returning to Plymouth. He had two brothers: Charles John (who predeceased him) and Mark Mordecai who became an engraver. In 1819, Solomon Hart moved to London and, at the age of only fifteen, studied at the British Museum. In 1923, he was admitted as a student of the Royal Academy and, three

Mrs Silverstone

[91] Susser, p.162.
[92] Jewish Chronicle, 5 April 1888.

years later, exhibited a painting of his father, entitled *Mr Samuel Hart, Professor of Hebrew Language*. He went on to paint many famous public figures and scenes. This included *Manassah ben Israel before Oliver Cromwell*, *The Eve of the Sabbath, Leghorn Synagogue*, and portraits of figures including Sir Anthony de Rothschild, and Alderman Salomons M.P, and Rt Hon. David Salomons, Lord Mayor of London (1856). Hart enjoyed rapid success such that a number of portraits were commissioned for display in public institutions. It had not always been so, and part of his early years were marked by financial struggle. In 1840, Hart was finally elected a full member of the Royal Academy. This may in part have been due to his achievement of the 14ft square masterpiece *Lady Jane Grey at the place of her Execution* which remained rolled up for forty years until he donated it to Plymouth in 1879.[93] Hart never married. He died at his home, 36 Fitzroy Square (London) on 11 June 1881 and is buried in the cemetery of the Western Synagogue. He bequeathed the bulk of his fortune to family in America, and a £1,000 bequest to the Plymouth Synagogue to be invested under the trusteeship of local Jews Eleazar Emdon, Aaron Lyons and Asher Levy. The Jewish Chronicle commented of him: 'art was his mistress to whom he paid a loyal and undivided allegiance to the day of his death.' After Hart's death, Lewis Hyman of Bank Street, Plymouth wrote another tribute in the Jewish Chronicle:

> 'In Hart's last visit to Plymouth he called on the late Jacob Nathan, the Jewish benefactor of the town and described him as one of Nature's Noblemen. His [Hart's] handsome bequest shows the kindly feeling after many years absence he entertained towards the House of Prayer in which his forefathers worshipped.'

Julia Weiner, an expert on Solomon Hart, commented: 'his greatest legacy was that the British art world had become accustomed to having a Jew in their midst.'[94]

Leon Solomon (1817-1879)

Leon Solomon married Rose Joseph (1829-1887), the daughter of Abraham Joseph II, in Plymouth Synagogue on 1 July 1846. Solomon originated from London, a jeweller by profession at 66 Jermyn Street and son of general dealer Solomon Solomon. It appears that Leon Solomon and Rose settled for a time in Plymouth because in November 1862, she gave birth to a son at 1 Clarence Place. Solomon eventually moved his family to Dawlish where they lived in a large house of 21 rooms, overlooking the sea. The house, 'Sunrise' at 7 West Cliff, was then the tallest building in Dawlish. Solomon led quite a lifestyle. He had his own carriage and horses, and was well-known for his entertaining. He and Rose had at least twenty-one

Rose, wife of Leon Solomon

children: Ernest, Adolphus, Sarah, Eliza, Hannah, Asher, Daniel, Meyer, David. Montagu, and eleven further sons. Their son Ernest Solomon emigrated to America and changed his surname to Simpson. It was his son Ernest Simpson (1897-1958), grandson of Leon Solomon, who married Wallis Warfield – Wallis Simpson of fame who embarked on a passionate love affair with Edward VIII and for whom he renounced his throne in 1936. After her divorce from Ernest Simpson in October 1936, her relationship with the new king caused one of the biggest constitutional crises ever to face the British monarchy.

Leon Solomon was an important benefactor to the Plymouth synagogue and gave money for its repair and the construction of the Ladies Gallery. When his second daughter, Hannah, married Lewis Samuel of Birmingham on 9 January 1872 there was a long account of the splendid occasion in the *Exeter & Plymouth Gazette*:

> 'On the wedding day the Post Office, hotels and principal shops, and parts of the town were decorated with banners and crowds collected at the house in which the marriage was performed. The munificence of the bride's family occasioned an intense effect in Dawlish. Mr Solomon presented

---

[93] Julia Weiner in *Catalogue of the Jews of Devon & Cornwall*.
[94] Julia Weiner, op. cit, p.48.

£10 to the vicar of Dawlish for distribution among the needy. A dinner was given to workmen, railway employees and ringers (who had peeled church bells loudly all day).'[95]

Local people were not the only ones to benefit from the celebrations of Solomon's daughter's wedding. At Westminster Jews' Free School in London, he paid for entertainment at the school. He was also a regular contributor to funds for Palestine. Leon Solomon eventually moved from Dawlish to London where he died at 60 Hogarth Road, South Kensington on 12 November 1879 at the age of 68.

Nelson Family

John Selig Nelson (born Libau c.1835) started his business at 181 Union Street, Plymouth sometime after 1851. His shop became a well-known landmark in the city. According to the 1851 census, he was living in Portsmouth with his brother Alexander; both as watchmakers. In 1868, John Selig Nelson married Esther Isaacs in Plymouth, the daughter of John Isaacs (b. 1803) who originated from Poland. John Isaacs and his wife Esther had a number of children: Isaac (b. 1841), Evelina (b.1846), Esther (b. 1849), Elizabeth (b. 1852) and Rachel (b.1855). They lived in Southside Street. Nelson was an oil cloth manufacturer (waterproof clothing). By the 1871 census, he and Esther were living at 89 Fore Street, his occupation noted as clothier & outfitter. At this time, they had a one-year old

Esther Nelson (née Isaacs, 1850-1891)

Hyman John Nelson

daughter, Evelina, and a 2-month old daughter, Beattie (Beatrice). All their subsequent children were born in Plymouth: Hyman (b.1872), Alexander (b.1876), Clara (b.1877), Alf (b.1880), Rachel (b.1881) and Florrie (b.1884). On 1 May 1889, Evelina married Philip Bernstein, jeweller of 2 Old Town Street. Two years later, Beatrice married Godfrey Kalischer, musician of London, on 16 September 1891. On 24 July 1904, Harry Nelson married Lena Titleboam Abrahams of 39 Catherine Street, Devonport, daughter of A. T. Abrahams (photographer and fine art publisher). The Nelson family remained prominently involved in the life of the Plymouth Hebrew Congregation into the next century.

Orgel Family

Eleazer Orgel (born in 1861, son of Chaim Orgel, a hawker) hailed from Austria. A furniture dealer, he settled in Plymouth in the 1880s and lived at 69 King's Gardens. On 12 April 1883, he married Esther Weinberg, daughter of Plymouth shopkeeper Calmen Weinberg and Rebecca Weinberg (née Cohen), of 100 Union Street. They had the

---

[95] Doreen Berger, p. 537.

Miriam Orgel

Tombstone of Lyon Lazarus, old cemetery

following children: Tilly, Hershell, Colman, Simeon (Simon/Sherle), and Miriam. Eleazer was active in the Jewish community, his name mentioned in connection with the Devonport Synagogue in 1903. His father-in-law, Calmen Weinberg, was buried in the Gifford Place cemetery in 1884. His mother-in-law, Rebecca Weinberg, moved to London after her husband's death. Eleazer and Esther Orgel's son Hershell married Sarah Deborah Robins, daughter of the late Gedaliah Robins in Plymouth on 10 June 1908. Community records show that Hershell was active in the Plymouth synagogue during the early 1900s.

Lazarus Family

Lyon, or Lippa, Lazarus married Mathilda Lyon (b. Bideford, 1801), daughter of Francis Lyon. An article appeared in 1832 in which Lyon Lazarus applied to the Bench for a summons against Hyman Isaacs of Cornwall, a converted Jew, who had previously made accusations against Lazarus that he had stabbed him [Isaacs].[96] An investigation took place which basically cleared Lazarus of the accusation of having stabbed Isaacs. Lazarus was assured that if Isaacs ever set foot in Plymouth, a summons would be issued against him. By 1836, Lyon Lazarus was working as an optician in Frankfort Street, Plymouth. In 1847, he was known to be at 27 Frankfort Street, occupation as general dealer.[97] Three of their children Abraham, Daniel and Solomon died in 1832, 1833 and 1836. Surviving children were Mosely (general dealer), Nancy (b. 1831) who married her first cousin Samuel Joyful Lazarus of Exeter, Fanny (dressmaker) who married a cousin Nathan Lazarus [Laurance] in Exeter in 1853, Isaac, Mike, Moses, Frank (merchant apprentice), Hezekiah and Phoebe. In the Lazarus household at that time of the 1851 census were Lyon Lazarus' niece, Hannah Lyons (dressmaker), and Juliana Marks of Portsmouth. Lyon Lazarus died 8 August 5609 [= 1849] aged 59 years and is buried in the old cemetery in Plymouth. Other members of the Lazarus family settled in Exeter and became involved in synagogue life there.[98] Others later emigrated under a new surname Laurance and went on to become internationally known opticians.

Jacob Nathan

Jacob Nathan is first mentioned in Congregational records in 1819. He is recorded as a goldsmith in English Goldsmiths in 1833. His brothers were Nathaniel (b. 1778-1865) and Henry (b. 1793-1864). Their sister Bila died in 1833. None of them married. The Nathans were owners of large houses. Jacob Nathan was active in synagogue affairs and that of the city such that, after his

---

[96] Woolmer's Exeter and Plymouth Gazette, 4 February 1832.
[97] Information provided by Giles Croft.
[98] Helen Fry, *The Jews of Exeter*.

death in May 1867, the epitaph on his tombstone described him as 'one of the worthies of his native town Plymouth. His path during life was upright, just and righteous. The name of Jacob Nathan was proverbial for deeds of kindness and acts of charity to the needy and unfortunate'.

Jacob served as president of the synagogue from 1858-1860. On his death, he became the largest single benefactor to the Plymouth Synagogue. He left the bulk of his estate of £14,000 for its maintenance. In his will dated 15 January 1864, he bequeathed at least twenty-one further bequests to charitable and social institutions. It made him 'one of the most liberal benefactors of modern Plymouth.'[99] The trustees were Abraham Ralph, Eleazer Emdon and Asher Levy. The will included an endowment for the establishment and running of the Jacob Nathan School and £500 free of duty for the Jews' Burial Ground. Other charities which benefited were the *Jewish Poor in Plymouth* for the provision of coal in the three winter months, and the *Poor of the Hebrew Congregation of Plymouth* to be distributed annually on the first day of Jewish New Year, eve of Day of Atonement, eve of Day of Tabernacles, eve of Passover and the eve of the Day of Pentecost. Also the *Ladies' Hebrew Benevolent Society* which provided for 'the relief of poor Jewish women in Plymouth in time of sickness, child-bed or other necessity.' Numerous non-Jewish charities received bequests: The South Devon and East Cornwall Hospital, the Plymouth Public Dispensary, the Plymouth Eye Infirmary, the Society for the Prevention of Cruelty to Animals (Plymouth), the Plymouth Lying-in Charity, the Plymouth Branch of the National Life Boat Association, the Plymouth Humane Society, the Plymouth Sailors' Home, the Plymouth Female Penitentiary, the Female Home in Plymouth, the Plymouth Industrial Society, the Plymouth Ragged School, the Plymouth Soup Kitchen, the Plymouth Benevolent Society and the Plymouth Blanket Society which lent blankets to poor people in the winter.

No familial connection has been found between the above Nathan brothers and Aaron Nathan who was also active in the city. In 1827, Aaron Nathan is known to have been situated at 17 Pearl Street, Stonehouse and became a Constable for Stonehouse. In 1837, he apprehended a gang of counterfeiters, and a silver snuff box awarded to him for this exploits is now in the Jewish Museum, London. In 1851, he was superintendent of the Watch Force and lived at Fore Street, Stonehouse with his wife Mary and daughters Haranitha (dressmaker) and Sarah (milliner). He died in 1858 and is buried in the old cemetery.

Abraham Emdon (1799-1872)

Born in 1799 in Plymouth, Abraham Emdon was the eldest son of Eliezer and Kitty Emden (Emdon). He married Rachel (Frumat bat Moses), daughter of Mordecai Benjamin. Rachel died on 13 May 1838 and is buried in the old cemetery. On 25 March 1840, Emdon married his second wife, Lydia, daughter of box-maker Mordecai Davis. Their children, all born in Devonport, were Eleazer (b.1841), Clare, Solomon, Clarence and Mark. In 1844, Abraham Emdon was listed as a pawnbroker in Cornwall Street, Devonport. In 1851, he was at 13 Ordnance Street. On 9 November 1870, he was elected Town Councillor of Devonport, and later a commissioner of Devonport and member of the General Purposes Committee. He was another early example in England of a Jew being elected to public office. He died on 20 May 1872 at the age of 73 and is buried in the old cemetery.

Wolf Emden (b. 1810) was a brother of Abraham. Wolf's marriage to Rebecca Franco, daughter of salesman John Franco, on 16 August 1837 is the first entry in the Marriage Register. On the 1841 census, Wolf and Rebecca were living at Duke's Street with Rebecca's sister Blum. On the 1851 census, they were at 19 High Street. Wolf's occupation was recorded as draper, assisted by his wife. His sister-in-law Blum Franco was still living with them in 1851. Wolf died on 15 March 1867 and is buried in the old cemetery. His wife Rebecca, who died on 9 March 1895, was buried in the other cemetery.

Eleazer Emdon II

Eleazer Emdon (born Devonport) was the eldest child of Abraham and Lydia Emdon. He was a pawnbroker of Ordnance Street. On 6 February 1878, he married Eliza, daughter of Abraham Joseph II. They had six children, all born in Devonport: Arthur, Leon [Frank], Rolfe, Herbert, Rose and Reginald. Eleazer Emdon's name appears on the synagogue indenture of 16 July 1873. He was another Plymouth Jew who played a prominent role in the civic life of the city. During the 1860s, he was elected a Poor-Law Commissioner. In 1872, he succeeded his father (the late Abraham Emdon) as representative of Morice Ward on the Borough Council, a post which he held for twenty-two years. In 1895, he was appointed Alderman. He died on 26 February 1900, aged 59, and is buried in the Gifford Place cemetery. His funeral was led by his brother-in-law, Rabbi R. Harris of Bayswater Synagogue, and also Revd. Dr Berlin (minister of Plymouth), Revd. J Posner and A. Greenbaum. Eleazer had 'taken an active interest in the public affairs of the Borough of Devonport for over a quarter of a century.'[100] He had become a father-figure in Devonport, known as 'the friend of the Poor'. Throughout his life, he had been a staunch supporter of the poor, a trustee of the synagogue and of charities connected to the synagogue. It was said that no poor person who ever knocked on his door was turned away. His grandson Bert later wrote in a memoir: 'a measure of his philosophical outlook on life may be gauged by the fact that when he was

---

[99] Transactions Plymouth Institute, VI, p.82.
[100] Jewish Chronicle, 2 March 1900.

Tombstone of Eleazer Emdon, old cemetery

offered the Mayorality of Devonport he refused because the office carried with it the post of Chief Magistrate, and he said he did not feel that he was paragon enough to sit in judgement of his fellow men.'

Eleazer's son Hugh became a founder of the Devonport Synagogue in 1904. Another son Frank married Rose Levy, daughter of Hyman Levy. They had four children: Ernest (b. 1914), Bertram (b. 1916), Ralph (1918-1945) and Edward (b.1920). These brothers served the synagogue faithfully during the 20th century.

Ralph Family

Links between Jews in Plymouth and Barnstaple were forged through the Ralph family. From the 1760s, Abraham Ralph I of Barnstaple, silversmith and oldest shopkeeper in the town, held synagogue services in his house for over forty years. He traded as a silversmith and dealer in Wearing Apparel. He and his wife were known to have had at least ten children: six daughters and four sons. Most of their names appear in Abraham Ralph's will, proved in London in January 1806. The sons were Lyon (or Lewis / Judah), Syman, David and Henry. The daughters were Rose (Lyon), Miriam (Jackson), Hannah (Levi), a daughter whose name is not decipherable from the will, but appears to be Kitty, and Catherine whose name appears on a family tree for Betsy Jacobs (née Levy) of Barnstaple.[101]

Three of Abraham Ralph's daughters married three sons of Betsy and Isaac Jacobs of Totnes. Miriam Ralph married Jacob Jacobs, Betsy Ralph married Abraham Jacobs, and Catherine married David Jacobs. The death of Abraham Ralph's wife in July 1794 was recorded in the *Exeter Flying Post*.[102] No record has survived of where she is buried, but probably the old cemetery on the Hoe. She therefore did not live to see the wedding of their eldest daughter, Hannah, to Isaac Levi of Bristol in 1798, which took place in Abraham Ralph's house in Barnstaple. It was a full Jewish ceremony and 'an elegant entertainment given to visitants'.[103] Abraham Ralph I died in Barnstaple in 1805. On his will, he signed his name in Hebrew: *Abraham ben Raphael* (Rafael) – Abraham son of Raphael. It is not known where he was buried, but most likely that his body was transported to Plymouth for burial and that he is in the old cemetery. His son Judah and descendants settled in the city, where they became active in synagogue affairs.

Henry, a son of Abraham Ralph I, lived and worked for a number of years in Penzance. He was a prominent member of the Penzance Hebrew Congregation and is mentioned several times in the Penzance Minute Books for the early 1800s, as well as being one of the signatories to the Penzance *Tikkunim* (Regulations) under his Hebrew name, *Moses ben Hayim ben Abraham*. Before he left Penzance for Plymouth, he donated several items to the Penzance synagogue for use in worship: two Ark curtains and two covers for the Reading Desk.[104] By 1814, he was known to be living in Plymouth as a Navy agent. Although the name of his wife is unknown, he was a married man because it is known that his son Raphael was circumcised by Joseph Joseph on Friday 7 July 1815. An entry survives in the Minute Book for the 1800s in which Henry Ralph apologizes to the congregation for slaughtering his own chickens and agreed 'to pay the fine which the Vestry have imposed upon him and further that he will ask the Rav [head of the Beth Din in London] for a ritual decision concerning the fitness of his vessels.'[105] Henry Ralph later moved to London.

Judah Ralph (1770-1824), another son of Abraham Ralph, was probably born in Barnstaple or Bideford. He was known under various names Lewis, Leape or Judah. He was a pawnbroker, silversmith and engraver. He took out an insurance policy with Royal Exchange on a property in High Street, Barnstaple on 25 October 1794. In 1782, he had made a silver pointer for the Plymouth Synagogue. He married Hannah Nathan (Gitla bat Zvi) of Plymouth and they had four known children: Samuel (1803-1867), Frederick (1804-1850), Abraham (1814-1890), Amelia (1812-1874) and possibly a fifth, George who died in 1877. Samuel's birth on 18 June 1803 is known because he was circumcised by Joseph Joseph. Judah may well have moved to Plymouth after his marriage to Hannah, or after

---

[101] Betsy Levy of Barnstaple married Isaac Jacobs of Totnes in 1774. Both are buried in the old cemetery in Plymouth.
[102] 10 July 1794.
[103] Exeter Flying Post, 7 June 1798.
[104] *The Lost Jews of Cornwall*, p.95.
[105] Minute Book entry, 7 June 1812.

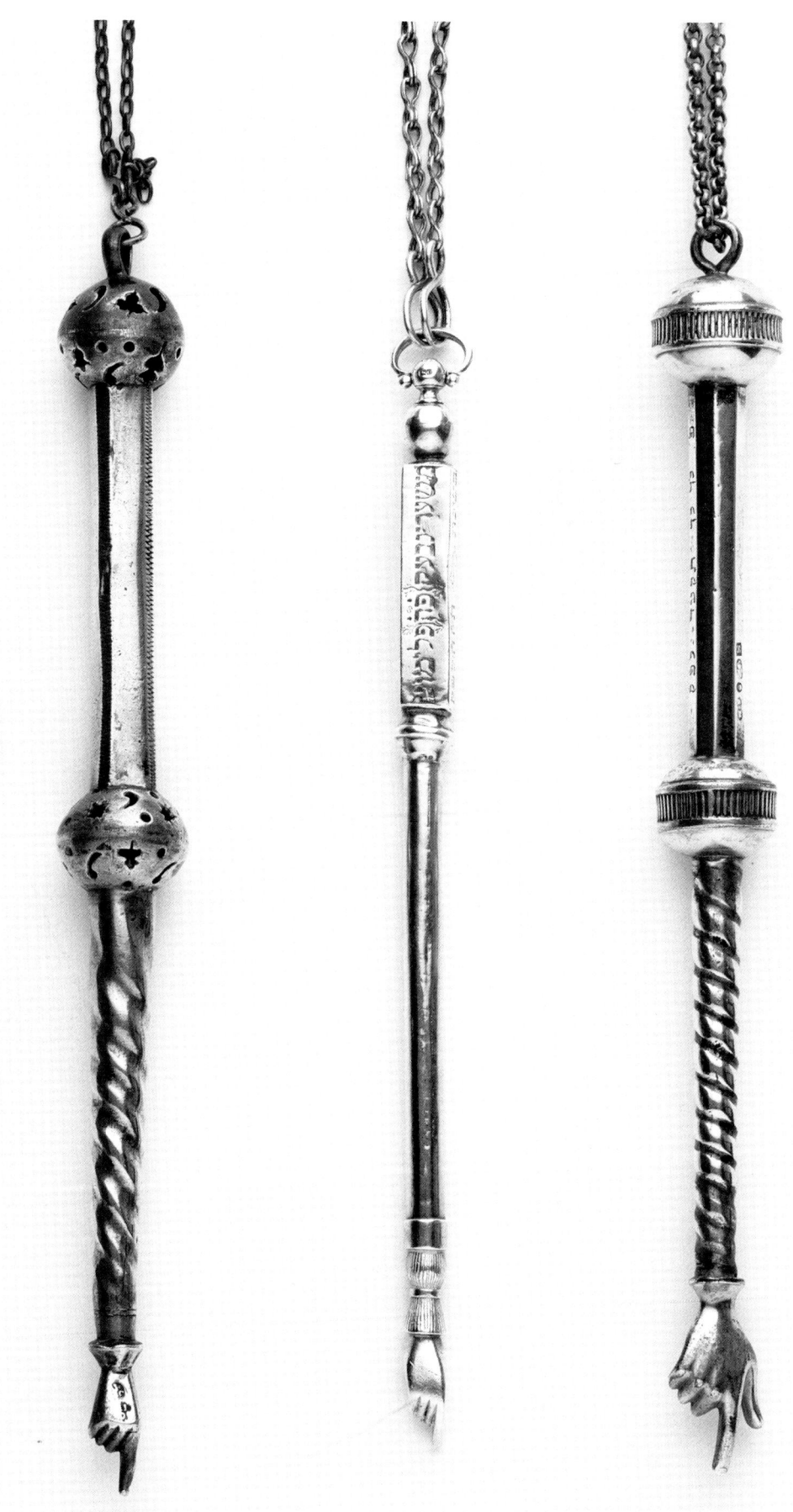

Silver pointers, (from left to right): silver pointer in memory of Judah, son of Abraham Ralph, 1792; silver pointer in memory of Yehuda Jacob son of CaHarar, 1745; silver pointer, 1813, made by Simon Harris of Plymouth Dock. COURTESY OF BONHAMS

THE COMMUNITY: 1800 - 1900

his father's death in 1805, when Jewish services in Barnstaple appear to have ceased. By 1812, he was registered as a Navy agent in Plymouth and known to have been secretary to a Masonic Lodge. He was a member of the Vestry committee of the synagogue and frequently named in the Minute Book for the period. In October 1812, he was appointed treasurer of the cemetery fund, alongside Emanuel Hart [Manasseh ben Zvi] who was the second treasurer on behalf of the Dock Minyan. The death of Judah [Lewis] Ralph was recorded in *Trewman's Flying Post*, 5 February 1824: 'Died on Sunday, at his house, in Catherine Street, Plymouth, Mr Lewis Ralph, aged 54.' There is no record of his burial in the old cemetery, however, given his active role in the synagogue, it is inconceivable that he is not buried in the Jewish cemetery. Judah was known to have financial constraints because, in one of the Minute Books, it notes that his brother-in-law Yehiel b. Zvi paid half a guinea for 'Judah b. Abraham of Barnstaple to become a Vestry member of the congregation'. In 1815, Judah was expelled from membership of the Burial Society for not paying his arrears. His wife Hannah died in May 1853 at the age of 87 and is buried in the old cemetery. Of their children, Samuel Ralph died on 17 March 1867 and is also buried in the old cemetery. According to the 1841 census, Frederick was a general dealer, living with wife Tressa at 4 Bull Hill with two children, Henrietta and Henry. In 1844, he was listed as a marine store dealer on Southside Quay. His tombstone inscription reads: 'Here lies Avigdor ben Judah: In memory of Frederik Ralph, who departed this life 15 October 5611 [= 1850], aged 46 years.' Amelia Ralph never married and died in 1874.

Abraham Ralph II (1814-1890) was named after his grandfather, Abraham Ralph of Barnstaple. He appears variously in the happenings of the Plymouth synagogue in the mid-1800s as member of the Vestry committee. After the death of his cousin Jacob Nathan, he was named in the will as a trustee of the Jacob Nathan School and one of the executors of the estate. According to the 1841 census, he lived Southside of Bedford Street with his 75-year old mother, sister Amelia and aunt Harriet Nathan.[106] His occupation was given as dealer in marine stores. In the 1870s, he was known to be living at 6 Union Terrace. When he died on 4 October 1890, at the age of 76, he was buried in the Gifford Place cemetery.

Bloom / Ullmann Family

Philip Bloom (b. 1873, Whitechapel) moved from Hanley, Staffordshire, where his father had a tailoring business, to Plymouth to set up his own business as a naval tailor/outfitter. He enterprisingly rowed himself out to meet incoming ships, getting orders from sailors. On 30 June 1897, he married Gertrude Augusta Ullmann (b. 1876, Plymouth) in Plymouth, the daughter of Wolfram

Gertrude Augusta Bloom, daughter of Deborah Ullmann

Pearl, Frank and Gertrude Bloom

Deborah Morris, 1893

Left to right: Philip Bloom, daughter Pearl, son Frank and Gertrude Bloom

---

[106] Harriet Nathan was born in Plymouth in 1773, listed in the Plymouth Directory of 1850 under 'gentry' and of Bedford Street.

Charles Samuels

Jacob Ullmann and Deborah Ullmann (née Morris).[107] They had ten children: eight girls and two boys. One son, Frank Bloom, was born at 35 William Place, Devonport on 28 October 1914. He served as a gunner in WW2. He died in Plymouth in January 1995.

Wolfram Ullmann (b. 1835, Driesen, Prussia), the father of Gertrude Augusta (above) came to England with his brother Solomon in 1848, and they settled in Plymouth as importers of sponges and leather. Wolfram married Deborah Morris on 22 May 1861 at 35 Cambridge Street, Plymouth. She was the daughter of Henry Morris and Brina Morris (née Joseph) who had married in Exeter Synagogue around 1830.[108] Wolfram and Deborah had nine children. Wolfram took up photography for a while and became a travelling photographer. He had a few other occupations: pawnbroker, outfitter and furniture dealer. His brother Solomon married Sarah Joseph of East Stonehouse, and they had twelve children, all but three of them born in Plymouth. Solomon later became a wealthy diamond and pearl merchant with a shop in London's Hatton Garden.

Francis Lyon

Another link between Plymouth and North Devon came through the Lyon family. Francis Lyon (1752-1837), a silversmith and watchmaker, whose Hebrew name was Avigdor ben Moses Isaac, lived in Bideford around 1790. In 1767, he was apprenticed as a clock and watchmaker to John Lakeman in Exeter, a non-Jew. There is an entry for Francis Lyon in Ponsford's *Devon Clocks & Clockmakers*: 'Francis Lyon, Bideford, silversmith & watchmaker. Long case reported.' By 1822, he was working as a watchmaker in Pike Street, Plymouth. He married Sara Fanny Lazarus, a straw hatmaker and daughter of Samuel Mark Lazarus. They had four known children, all born in Bideford: Judah (1794-1852), Fanny, Solomon (1797-1838) and Mathilda (b.1801).[109] Francis Lyon died on 28 January 1837 and was buried in the old cemetery, as are many members of his family, including his wife Sara who died in March 1849. Judah P. Lyon, Solomon Lyon and Fanny Lyon stayed in Plymouth. Judah became a watchmaker and jeweller at 7 Union Street. He is also mentioned in Ponsford's *Devon Clocks & Clockmakers*: 'Lyon, Judah. Plymouth. Watch & clockmaker & silversmith, Bedford Street, 1830-6; 7 Union

---

[107] Philip Bloom died in February 1934, and Gertrude in April 1949. Both are buried in the Gifford Place cemetery.
[108] Brina on 28 August 1867 and is buried in the old cemetery.
[109] Mathilda (born Bideford, 1801) married Lyon Lazarus. Lyon Lazarus died in 1849 and is buried in the old cemetery.

Street, 1850-6.' He married Fanny Michael of Swansea, daughter of Levi Michael.[110] They settled in Swansea, before moving back to Plymouth in 1847. Judah died on 18 February 1861 in Plymouth, thought to be buried in plot B74. Lyon's sister, Fanny, appears not to have married.

Solomon Lyon married Feigela bat Mordecai. He worked as a silversmith; his wife as a straw hat maker in Pyke Street. Tragically, she was one of the victims of the plague of 1832. The Exeter Flying Post recorded: 'Died last week of cholera, Mrs S. Lyon, aged 29, wife of Mr Solomon Lyon, silversmith, Frankfort Street, Plymouth.' Her tombstone reads: 'My wife Feigela bat Mordecai, wife of Isaac ben Avigdor, died on account of the plague, Tuesday, 2nd day of Rosh Hodesh Elul 5592 [= 28 August 1832].'

Gabrielson / Gittelson Family

Samuel Gittleson (born Riga, Latvia, 1862) came to England in the mid-1880s and settled first as a general dealer at 113 West Street, Fareham in Hampshire. From there, he came to Plymouth and once settled, brought over from Latvia his brother Conrad, his sisters and father.[111] During his brief time in Plymouth, he met Charlotte Gabrielson (b.1866, London) who was living with her family at 41 Union Street. She was a daughter of Austrian-born Morris Zeitung (a picture dealer), and Harriet Zeitung (neé Prager, born Cracow). On the 1881 census, her siblings are listed as Emily, Lewis, Eva and Miriam, the latter born in Plymouth. The family had already anglicized their surname from Zeitung to Gabrielson by the time Charlotte married Samuel Gittleson in Plymouth Synagogue on 22 September 1886. Subsequently, Samuel Gittleson moved to Exeter with his new bride and anglicised his name to Charles Samuels. He went on to become president of Exeter Synagogue for over 60 years.

New Wave of Immigration

The 1880s saw a wave of Jewish immigration into Plymouth, but concern over the fate of Russian Jews was not limited to the Jewish community. In February 1882,

Outside the synagogue, date unknown

---

[110] The Cambrian, 11 April 1840.
[111] The only exception was sister Freda who remained in Latvia and later perished in the Holocaust.

the Mayor of Plymouth, Mr Burnard, held a public meeting in the Guildhall attended by a thousand people, including Christian ministers and private individuals. A number of speakers gave eloquent speeches which expressed their sympathy for Russian Jews and a condemnation against the persecutions. Revd. Prebendary Wilkinson put forward a motion that: 'this meeting deeply laments the outrages which the Jews in several parts of the Russian dominions have for some time suffered, and considers them as an offence to humanity and civilization.' A vote of thanks was proposed to the Mayor by Asher Levy and seconded by Lewis Hyman. The meeting demonstrated a very important solidarity between the Gentile and Jewish community that was not always paralleled elsewhere in England. It demonstrates again how Plymouth continued its tradition of tolerance for peoples of different religions.

In 1897, new refugees from persecutions in Russia arrived in Plymouth aboard the liner *SS Paris*.[112] Moored in the Plymouth Sound, they were transferred to the Dunstan & Co tug and taken to Millbay Docks for disembarkation. There were 400 Jewish women and children who arrived with nothing except the clothes they stood up in. They were met at Millbay Docks by the Mayor and Chief Constable, Mr Sowerby. James Abrahams, son of photographer Titleboam Abrahams, was eight years old at the time and witnessed his father helping the refugees, along with the synagogue's minister, Revd. Berlin. A committee and group of helpers formed by the Plymouth Hebrew Congregation gathered enough food and drink for the 400 refugees waiting in the yard at the local police station. In the coming days, the refugees were found new homes from larger centres of Jewry in London, Manchester and Leeds.

By the end of the 19th century, Jewish religious life in Plymouth remained strong and the community continued to grow. The Jewish community would continue its contribution to public life in Plymouth into the next century.

---

[112] Digest, November 1972.

CHAPTER 7
TWENTIETH CENTURY

AS A NEW century dawned, Plymouth emerged as the only viable Jewish community in the South-West. Exeter was in temporary decline, and the two Cornish communities of Falmouth and Penzance were defunct. Membership of Plymouth Hebrew Congregation stood at around 230 individuals. The beginning of the twentieth century saw a rise in membership to 300 by 1906 and 400 by 1936. The community remained extremely active; a measure of that is glimpsed in reports in the Jewish Chronicle. It noted, for example, that in spring 1904, the Jewish Literary and Social Society of Plymouth held a successful Purim ball. The programme was arranged by Isaac Bromberg and Isidore Cohen. Refreshments were provided by the ladies committee: Mrs Lempert, Mrs I. Roseman, and Mrs B. Cohen. Thanks were also given to the Committee: Mr H. Orgel, Mr M. Feather, Mr A. E. Roseman and Mr I. Fredman.[113] In 1909, the Plymouth Hebrew Board of Guardians was founded, due to the efforts of Myer Fredman. In its first year, the Board undertook a number of charitable acts that included assisting a Russian stowaway by paying his fare to London to board a ship to America to join friends there. It paid fares so a father could take his son to London for an operation. It also obtained special leave for Passover for Jewish soldiers and sailors, obtained pedlar's licenses, and granted coal, matzos and financial assistance to local Jewish poor. At the end of May 1911, the synagogue received a visit from Dayan and Mrs Hyamson of South Wales. They were greeted by ministers Revd. Jacobs and Revd. A. Slavinsky, along with Myer Fredman (President), A. Conick (Treasurer), M. Solomons (Secretary) and other gentlemen. Dayan Hyamson inspected the Hebrew schools of Devonport and Plymouth.

Plymouth's Jews kept abreast of the changing technological times. The firm of Joseph Sanger went from trading in gas fittings to electrical fittings from premises at 7 Cornwall Street. Tobias Brand at 42 Frankfort Street traded as a wholesaler in gas fittings and sold the first refrigerators in Plymouth. His shop was memorable for its green painted window. Close to the old railway arch, near King Street, Moshe Sanger sold all kinds of electrical goods, including the latest new gadget – the wireless set. From an adjacent office, he operated the "Whitehall Finance Corporation", a loan office that went on to become incredibly successful. Almost immediately opposite on the corner of Well Street was Louis Robins' pawnbroking business called Manchester House. Here he also sold jewellery, optical instruments, soft furnishings, bedding, clothing for workers, boots and shoes. Nearby was the furniture business of the Conick family. In King Street was another furniture business, new and secondhand, run by Mr. Gold. Behind these shops in one of the many narrow streets was *The Globe Upholstery Co*, a wholesale furniture and cabinet-making business run by Sam Owen. Off King Street, in Tracey Street, was Goldstein's master tailors whose team of seamstresses and machinists made bespoke outfits. The Cohen and Fredman family businesses were located in the narrow Old Courtenay Street. Mr. L. Cohen ran Courtenay House Stores, whilst Misses Beatrice and Lily Cohen managed a toy shop. Miss L. Pearl ran a costume business known as Courtenay.

Eva and Ruth Field

---

[113] Jewish Chronicle, 11 March 1904.

Frankfort Street became one of the central trading areas for Jews. Here was the ladies gown shop, *Jennie Lee*, the trading name of Mrs Jennie Greenburgh (wife of Joseph Greenburgh), and the premises of *The Artistic Furnishing Company* of the Lazarus family. The Fredman business fronted onto Frankfort Street, but around the back in Willow Street was their furniture repository. In the 1920s, Mr. L. Cohen ran *Novelty Stores*, and George Lazarus had an estate agent business at 35 Frankfort Street. There was also pawnbroker, Abraham Cohen of 45 Frankfort Street. He and his wife Henrietta had three sons: Isidore, Moses and Herman. Isidore continued the business in the period between WW1 and WW2, founded as it was on the traditional pawnbroker industry that blossomed into a jewellery and fancy goods shop. The family traded in Frankfort Street until the business was destroyed in the blitz. Samuel Davies was a wholesale dealer and importer of horological and other goods. Then there was tobacconist, Mr Conick, another pillar of the community who traded in Tavistock Road, on the corner of Russell Street and Frankfort Street. There were two Jacobs families in the city, one living on the Barbican, the other near the Market. To differentiate between the two families, one was known as "Barbican Jacobs", the other as "Market Ally Jacobs". Then there was Ephraim (Frank) Holcenberg (b. 1867 in Wyszograd, Poland) who was one of five children of Pincus Holcenberg and Ruchla Herszt. He and his wife Eva came to England around 1909. They settled in Plymouth with their two children Rose (Peggy) and Gussie, where Ephraim (known as Frank) traded as a furrier. From Plymouth, he expanded his trade and travelled to markets all over Devon, Cornwall and even Wales. Whilst he travelled for his work, his wife and daughters ran a successful family business *Imperial Fur Company* from Frankfort Street from around 1913. It was so prosperous that, in 1925, they moved to premises in George Street and became the city's leading furriers. Frank Holcenberg died in 1934. His widow and daughters continued the family business and became so successful that two years later, in 1936, they opened *Woodhills*, a fashion shop. The daughters eventually married and the family was involved in redeveloping the blitzed city of Plymouth after the Second World War.[114] Daughter Peggy married Isidore Joseph, also a member of an old Plymouth family, and lived most their business life in Torquay. Isidore became the first Jewish Mayor of Torquay. Peggy and Gussie endowed Plymouth Central Library with the Holcenberg Collection - the largest collection of books of Jewish interest in any British provincial public library.

Marlborough Street in Devonport was also a buzz with Jewish traders, including Joe Spark, a master tailor of the old school. Sidney Aloof once recalled: 'He made me my first ever Plus Fours suit when that type of men's garb was fashionable in the 1920s and 30s.'[115] Here too was King Field who traded in the street for a while. In 1928, Field opened a watch and clock repairs and sales shop at the top end of the street, just a few doors away from Abraham's Photo shop and almost opposite Roseman's furniture shop. Elias Ellis, the congregation's president in 1921, ran a butcher's shop in Russell Street before he left for South Africa. It was from here that local Jews could purchase

Synagogue school outing, 1932

---

[114] A trust was founded in Plymouth called The Holcenberg Foundation Trust Fund.
[115] Plymouth Hebrew Congregation Digest, March 1970.

kosher meat that had been slaughtered in an abattoir in Library Lane. Also in Russell Street was Da Costa's antique emporium known as Andrade. Adjacent to him was the London Fruit Stores, run by Mrs Wolestein, a relative of Mr. Pinkofsky whose tailoring establishment was located around the corner. Another man, about which little is known, was Mr. Maunchester of 17 Lisson Grove who appears to have had some standing in the congregation. In 1895, he was one of the committee members of the Jacob Nathan School. In Richmond Street, Abraham Robins established himself as a pawnbroker, a trade also carried out by his brothers. At the lower end of the entrance to the Meat market stood a china and glassware shop, belonging to Joe Jacobs which carried a competitively priced range of goods. Nearby was the *London and Garceston Boot Company*, run by Mr. Leskin. In the Pannier Market were some small Jewish-run stalls, one run by Bert Emdon's father in miscellaneous items, another in imitation jewellery run by Mr. Spurling, and a handbag stall under the ownership of Miss Bella Wykansky.

A Plymouth Jew from this period who became famous on the political scene was Leslie Hore-Belisha. Born in Devonport on 7 September 1893, he was the only son of Jacob Isaac Belisha and Elizabeth Miriam Belisha (née Miers). His father died in 1894 when he was a few months old. In 1912, his mother married Sir Charles Adair Hore, Permanent Secretary of the Ministry of Pensions. Leslie Hore-Belisha was educated at Clifton College, Bristol, based at Polak's House, and later studied at Oxford University. In 1923, he qualified as a barrister, then in 1923 was elected the first Liberal MP for Devonport.[116] From June 1934 until May 1937, he served as Minister for Transport, in which capacity he became famous for the introduction of Belisha beacons on zebra crossings. He also restricted the speed limit on built-up roads to 30 mph. From May 1937 until January 1940, he served as Secretary of State for War in the government of Neville Chamberlain. He died in Rheims, France in February 1957.

Nelson family

The Nelson family, already settled in the city since the 1800s, continued to enjoy prominence in the twentieth century. On 7 and 8 March 1902, the new King Edward VII and Queen Alexandra visited Devonport and issued a royal summons to the Nelsons:[117]

> 'Messrs Nelson & Sons of Trafalgar Square, Union Street, Plymouth had the honour conferred on them of a Royal Command from HM Queen Alexandra and Princess Victoria to call on the Royal yacht with an assortment of antique silver. Her Majesty and Her Royal Highness made a large selection of quaint and interesting pieces and seemed delighted with the display shown by Hyman and Alec Nelson.'

Nelson's shop

Nelson's shop

Alice Nelson

Two years later, the community mourned the death of John Nelson, resident of 181 Union Street, who died on 6 March 1904. His wife Esther predeceased him at the age of 39 in March 1891. John Selig Nelson was a prominent Freemason and member of Lodge Charity. It was reported that he was 'for 50 years was one of the best known tradesmen of Plymouth and Devonport... His benevolence was not limited by race or creed.' The funeral took place on a Friday and was reported to have been attended 'by fully 5,000 persons.'[118] A few months later, his son Harry married local Jewish girl, Lena Titleboam Abrahams of 39 Catherine Street, Devonport, daughter of A. T. Abrahams (photographer and fine art publisher). Three years later, on 10 February 1907, John Nelson's daughter Rachel married widower, Michael Jacobs, an outfitter, of 19 Buckland Street.

---

[116] Hore-Belisha was not the only Jewish MP in Plymouth's history. There was Sir Sigismund Mendl, MBE who was elected for Plymouth 1898-1900.
[117] Jewish Chronicle, 14 March 1902.
[118] Jewish Chronicle, 11 March 1904.

The Brock family

The Brock family connections with Plymouth stretched back at least a hundred years. Eleazar (George) Brock was a tailor in the city by the turn of the 19th century. When his son George married Sarah Levy, daughter of Lyon Levy, on 3 January 1838, it was the second wedding to be entered in the Synagogue Marriage Register. George and Sarah's son Lewis became a hairdresser and, in January 1860, married Henrietta Nathan, daughter of Aaron Nathan (a police constable). Lewis and Henrietta had five sons: Henry, Charles, Alfred, Jacob Nathan (John) and Ernest. The family had musical talent – father and sons formed a band locally, known as Brock's Band. Jacob Nathan became a watchmaker at 21 Union Street. In April 1890, he married Eva Lavinia Atkins under the auspices of the Plymouth Synagogue. Charles Solomon Brock went on to open a nightclub in the city and by the time of his death in 1947 left around £25,000. Alfred Brock became the first electro-plater in the South-West and left £1,400 when he died the previous year in 1946.

Ernest Brock's business was met with even greater success. He began with a clothing factory which employed several hundred workers which continued until destroyed in the blitz on Plymouth. He turned his hand as a bookmaker and property developer. In 1923, he married Lilian Ada Harvey (b. 1882), known to everyone as Cissie. They both served as Aldermen on Plymouth Council. Cissie was a member of the Council for 34 years, from 1928 until 1964, the first woman on the City Council to become a Party Whip. She was the first female chairman of the Watch Committee (then responsible for the Police and Fire Services). In 1966, the first Plymouth Fire Boat was named Cissie Brock in her honour. She served as a trustee of Rowe's Charity and always supported Jewish charitable appeals. On Ernest's death in 1950, he left a considerable estate worth £125,000, part of which was used to establish the Ernest Brock Almshouses for 'the aged and deserving poor of Plymouth'. A stained glass window was donated to the synagogue in his memory by his widow. Cissie died on 20 May 1978 at the age of 96.

Ernest's older brother, Jacob Nathan Brock married Miriam Frances Bash on 6 April 1952. He was a widower; she was a spinster of 57, the daughter of diamond polisher Samuel Bash. Jacob (John) died on 13 March 1959 at the age of 91. He was predeceased by his wife who died just eight months after they had married. Today, there is a plaque in the synagogue in memory of Miriam Brock, which reads:

> Miriam Frances Brock
> A native of this city
> and a member of this congregation
> who died 27 December 1953 – 5714, aged 58
> 'Many daughters have done worthily
> But thou excellest them all'

She bequeathed the residue of her estate (exceeding £12,000) for the benefit of the Plymouth Hebrew Congregation

The Brocks are buried in the Gifford Place cemetery.

Fredman Family

The Fredman family played a very important role in the civic and Jewish life of the city for several generations from the late 19th century into the mid-twentieth century. Jacob David Fredman was the first of the family to settle with his wife Rachel in Plymouth by the 1860s. They both originated from Russia. Their first daughter Leah was born in Birmingham in 1862. They moved to Devonport where, in 1863, their daughter Phoebe was born. After Phoebe came other children: Amelia, Rebecca, Janette, Annie, Hannah, Samuel, Israel, Joseph and Esther, all born in Devonport. Jacob established a successful business as a clothes dealer in Queen Street, Devonport.[119] Around 1866, when a vacancy arose for Beadle in the Plymouth synagogue, his brother Levy Fredman came over from Saki to take up the post. By the 1881 census, Levy Fredman was no longer Beadle of the synagogue but a general dealer at 11 Hoe Street, not far from the synagogue.[120]

Lili Fredman

---

[119] Jacob Fredman died on 2 December 1898, aged 64 and is buried in Gifford Place.
[120] Levi Fredman died on 17 January 1886, aged 54 and is buried in Gifford Place.

Other family members soon emigrated to Plymouth, including a brother (Samuel) Wolf Fredman who was a traveller, and Levin Fredman who started humbly as a hawker of sponges and leather. Levin Fredman, his wife Hetty and two children shared a house with Jacob Roseman and his family at 98 Pembroke Street. Wolf Fredman, his wife and four children lived at 3 Canterbury Street in Devonport, with his married daughter Rachel Roseman and her husband Israel Roseman. This was not the only inter-marriage between the Fredman and Roseman families. On 26 February 1890, Myer Isaac Roseman of 30 Union Street (the son of Levy Roseman) married Amelia Fredman, daughter of Levin Fredman. By this time, Levin had moved on from being a hawker of sponges and leather to become a successful property dealer. Levin had another daughter, Fanny, and three sons: Myer, Aaron and Israel. Myer entered politics (see below), Aaron served on the Board of Guardians, and Israel Fredman served on the local Borough Council. By 1881, Levin was living with his family and one servant at 4 James Street, Devonport, occupation listed as an outfitter. He, like so many of Plymouth's Jews, had moved from itinerant lower class to middle class respectability. By the time of his daughter's marriage in 1890, he was living in Catherine Street, Devonport.

Levin Fredman's daughter Fanny married Revd. Reuben Tribich (Lincoln), minister of Bradford Hebrew Congregation, in the Plymouth Synagogue on 23 January 1907. The wedding created considerable interest in the three towns 'as the bride and her family have for many years past taken great interest in public work.'[121] The couple received over 300 presents, and the wedding was attended by non-Jews, including the Mayor and Mayoress, Deputy Mayor and several ex-Mayors, county Councillors and magistrates. The service was conducted by Revd. M. Abrahams of Leeds, assisted by Plymouth's minister Revd. D. Jacobs. They were married under a new canopy given by Fanny's parents and designed by her brother Myer Fredman. Her nieces Hilda, Dorothy and Freda Fredman were bridesmaids, and David Fredman pageboy. It was reported that the bride wore: 'a charming white silk hand-embroidered robe with full court train trimmed with Honiton lace and a beautiful coronet of orange-blossoms.' The approaches to the synagogue were decorated with flags and bunting for the occasion. Afterwards, a reception was held at the Guildhall, Devonport. Revd. Tribich later became minister of a congregation in New Jersey, America. Fanny and Reuben's children were Wolfe, Ellis, and Ashe (Fredman Ashe) Lincoln QC who served with distinction in the Royal Navy in the Second World War.

Levin Fredman was active in both the main Plymouth Hebrew Congregation and the Devonport Synagogue. He served as President and Treasurer at the main synagogue in Catherine Street, to which he walked every Sabbath until ill health prevented him. He gave generously to synagogue funds and to the local poor. He had been involved in the opening ceremony of the Devonport synagogue in 1907. In politics, he was a Conservative and, as such, engaged with local issues. He contested local Council elections, losing by only a few votes. It was to be his son Myer Fredman who would make history by becoming the first Jewish Mayor of Devonport. Levin's wife Hetty died on 22 February 1910 at the age of 77 and is buried in the Gifford Place cemetery. Two years later, in October 1912, Levin himself died. The Jewish Chronicle paid tribute to him:

'Mr Fredman settled at Devonport about half a century ago, and from very humble beginnings he rose by reason of his business acumen to become one of the largest property owners in the West of England… He worked tirelessly to solve the problems of housing of the working classes. For over 40 years he had improved some of the poorest quarters of Plymouth.'[122]

Levin Fredman was a popular and well-respected man. His funeral at Gifford Place was conducted by Revd. D. Jacobs and Revd. A. K. Slavinsky.

Myer Fredman

Myer was the eldest son of Levin and Hetty Fredman, born in Devonport. He married Rebecca Levy from London, the daughter of Mr and Mrs Isaac L. Levy. Myer and Rebecca had two children: David (b. 1898) and Hilda. Myer continued in the family business and rose to a prominent role in local politics, first as a Councillor and then, in 1909, elected JP for Devonport Borough Council. He served as Chairman of the Mercantile Association, Chairman of the Swimming & Humane Society, Executive of the Conservative Association, Chairman of the Tramways Committee and Chairman of the Plymouth Jewish Board of Guardians. Myer Fredman became the first elected Jewish Mayor of Devonport. On 19 November 1911, in his capacity as Mayor, he accompanied magistrates and members of Plymouth Corporation on a special visit to the synagogue. On 3 July 1919, Myer's wife Rebecca died at the age of only 44. The Jewish Chronicle reported that her untimely death was 'mourned far and wide. She was in ailing health for a number of years, but bore her suffering with resignation and cheerfulness… Plymouth Jewry has sustained an overwhelming and irremediable loss.' The funeral and prayers were led by Revd. Slavinsky and Revd. Zeffertt.

Myer Fredman died on 5 August 1927 at the age of 57. His funeral in Gifford Place cemetery was attended by the Mayor, other civic dignitaries and the whole Jewish community. Revd. Zeffertt said 'he was the moving spirit in the congregational life… Whether in office or out of office, he displayed the same deep interest in all communal

---

[121] Jewish Chronicle, 1 February 1907.
[122] Jewish Chronicle, 25 October 1912.

Myer Fredman, first Jewish Mayor of Devonport

Rebecca, wife of Myer Fredman

affairs.'[123] Joseph Sanger, then President of the Plymouth Synagogue, called him 'a sincere and kind-hearted friend, beloved by rich and poor alike. We shall remember him still more for the countless kind and thoughtful acts which have helped to lighten the load of the sorrowful and suffering.' A tribute came from the President of the Devonport Synagogue, Solomon Robins, who said: 'his death has deprived the Devonport Jewish Community of a highly esteemed and beloved friend.' Fredman's tombstone describes him as 'honoured citizen of his native city.'

Myer Fredman's children both married. In August 1920, Hilda married Lesley Israel Cohen of Plymouth, in a ceremony conducted by Revd. S. Lipson and Revd. M. Zeffertt in the synagogue. They had five children: Rivka and Levin (twins), Doreen, Ruth and Sally. The family stayed in Plymouth until WW2, then during the blitz moved to Coffinswell near Newton Abbot. On 9 December 1921, David Fredman married Lili Shaffer in Blackpool, the youngest daughter of Mr and Mrs Mark Shaffer of Blackpool. David Fredman went on to serve in both world wars, after which he continued in the property business. He and Lili had two children: Baba (b.1924) and John (b.1927), both born in Plymouth. At the age of 13, John celebrated his *bar mitzvah* in the Plymouth Synagogue. Baba married Jack Clarfelt in London.

Roseman Family

By the 1870s, several members of the Roseman family had come over from Poland. The men originated from Sakie and were hawkers of sponges and leathers. One was Abraham Roseman, a lodger at 53 Mount Street, aged 20. Thirty-one year old Jacob Roseman lived at 98 Pembroke Street with his wife Mary (also born in Poland) and two children, Norman and Myrah (the latter born in Devonport). At 44 Marlborough Street was Myer Israel Roseman (son of Levy Roseman), a furniture dealer who had married Amelia Fredman in 1890. Amelia was a daughter of Levin Fredman who also hailed from Sakie. During the First World War, Myer Israel Roseman served in the Special Constabulary and as Munitions Director in the Devonport Dockyard. Because of his capabilities in this role, he was transferred to the Albert Docks in London as director from 1915-18. He also served on the Refugee Committee. He died on 15 February 1935 at the age of 68, having served as synagogue president and treasurer, and been a member of numerous committees that included The Board of Deputies, Jewish Board of Guardians, Zionist Society and the Burial Society. His obituary commented: 'he evinced a keen interest in the disused cemeteries, and was solely responsible for obtaining for the West of

---

[123] Jewish Chronicle, 12 August 1927.

TWENTIETH CENTURY

Rachel, wife of Israel Roseman, COURTESY HILDA MARKS

Israel Roseman, COURTESY HILDA MARKS

On 25 June 1913, Rosa (Beatrice) Roseman, married Sonny (Solomon) Gordon, son of Michael Gordon. Sonny ran a grocery shop in the Pannier Market, and Rosa a Ladies Fashion business.

Black Family

By the late nineteenth century, the Black family arrived in the city and inter-married with other prominent Jewish families. On 14 March 1923, Eli Black's son Harry (Hyman) married Esther Roseman, the youngest of ten children of Israel Roseman. Harry and Esther had two children: Hilda and Israel (Bertie). Harry Black was the founder of the Mutley Property Group of companies. His wife Esther was very active in the Jewish community, charitable causes, and in giving hospitality to American and British Jewish service personnel during the Second World War. The Black's home was always open, frequently entertaining people for Friday night Shabbat dinner. Esther was founding a member of the Plymouth Jewish Ladies' Guild. After Harry's death in January 1956, his widow Esther and the children, paid for a new prayer house to be built in his memory at the Gifford Place cemetery where he is buried. In 1962, she returned to the city again to unveil a plaque at the opening of Mutley House in Armada Way, a new self-contained modern office block that housed the

England special grants for the disused cemeteries of Devon and Cornwall.'[124]

In 1871, at 3 Canterbury Street, lived 20-year old Israel Roseman with his wife Rachel. By 1891, he was living at 30 Union Street, trading as a pawnbroker, with one servant and 9 children: Ernest, Rebecca, Myer, Samuel, Deborah, Isaac, Bertie, Joseph and Beatrice (all born in Devonport, except Beatrice who was born in East Stonehouse). A number of Roseman weddings took place in Plymouth. In June 1893, Rebecca Roseman married Elias Plaskowsky, the son of Lewis Plaskowsky. On 7 March 1906, Deborah Roseman married Gedaliah Lechovitchkey, a furniture dealer of Lower North Street, Exeter, in Oddfellows Hall in Devonport. On 11 December 1911, Joseph Roseman, who worked at his father's business at 30 Union Street, married Katie Stein of 21 St Aubyn Street, daughter of M. Stein.

[124] *Jewish Chronicle,* 14 February 1936.

Wedding of Doris Lewis to Bertie Black, 1953, outside Plymouth Synagogue

Dora (née Black) and husband Phil Harris

Wedding of Hilda Black to Sam Marks, 1946, outside Plymouth Synagogue

Opening of Mutley House, Plymouth in memory of founder Harry Black

Esther and Harry Black

Mutley Property Group and dedicated to the memory of Harry Black. The high profile opening was followed by a lunch reception for 100 guests at the Guildhall, hosted by the Lord Mayor H. G. Mason. After the lunch, Esther Black presented the Lord Mayor with cheques for the Christmas Fund, the Guild of Social Service and the National Spastics Society (as it was then known). In a speech, Sam Marks paid tribute to the contribution of Lord Mayor Mason in the rebuilding and reconstruction of Plymouth. Bertie Black commented in his speech that it was 'a day of great pride and deep joy.' When Esther died in September 1967, her body was brought back to Plymouth for burial in Gifford Place cemetery in a ceremony conducted by the Revd. Alec Ginsburg.

Bertie Black served the synagogue as well as his parents. He became its secretary at the age of just 21. He went on to become its treasurer, then president in 1955. On 20 October 1953, he married Doris Lewis of Wales. They had two children, Isabelle and Harry. During the 1960s, Bertie became a highly successful property developer, his offices in Mutley House which had been opened by his mother in 1962. The Black family's philanthropic work extended beyond Plymouth. In 1980, Bertie began a long-standing partnership with the University of Exeter and funded the first of seven endowed departmental prizes. For over thirty years, he supported a broad range of research interests, as well as undertaking an active role on University Council and Court. In 1995, he founded the Bertie Black Chair in Business and Economics. Between 1998 and 2000, he financed research into the causes of diabetes at the Peninsula Medical School. Many of the charities which he and Doris supported were not always high profile, but small charities which could not have carried out their work without them.

Doris Black recalls of those days: 'we were a caring provincial community, small, so we looked after each other. When a family was in mourning during the *shiva* we took food to that family for the whole week.' In 1968, the rest of the Black family left Plymouth for Bournemouth. The Shabbat before they left, Revd. Ginsburg expressed regrets that they were moving away and thanked them for their 'unstinting work and devotion to the welfare of the congregation.' After the service, president Arthur Goldberg presented Bertie Black with a certificate for 70 trees in Israel and an inscribed silver wine coaster on behalf of the General Purposes Committee. For her work with the Ladies' Societies, Doris was presented with an onyx ink-stand by Rose Owen. The family's ties to Plymouth remain deep and they continued as generous benefactors of the congregation.

Rose Owen (née Fredman)

Rose Owen (née Fredman) grew up in Devonport, the daughter of Myer and Fanny Fredman. In March 1911, she married Solomon Owen, an upholster of 107 Union Street. Both were active in synagogue life. Rose remained fearless and outspoken for the causes that she held dear, especially votes for women in congregational affairs. She recalled her upbringing in Devonport as the fifth child of an ordinary middle-class Yiddisher family in which her mother spoke virtually no English. Rose's wider family contributed much to the city's life. Her cousin, Myer Fredman, became the first Jewish Mayor of Devonport in 1911 and on his induction, a speech was given in the synagogue. Rose once recalled: 'his brother-in-law, Reuben Lincoln (father of Ashe Lincoln), was then a retired minister from Bradford, and donning canonicals gave a very inspiring address in the Plymouth synagogue which was filled to capacity by the civic dignitaries from Devonport and Plymouth.' She died on 1 February 1969 and is buried in the Gifford Place cemetery. Her husband, Hyman (Solly) predeceased her in November 1955 and is buried in the same cemetery.

King Field / Pearl Family

King Field (1881-1958) came from Russia/Poland, the son of Scholem Israel Flichtenfeld. King was a skilled clockmaker who had learned his trade in Vienna. He came to Plymouth where, on 5 February 1902, he married Eva Stern (1878-1967), daughter of Isaac Stern, in Oddfellows Hall, Devonport. A daughter, Ruth, was born on 17 December that year. There is an anecdote about King Field which has survived which says that, on Yom Kippur, he used to pass smelling salts and snuff around the congregation. Another tradition says that, on one occasion, he won £1,000 in a Daily Mirror Competition. He was so thrilled that he left his shop, grabbed a police officer

From left to right: Ethel Robins, Maurice Kopp, Marjorie Robins, Bill Robins, Phyllis Kopp, Valerie Woolf, Clara Robins, Joy Robins, Michael Robins. COURTESY OF JOY GERZI

outside the Palace Theatre and did a little jig, much to the surprise of the officer.

King and Eva's daughter, Ruth, married Joshua Pearl, a radio dealer and son of Rabbi Saul Pearl. They married in Plymouth Synagogue on 14 September 1932. They had one son, Brian, who was born on 24 July 1933.[125] The marriage was a brief one, and they separated when Brian was still a baby.[126] Brian grew up at 54 Union Street (Stonehouse) with his mother and maternal grandparents. He recalls:

> 'My mother was an enterprising lady; she had to earn a living, apart from my grandfather's trade. We lived over the shop at 54 Union Street. Her business in the 1920s and 30s was selling radios, radio components and parts, which was a very 'hi tech' trade in those days. She had a manager/ engineer who dealt with constructing, repairs, and was experimenting with television in her workshop at the time as well. As well as direct retail, she also had a mail order business, and advertised nationally.'

The outbreak of war in 1939 saw an end to Ruth Pearl's business and she opened a naval supplies business, selling uniform items to the large naval population. King Field and his wife Eva are both buried at Gifford Place cemetery. Their daughter Ruth died on 10 October 1978 and is buried in Bushey Jewish cemetery.

Brand Family

Tobias Brand, who traded at 42 Frankfort Street and sold the first refrigerators in Plymouth, served as president of the synagogue in 1929 and 1930, and treasurer in 1933. He was remembered as a short, rather portly figure, who lived in the quiet, select Portland Villas. On 4 March 1908, his son Arthur married Esther Rose Robins, the youngest daughter of the late Gedaliah Robins. The ceremony was conducted by Revd. D Jacobs and Revd. E Shvenski. It was reported:

> 'The Bridal party stood beneath a canopy of white brocade tastefully decorated with flowers and trails of smilax. The bride was given away by Mr Abraham Robins, her brother and wore a dress of white Oriental satin in Princess-empire style, embroidered in true-lovers' knots in silver and having a yoke of fine lace, while her tulle veil covered a spray of real orange flowers in her hair.'

The bridesmaids were Emily and Lena Brand, sisters of the bride, and niece Miss Phyllis Robins. The two younger bridesmaids wore white muslin dresses with sashes of pale pink silk, with wreaths of lilies in their hair. Emily Brand, the eldest bridesmaid, wore a dress of shell pink silk and a large hat of white straw with plumes. Mr E. Orgel acted as best man. After the service a reception was held at the home of the mother at 10 Eliot Street. The newly-weds

Synagogue school outing, 1930s

honeymooned in Bournemouth and received numerous presents which included 'a quantity of valuable jewellery and silver.'

On 18 June 1919, Tobias' daughter Emily married Joseph Reese, a manufacturer of Pinner. In August 1927, Eva Brand married Morton Morris, a master tailor from Bromley. Two years later, Lena Brand married Isidore Gasson, an optician of 187 Union Street, Plymouth. On 15 June 1932, Arthur and Esther Brand's eldest daughter, Ruby (granddaughter of Tobias Brand), married Dr Herman Harry Cohen in Plymouth Synagogue. He was the youngest son of Mr and Mrs B. Cohen of Ebbw Vale (Wales). The ceremony was conducted by Revds. Wolfson and Wykansky. The Western Evening Herald reported that the synagogue was 'effectively decorated with flowers and palms.'[127] The bride wore a gown of 'ivory-tinted satin made on sheath-like lines with a train of the same material heavily embroidered with pearls and crystals falling from the shoulders.' She was attended by her sister Doris Brand, aunt Miss Rosie Brand and young cousin, Pamela Robins. On 4 January 1939, another daughter, Doris, married Samuel Reuben Saunders, a doctor from Southampton.

Tobias Brand died on 16 February 1936 at the age of 71 and is buried in the Gifford Place cemetery. So too, are other members of the Brand family, including Arthur Brand who died in June 1960.

Robins family

The Robins family was amongst the founding members of the Devonport Synagogue in the 1890s. Other members worshipped at the synagogue in Catherine Street. Gedaliah Robins and his wife Louisa originated from Poland, and by 1891, he was trading at 80 Pembroke Street, Plymouth. Two of their children, Lewis and Solomon, were born in Poland before the family emigrated. A daughter Sarah, who was born in Bristol, went on to marry Hershell Orgel, son of Eliezer Orgel of Plymouth. Siblings Phoebe, Rosie, Esther and Ernest were all born in Devonport. Esther

---
[125] Joshua Pearl was the son of Saul and Leah Pearl.
[126] Although separated for a long time, the marriage ended in divorce in 1947.
[127] Western Evening Herald, 15 June 1932.

Hester Robins

Hester Robins became the first Jewess in Plymouth to be elected Councillor in Municipal Elections in 1928. Born Hester Sugarbread, she married Solomon Robins, President of the Devonport Hebrew Congregation. In June 1932, she was amongst those councillors presented to the Duke and Duchess of York on their visit to Devonport and Plymouth. As a member of City Council, she served St. Aubyn's Ward for seven years, and on the following committees: The Public Assistance, Finance and General Purposes Committee, Public Health, Child and Maternity Welfare, Gas, General and Tenders, Voluntary Hospital, Didworthy Sanatorium, and Port Sanitary Committee. Her tireless work for the greater good of the people of Plymouth earned her an OBE. On her death in January 1936, the Jewish Chronicle reported: 'Her work among the poor will always be remembered, and her memory will be treasured far and wide. She was a staunch supporter of every Jewish cause and organised in her home a special charity function in aid of the German Women and Children's Fund.'[129] By all accounts, she had an impressive funeral at the Gifford Place cemetery. The cortege was followed by a number of dignitaries: the Lord Mayor, Sir William Mountstephen; Leslie Hore-Belisha (Minister of Transport) who had travelled down from London specially for the ceremony, the Chief Constable, representatives of the City Council, and Mr A. E. Field (chief Liberal Agent for Devonport). Leslie

Ethel Robins

Robins married Arthur Brand; Phoebe married Isidore Cohen, and Ernest Robins married Ethel Parker from London. Ernest and Ethel had five children: Phyllis, Valerie, Marjorie, Vivian Abraham and Roland.[128] Ernest Robins lived with his family in an old house in Thornfield. He had a business on Southside Street as a credit trader, as well as running a watch repair business at the back of the premises. Uniforms for the Navy and farmer's boots were bought on credit. His granddaughter, Joy, recalls growing up in Plymouth: 'It was a very close community and lots of fun. Services were full, especially around High Holy days. Children sat in the window seats it was so full. The League of Jewish Women was always active, like volunteering at Greenbank Hospital to make sandwiches and tea for visitors.'

Roland Robins married Clara Solomon in Newcastle in 1947. They raised their children in Plymouth: Joy, Nicole, Michael and adopted daughter, Emma. Roland served in the Royal Army Medical Corps in WW2. After the war, he went into his father's business. In retirement, he moved to Bournemouth. He and his wife Clara are buried there. Gedaliah, the original ancestor who came to Plymouth, died in 1907 and is buried in the Gifford Place cemetery.

Tombstone of Hester Robins, OBE, Gifford Place cemetery

---

[128] Phyllis married Morris Klopplovitz. Valerie married Raymond Woolf. Marjorie married Bill Robins (Rubenstein), and Vivian married Doreen Shevlov. Vivian died in 1992 and is buried in the Gifford Place cemetery, where other family members are buried.
[129] Jewish Chronicle, 10 January 1936.

Hore-Belisha, who knew her personally, wrote: 'she had no personal interest to pursue but was drawn into activity by her very genuine love of the people and understanding their needs... Whenever I was in Devonport I was accustomed to having the Friday night meal there and it was one of my keenest pleasures to feel the historic sanctuary of such an atmosphere. She was deeply interested in me and all my work and inspired me invariably to do good.'

Greenburgh Family

The Greenburghs became well-established as famous Navy agents and tailors with branches in Plymouth, Malta and Gibraltar. Jacob Greenburgh and his wife Bessie arrived in the 1870s as penniless refugees from the pogroms of Czarist Russia. Their children were Joseph, Henry, Solomon, Arthur, Hyman, Annie (Mrs J. Goldberg) and Esther (Mrs Bass).[130] Jacob trained as a master tailor in London. His skills were many and covered all kinds of garments – Morning Coats, Greatcoats, uniforms, Mess jackets and even cassocks for clergy. Wishing to better his life, he decided to move his family to the South-West, first Exeter and then Plymouth. In 1903, he obtained employment with Gieves, the Naval outfitters in Fore Street, Devonport and soon became head of the workshops. He took this opportunity to teach his sons the trade, especially whenever they had a customer who was a difficult fit. He made

THE FIRM WITH THE REPUTATION FOR

SERVICE!

We have given 50 years Service and Satisfaction to hundreds of thousands of Naval Men in their Uniform and other requirements. Our Uniforms excel in materials, fit and workmanship, and our Civilian Department can supply your every need from a complete outfit to Gifts for every member of your family, all of which are available at lowest cash prices through our Allotment Accounts. Avail yourself of this Service, and obtain particulars at once from :—

GREENBURGH BROTHERS LTD.
14 WILLIAM STREET, DEVONPORT
(HEAD OFFICE PHONE: DEVONPORT 379)
Branches at MALTA, PORTSMOUTH and CHATHAM

uniforms and Mess jackets for Naval Officers, highly skilled work that included the use of a lot of gold braid and demanding a high standard of finish. By 1905, Jacob had become successful enough to start a business of his own called *Greenburgh Bros*, which became world famous in Naval circles. They specialised in producing well-tailored suits for the lower deck, catering as far as naval regulations permitted, for the individual personality of the customer. Greenburgh's "Tiddly Suits" (uniforms purchased privately because of their superior fit) were worn whenever a sailor wanted to look his best. By the outbreak of WW1, Greenburgh Bros had branches in Portsmouth, Chatham and Malta. The outfitting trade expanded enormously during WW1. The basic material used was blue serge which the company ordered in huge bales direct from the wool mills in Huddersfield and other places, sometimes as much a £500 worth at a time. It was manufactured in several grades and qualities, but a cloth known as a No.3 Canadian serge was the most popular. In addition to blue serges, white duckcloth was in demand for tropical wear. Demand began to outstrip the capacity of their own workshops, so outworkers were employed, always with strict production and quality standards. Before WW1, Naval cap-making was largely a different trade, produced by many well-known Devonport Jewish families: Mr Milner, Mr. Leskin, Mr. Melichan, Mr. Morris and Mr. Erlich. From WW1, it came within the ambit of Naval outfitters and in many cases, special departments were established to cope with it.

Bessie and Jacob Greenburgh lived at 17 Tamar-Terrace in Devonport. Bessie predeceased her husband in September 1936. Jacob died in November 1942. Both are buried in the Gifford Place cemetery. Their eldest son

Leila Rutman (née Greenburgh)

---

[130] A daughter Fanny died aged 11 and 9 months in 1911.

Joseph and second son Harry (born in the East End in 1888), looked after the family business in Devonport, while the younger brothers took charge of the branches in Chatham and Portsmouth. The brothers shared responsibility for the Malta branch. In Devonport, Harry and his wife Minnie (née Burns) entertained many Jewish sailors for Friday night meals. With the outbreak of another war just 21 years later, the family again served the Navy with honour. The Maltese branch received official recognition of its role in receiving a letter of thanks from the Governor General. Harry was a founding member of the Devonport Synagogue, and later a regular attendee at the Plymouth Synagogue after the bombing of the former.

In June 1923, Joseph and Harry's sister, Esther Greenburgh, married Charles Bisberg. In June 1937, Harry's own daughter Ethel married Philip Levy. Joseph Greenburgh married Jennie Ellison. They had at least two children: Leila and Harry (b.1917). In January 1939, Joseph's daughter Annie Leila married Morris Rutman, a commercial traveller of Spitalfields, London. Joseph himself died at the age of 56 in 1943. In 1938, Harry qualified from Guy's Hospital, London and became an eminent doctor. In WW2, he joined the RAF as a flying officer, was later promoted to Squadron Leader and served in South Africa. After the war, he returned to Guy's Hospital and trained as a pathologist, specialising in haematology. He received recognition and renown in the medical world. He returned to Plymouth in 1955 to nurse his gravely ill mother. After her death, he remained in the city, working in the Pathology Department of Freedom Fields Hospital and became head of department in 1972. Harry aided police in the most important murder investigations in the region. In 1971, he married Helene Rindl. He died in March 1985. Many members of the Greenburgh family are buried in the Gifford Place cemetery.

Royal Visit

CHAPTER 8
TWO WORLD WARS

CONTRARY TO POPULAR myth, the Jews of England have always played their part in the British Armed forces through successive campaigns and wars. A call to arms in 1798, raised volunteers from amongst the Jews of Plymouth, Exeter and Penzance when they enlisted in Volunteer Companies.[131] The Plymouth Hebrew Congregation is proud of the part its men and women played in both world wars. Prominently displayed in the entrance lobby of the synagogue are two framed memorial lists with names written in calligraphy of those who served their country in WW1 and WW2. There are twenty-nine names for WW1 and fifty-eight for WW2, many of whom served with distinction. Philip Harris served in the Auxiliary Fire Service and in 1942, he was called up for National Service in the Royal Marine Police, based at Devonport Dockyard. One local Jew received several decorations for bravery. Capt. H. Zeffertt saw action in South Africa, served in the Zulu Wars, and later took part in the relief of Ladysmith during the Boer War. During WW1, he took part in fighting in German South-West Africa and 'was honourably mentioned for having saved the life of Colonel Godfrey Halbert by carrying him out of danger zone on 13 November 1914. Captain Zeffertt is a native of Devonport.'[132]

World War 1

During the First World War, the Jewish community remained active and held regular services. According to the late Bert Emdon, the community's kosher meat at this time was slaughtered in an abattoir in Library Lane, a tiny street which ran up from Russell Street behind Cornwall Street. In November 1915, the congregation set up a Fund for the Relief of the Jewish Victims of the war in Russia. A committee was formed to collect weekly subscriptions and consisted of the following members: Elias Ellis,[133] Israel Fredman (of 11 Elliott Street) and Hyman Roseman of 13 Acre Place, Devonport. At the end of the war, the synagogue held a special service entitled *Restoration of Peace after the Great War*.

During the war, Plymouth's Naval connections became personal for the Jewish outfitters and Navy agents. Losses at sea became very personal losses because the trade knew most of the sailors. The war was scarcely a month old when the cruisers *Aboukir*, *Hague* and *Cressy* were lost off the Dutch coast. This was followed very quickly by the defeat of Admiral Craddock at the hands of the superior forces of German Admiral von Spee in the South Pacific at the Battle of the Coronel Islands. The loss of the *Monmouth*, a Devonport manned ship, cast an atmosphere of gloom over the port. The *Invincible* and *Inflexible* were dispatched to Devonport Dockyard for a special mission, to be ready by

Henry Peck

---

[131] *The Lost Jews of Cornwall* (ed. Keith Pearce & Helen Fry).
[132] Jewish Chronicle, 31 December 1915.
[133] Ellis married Rebekah Roseman. They left Plymouth and he became the first minister to the Nairobi Jewish congregation.

Jewish Battalion, Crownhill, WW1

13 November. Winston Churchill, then First Lord of the Admiralty, issued orders that they were to be ready for 11 November. This caused some panic amongst Plymouth's Jewish outfitters who worked with urgency to get the sailors' uniforms prepared. The mission turned out to be highly significant because *Invincible* and *Inflexible* were to intercept the German Fleet as it sailed up the South Atlantic towards its home waters, and destroy it. The Battle of the Falkland Islands that resulted became one of the celebrated moments in British Naval history. Then came the sinking of the *Formidable* off Start Point (South Devon) with the loss of 500 men. The lowest ebb in Devonport's Naval history came in 1916 with the Battle of Jutland which was an unmitigated disaster. A large number of ships lost in that battle were Devonport manned. Behind the stories of all these ships were the outfitters, usually Jewish, who looked after the sailors and provided their new uniforms before they set sail.

Plymouth was not only known for its Naval history in WW1. It was here that the first Jewish unit was raised as the 38th and 39th Battalion of the Royal Fusiliers, stationed at Crownhill. The local Jewish community gave the soldiers hospitality. In return, the Jewish soldiers gave concerts and shows at their barracks. Their chaplain was Revd. Lipson. Every Friday night, one or two soldiers would partake of Shabbat meal with a local Jewish family. Rose Owen once recalled:

'At Simchas Torah, quite a number came to the synagogue. They were given the Seforim (scrolls) to take around, after which they lined up in front of the Ark and sang *Hatikvoh*, the building reverberated with their stirring voices. In the back of my mind, I think Ben Gurion was here, as was Jabotinsky. They were ardent Zionists, their only talk was about Israel. They helped to form the Zion Mule Corps and our minister at the time was the Revd. L. Falk, also a keen Zionist, and he eventually

Caple Peck (1886-1960)

joined this Corps and led them out to Palestine, leaving a young wife and family with us.'[134]

The links of Morris Pincus (originally Pinkofsky) to the synagogue began when he first came to Plymouth in 1916/17 and was posted at Crownhill with the Jewish Battalion. He, with many of the other soldiers, attended services before being posted to Palestine. His parents, Mr and Mrs Barnet Pinkofsky, left the Zeppelin Raids on London with their large family and came to Plymouth. They were tailors and opened a workshop in Old Richmond Street. Morris Pincus only returned again to Plymouth from Palestine for the funeral of Myer Fredman in 1927. He remained in Palestine after WW1 and in 1920 joined the Palestine Police. He served with distinction, rising to the rank of Chief Superintendent. He died in Israel in 1983.

The Inter-War Years

In the inter-war years, a number of Jewish families prospered in their trades. Apart from those mentioned in the previous chapter, there was also David Lubell, a relative of the Ehrlich family who became somewhat of a legend in his lifetime. Bert Emdon reminisced on the Jewish characters that graced the scene:

> 'Known as the Chocolate Kid, David Lubell was affectionately remembered by the vast number of the older members of the population to whom he sold chocolates and sweetmeats at amazingly low prices, and provided hours of free entertainment into the bargain to his large audiences ever week. There was Sammy Caplan, the Lancashire Stock buyer – surely one of the most entertaining and inexpensive purveyors of Lancashire goods that have ever earned the grateful thanks of the Plymouth housewife. Who could forget Mr Phil Strong, otherwise Phillip Emdon (no relation of mine) whose polished "lectures" delivered as he sold his "patent medicines" entertained thousands. As an entertainment artist he was in a class of his own.'[135]

Plymouth Market became a platform for citizens to voice their opinions, including Manny Shinwell, Hore-Belisha and Mr Robins. It was a kaleidoscope of characters who made up something very distinct.

Dr Herman Harry Cohen settled in Plymouth in 1927, having come from the mining valleys of South Wales. He trained in medicine at the London Hospital Medical College in the East End of London. After a spell as a ship's surgeon on the North Atlantic route, he arrived in Plymouth as a House Physician at South Devon & East Cornwall Hospital (Greenbank). In 1928, he entered General Practice and served the city for 51 years. In 1932,

Morris Smith with son Eric

he married Ruby Brand, daughter of Arthur and Rose Brand. They had two children, Robert and Barbara. Dr Cohen became Chairman of the Plymouth Division of the British Medical Association (1967-8) and the Plymouth Medical Society (1954-55). During the war, he served as a Captain in the Royal Army Medical Corps in England and East Africa. He died in 1984 at the age of 81 and is buried in the Gifford Place cemetery. Another long-standing member of the community was Esther Leskin who also died in 1984. She was born in London in 1891, daughter of Jacob Greenburgh, a family that was a pillar of the

---

[134] Digest, August 1966.
[135] Digest, September 1978.

Chief Rabbi Dr Herz visits Plymouth, June 1936

Devonport Synagogue. Her first husband was Charles Bass who died in the 1930s. She spent the intervening years, until her second marriage to Morris Leskin, caring for her parents. She never had any children, but remained a staunch member of the Jewish community, brought up in a home of traditional Orthodoxy.

In the inter-war period, Plymouth's Jews obtained its kosher supplies from a number of sources. In the 1930s, J. C. Edwards in the market advertised as a poulterer and licenced game dealer and 'kosher poultry specially catered for all Festive and ordinary occasions, Jewish Boarding Houses supplied on reasonable terms.' Mrs Wright at 40 The Fish Market advertised that she sold Jewish delicacies from Barnett's of London under the seal of the Beth Din, and added 'Kosher Frying Oil'.[136]

Second World War

Hitler's annexation of Austria in March 1938 and Czechoslovakia in March 1939 slid Britain closer towards another war. On 9/10 November 1938 came news of the pogroms against the Jews of Germany and Austria when Jewish businesses were destroyed and thousands of Jews arrested and taken to concentration camps, in what became known as *Kristallnacht*. On Sunday 10 November, Plymouth Synagogue held a special service of Prayer and Intercession for the Jews of Germany. The fate of Europe's Jews continued to be of source of concern.

Plymouth bore the brunt of the Luftwaffe bombing of the South-West. It was at Millbay Docks that thousands of French and Belgian refugees arrived after German forces overran the Low Countries in May 1940. Only the narrow waters of the English Channel separated the coast from the Nazis. So too, Plymouth docks became the scene of lots of vessels and small ships arriving with evacuated British troops from the beaches of Dunkirk. After the Germans occupied the Channel Island from 1st July, Plymouth became a front line town and the most important Naval base for Allied operations in the Atlantic. The first bombs fell on the city just six days later. The first civilian fatalities of the blitz on Plymouth were from the Jewish community. Mary Smith and her daughter Esther died on 10 July 1940 and are buried in a double plot in the Gifford Place Jewish cemetery. Brian Aloof has vivid memories of Plymouth as a child during the blitz:

'We lived at Portland Square which was heavily bombed in the war. I remember spending nights in

---

[136] *Digest*, April 1979.

Esther Smith, first civilian victim of the blitz

the cupboard under the stairs and hearing the bombs falling on the city. Some nights we hid under the table. Three weeks before a major raid on Portland Square we had moved to 3 Torrington Place. Had we stayed in Portland Square we would not have survived the blitz. We then moved to Thornhill Road but we were bombed out of there – we were literally dug out of the rubble. I also recall walking down the street one day and it not being there the next.'

Plymouth became a base for forces-in-exile, and that included Poles. One particular Polish sailor was wounded and his uniform dishevelled from a near miss with an incendiary device when it fell close to him. He came to the attention of Naval outfitter, Mr Angel, who took him in, gave him breakfast and renovated his uniform. Angel's daughter Leibe spoke Polish and conversed with him to find out that he was serving on the Polish ship *Gdynia*. Hereafter, Angel's shop became a focal point for Poles in the city. Another story connected with Mr. Angel concerns the Nazi attempt to wreck Britain's economy by flooding it with forged £5 notes. An oral tradition suggests that Plymouth was used as the first place to bring in the forged currency. The idea was to use Polish immigrants, especially dissidents, as an easy vehicle. Some of the £5 notes were passed to Mr. Angel in exchange for goods, and he fortunately spotted them and told the authorities before the money got into circulation. Although wartime offered an outlet for the city's Jewish naval outfitters, it also marked its sudden decline, due to a number of factors. Much of the heart of Devonport was ripped apart in the Luftwaffe bombing and that affected the businesses like that of Mr. Angel and Harry Greenburgh whose premises lay in rubble. Greenburgh had a lucky chance when a store of precious serge in the roof space of his garage in Tamar Terrace was saved when an incendiary device failed to go off. The trade was finding it difficult to obtain the special kind of serge asked for by the Australians for their new fashion of a skin-tight V-fronted tunic. Many naval outfitters started again in new premises in Albert Road, but could not stem the flow of decline. New wartime building regulations prevented them converting their premises as needed, coupled with severe wartime clothes rationing, led to an irreversible decline. Post-war, this would eventually be followed by mass-tailoring, which placed the final nail in the coffin of the hand-made business which had flourished in the city for over 200 years.

There was concern that the synagogue could be a casualty of the heavy bombing. In a precautionary measure, the minister, Revd. Wolfson, took the scrolls from the Ark and deposited them in the Guildhall. A few days later he had premonition to remove them from the Guildhall and return them to the synagogue. The scrolls were saved because, a short time later, the Guildhall was hit and received extensive damage. Nearby streets were razed to the ground by a night of heavy bombing, turning the area into something like a biblical Apocalypse. Three buildings miraculously survived and were the only ones standing in this part of the city: the Synagogue, the Guildhall and St Andrews Church. The synagogue survived again when an incendiary device fell on its roof, but fortunately failed to go off. One of the community leaders, Hyman Aloof, climbed onto the roof and kicked it off. In another incident, Revd. Wolfson and the caretaker fought a fire caused by an incendiary device that caught the *succah* alight. They carried buckets of water from the ritual bath (in the vestry), which was always full of water, to put it out, thus saving the synagogue. Dr. Mark Gordon once recalled: 'after the terrible night of the fire, 23 Sifrei Torah [scrolls] were dispersed to various members homes over a wide area. The *Pinkas*, the book which records the early history of the congregation, was sent to the Jewish Museum, London where it was stored in a vault, and returned after the war.' Throughout the difficult war years, the synagogue remained open for worship. Brian Pearl recalls:

'The early war years were pretty scary. Plymouth was the object of massive and sustained nightly bombing raids, and most of the central city was totally destroyed. We lived right in the middle, and spent most nights, first sleeping under the stairs and then in a dugout shelter in the garden. We were

Blitzed city centre

Bernard Harris

pretty lucky, as most of the surrounding properties, as near as two doors away, were hit and destroyed either by high explosive or incendiary bombs. It was also a difficult time because my grandfather had several brothers who lived in Belgium. I remember hearing that all of them had been taken to the concentration camps and murdered.'

Baba Clarfelt (née Fredman) was aged fifteen at the time and at school in London during the blitz. Her parents had moved the family to London from Plymouth when she was eight years old. She returned to Plymouth during the war to visit her aunt Hilda. She recalls: 'Although we lived in London, my mother took a house in Yelverton during the war and we lived there for a while. In 1941, I travelled to Plymouth by train to sit my exams and received quite a shock by all the devastation. The whole area was flattened as far as the sea.' At the age of 17, Baba served in the Red Cross and was posted near London. On Sunday 13 December 1942, the synagogue held a service of *Fasting, Mourning and Prayer for the Victims of Mass Massacres of Jews in Nazi Lands*. Four days later, the subject received the full attention of Parliament when Anthony Eden read the Allied Declaration to a packed House of Commons. The Declaration condemned: 'in the strongest possible terms of this bestial policy of cold-blooded extermination… None of those taken away are ever heard of again. The infirm are left to die of exposure and starvation or are deliberately massacred in mass executions.' During a service in Plymouth Synagogue in 1944, two extra prayers were recited for victims of Nazi persecution. The first was *Supplication for our Surviving Brethren in and From Nazi Lands*, and the second, *Memorial Prayer for the Victims of Mass Massacres*. The Bishop of Plymouth made his own plea on behalf of Europe's Jews when he spoke at St Marys Church, Devonport, and said: 'A million Jews are persecuted every day and we don't turn a hair. Most of our music, art and science can be traced back to Jewish origin.'[137]

There was an influx of refugees from Nazi Germany into Plymouth, who found shelter in local homes through Rose and Hyman Owen. One such person was Chana Rothschild-Lesser who was taken in by Isidore and Phoebe Cohen for three years. Later, Rothschild-Lesser wrote a letter of thanks to the community and said: 'sincerest appreciation to all my other good Plymouth friends for the many kindnesses you have shown me while I was in your

---

[137] *Jewish Chronicle*, 8 February 1944.

midst.'[138] Another was Helga Kramer, a 12-year old refugee from Frankfurt-am-Main, who was taken in by Simon and Etta (Hetty) Roseman. Kramer achieved the distinction of being top in algebra, arithmetic, French, English, history, geography, domestic science and biology at Devonport Public Central School for Girls. In 1940, she received the Form Mistress's Special Prize and in her spare time, aided Hebrew classes for the local Jewish children.

Jewish Service Personnel in the Area

The Plymouth Hebrew Congregation did everything it could for Jewish service personnel stationed in the area, both naval and army. As early as February 1940, a concert was arranged in the Hippodrome Cinema, Devonport for members of all sections of HM forces stationed in the city. It was attended by 2,000 personnel, sponsored by David Jordan, a former president of Plymouth Synagogue, and under the patronage of Sir Martin Dunbar-Nasmith, Commander-in-Chief of the Royal Navy. In March 1941, a special service was held in the synagogue, conducted by the Revd. Wolfson and Revd. Goodman. Afterwards, a reception was held at the Abbey Hall when 'a large number of Jewish men in the services were entertained to a tea and concert by the Plymouth Ziona Society.' The chairman, Cecil Brand, extended an invitation for the servicemen to attend entertainment every week. Councillor Arthur Goldberg, as President of the synagogue, welcomed the troops. A concert was organized by the Troops Entertainment Committee. Hilda Marks (née Black) remembers what the community did for the soldiers:

> 'On Yom Kippur, we had around 400 Jewish soldiers for the services led by Revd. Wolfson and Revd. Goodman. Half the ladies gallery was needed to accommodate the soldiers for services. Revd. Wolfson took a walk up to the Citadel and arranged for the Jewish soldiers to break the fast of Yom Kippur. The ladies of the Jewish community were able to take fish and salad into the Citadel. Revd. Wolfson arranged for us to receive 5 gallons of oil so that we could fry the fish. The American soldiers had their Commanding Officer who was Colonel Hornstein from New Jersey. The first year that the Americans came to Plymouth, at our Passover seder we cooked for 90 soldiers. I remember all the potatoes we had to peel to make the latkas.'

London-born Leslie Jackson was stationed off Plymouth with the Royal Navy. He recalls this period in his autobiography, *Pawn on a Chessboard*. By the time he arrived in Plymouth in the summer of 1940, the city had already been the target of heavy Luftwaffe bombing:

> 'Fresh water now had to be supplied through canvas fire hoses laid in the street gutters. Homes were without their supply of gas and domestic cooking

Two Jewish soldiers, WW2

> was carried out on small Calor gas stoves. Every night half the population, packed into open lorries and overcrowded buses, would migrate to Dartmoor, induced to leave either through fear of renewed bombing or because they had been rendered homeless. The minesweeping flotillas were based in Millbay Docks, which in happier times had been the point of departure for the tenders that ferried passengers and their luggage to the transatlantic liners anchored in Plymouth Sound. The task of *Sir John Lister* was to sweep the war channel, starting at the Eddystone Lighthouse and ending in Plymouth Sound. To the east we were responsible for the channel as far as Dartmouth and to the west to the Cornish port of Falmouth.'

On 18 August 1943, Leslie married local Plymouth Jewish girl Henrietta Cohen.

The city became an important base for US troops, as Brian Aloof recalls: 'the synagogue was often full of American servicemen. They gave us big bars of chocolate and our parents hosted them for meals.' One of the lasting memories of this period is the sheer amount of hospitality which local Jewish families showed to both British and

---
[138] *Digest*, September 1969.

Synagogue members with British and US Jewish servicemen, Revd. Goodman and Revd. Wolfson, 1943. COURTESY OF STUART GOODMAN

Shabbat meal for British and US Jewish servicemen in the Vestry during WW2

American service personnel. Tea dances, talks and social events were arranged, with anything from 30-100 soldiers in attendance. A snapshot of that generosity has survived in letters which were written to Mrs Esther Black.[139] The letters make for moving reading, especially in the context of the fact that these soldiers were about to take part in the invasion on the beaches of the Normandy. Esther's daughter, Hilda, remembers the soldiers going off for D-Day: 'The Red Cross man said to me, "there won't be many coming back." Of course he was right.' The Americans would sustain 94% casualties or fatalities on those beaches on the first day. On 10 May 1944, less than a month before D-Day, one American Jewish soldier, Abraham Butler, wrote to Esther Black, expressing his disappointment that he could not even say goodbye to her:

> 'As you have probably guessed, I am no longer in your vicinity, nor near enough to visit you again. I was all ready to come in on Thursday last, as I said I might, and was then told that I must stand by orders. I am so sorry that I had to go off without a word, but the amenities can hardly be reconciled with military necessity. I shall not undertake to describe the immensity of my disappointment. I was beginning to regard your home and family as being closely akin to my own. Your generous hospitality and the open-hearted manner in which you received me made me feel most comfortable, and enabled me to enjoy every moment that I spent with you.'

He ended his letter by saying that he had enclosed 20 shillings: ten shillings for the Jewish congregation and ten shillings to be donated to a charity of Esther Black's choice. American soldier, Louis Sandell, wrote to Esther Black two months after D-Day: 'Sorry I was unable to see you before I left Plymouth, but like all military movements, only the commanding officer knew until the last moment. I had intended to see you at the dance, but left yesterday. Even that is impossible now... I want to thank you very much for all the kindness and hospitality you've shown me since I met you. I'll always remember the very nice times I had at your homes and the favours you did for me... Best regards to Revd. Susman and the rest of the folks at the "club".' In January 1945, Esther Black received a letter from another American serviceman in a US Army Hospital, in which he thanks her for her support. He spoke about 'praying hard that this mess [war] will end. I do it wholeheartedly at the services in the hospital. I attend the service every Friday. There isn't a Chaplain here, we get together a handful of Jewish soldiers and perform a quintet and un-orthodox service.' At the end of the war, Esther Black received a letter from US soldier, Sgt A. Rosencrantz, from a military hospital in France, having been wounded in action. 'I am the soldier of Plaster Down near Tavistock that enjoyed your hospitality last Passover which I can yet taste the delicious chicken dinner – Well, at that time, I said I would give you, your sister and Hilda, a mezuzah – enclosed you will find the three mezuzahs that I hope you will enjoy. I couldn't deliver it personally as I had wanted to, for obvious reasons.'

In March 1945, the Plymouth Synagogue was presented with a special plaque from the US forces as thanks for all they had done. It was presented in the presence of the Lord Mayor of Plymouth, Revd. Goodman and Revd. Susman. On 7 May 1945, Germany signed the official surrender and war was over. The community celebrated with a special service in the synagogue for *Thanksgiving for the Allied Victory in Europe*. Its men and women had served their country with distinction. One member, Major Gerald Robins, was awarded the OBE by King George VI.

Presentation of plaque by US servicemen to the synagogue, in the presence of the Lord Mayor, Revd. Goodman and Revd. Susman. COURTESY OF STUART GOODMAN, MARCH 1945

Plaque given by US servicemen to the synagogue

---

[139] Letters lent to the author by Hilda Black and Rochelle Selby.

Smith Family

The Smith family settled in Plymouth immediately after the First World War. Morris Smith had served in the Jewish Battalion of the Royal Fusiliers and was stationed for a time in Plymouth before being sent to Egypt and Palestine. After being wounded in action, Morris was shipped back to a military hospital in Plymouth. He liked the city so much that after his recovery, he decided to settle in the city. He brought his family from London to Plymouth, including his widowed mother Mary, three brothers Nathaniel [Nat], Hyman and Joseph, and sisters Esther and Hetty, and Hetty's husband, Saul Solomon Silver.[140] Nat, Joseph and Hyman all served in the army in WW1 and returned safely from action in France. Tragically, they came home to discover that their father had died from the Spanish Flu epidemic.

Florie Smith, Irene Silver, Mary Smith and sister Rebecca Harrison

Morris Smith. COURTESY OF ERIC SMITH

It is believed that the family originated from the Russian/Polish border and came to England because of the pogroms of the 1880s. They lived initially in Old Castle Street in the East End. It is thought that they anglicised their surname from Schmidt to Smith. Morris Smith married Sarah [Sadie] Caplan from a strictly Orthodox background, one of the daughters of an East End kosher poulterer. Sadie's brother, Harry Caplan, sent poultry from the East End to the Plymouth Jewish community. Sadie's sister, Polly Caplan, married Abe Milner on 27 March 1940. Morris and Sadie Smith had two sons, both born in Plymouth: Eric in 1931 and Cyril in 1934. Eric recalls: 'It was Revd. Goodman who performed my circumcision when I was 8 days old. He never let me forget it when I was older. When I attended cheder, he would squeeze my cheek and say "you were my first circumcision." We had a busy religion school. I remember that we collected stamps and stuck them on a tree for the Israel Appeal.' The Smith family were active members of the synagogue. In the city itself, Morris Smith was quite a character. He opened an emporium called *Savoy Stores* at 79 Union Street which sold fruit, confectionary, and also had a barber's section for ladies and gents hairdressing. At the back of the shop was a Turkish bath, open until midnight. His son Eric comments:

> 'People coming out of the Palace Theatre late at night could pick up fruit, sweets and cigarettes. We had spare rooms above the shop which we let to people who were performing at the Palace Theatre just down the road. We let a room to the likes of Archie Pitt (Gracie Fields' husband), Lesley Holmes of the "Two Leslies", and opera singer impersonator Afrique, and many others. We had a huge yard at the back of shop. Here my father kept a stable for ponies, a racing pigeon loft and 2 or 3 vintage American cars. He was well-known all over Plymouth. If anyone wrote to my father, they addressed the envelope 'Fatty Smith, Plymouth' and it got to him! He was a betting man, which he did under the name 'Fatty Smith' at the Greyhound Stadium, Pennycomequick. On the evening that I was born, he had already commenced betting in his

---

[140] Mary Smith had been widowed in 1918/19 when her husband contracted Spanish flu.

bookmaker's pitch. Suddenly the betting board was changed and up came a message "Fatty Smith & Son" and he knew his wife had given birth to a son!'

Eric has many fond memories of his days in Plymouth. In 1936, his grandmother came from the East End to stay with them. She used to sit in the front room and look down Union Street and watch everything going on. Eric recalls: 'Our front room was the best room in the house. We didn't really use it. I always remember a big bowl of fruit in there which we weren't to touch. One night as I crept up to bed, I passed the front room, went in and took a pear. I heard this voice say in a European accent "Eric, das ist thieving." My grandmother was quietly sat in there, hidden from view. My father came running in and threatened to give me a clip around the ear, but he never carried it out.'

Prior to the Second World War, Morris's shop took about £1 a day. Even on such modest takings, Morris and Sadie were able to employ a maid. Sadie worked hard in the shop too. The outbreak of WW2 temporarily changed their fortunes for the better. The shop went from taking £1 a day to £100 a week. All aspects of the shop did extremely well and remained open until midnight. By now, Morris was also selling memorabilia from the Great War, badges, soldier's canes and caps. Eric comments: 'It lasted about 6 months. Then the bombs came down and it was all over. We went from rags to riches, riches to rags.' As mentioned, tragedy struck this family when Mary Smith and daughter Esther became the first civilian fatalities of the blitz on Plymouth. Today, their names are inscribed on a window at the Ford Park Cemetery, Gifford Place, alongside other victims of the blitz. Bombed out of the city in 1941, Morris and Sadie left for Exeter with their sons and settled there with Morris's sister Hetty and Saul Silver. Bombed out again, they moved to Barnstaple where Morris opened an emporium.[141] In May 1946, he died in Barnstaple. His body was brought to Plymouth for burial in the Gifford Place Jewish cemetery.

Polly Milner

The well-known scrap-metal business in Plymouth, *Davies and Cann Ltd*, was purchased by the Smith family. Purchased through the company M.C. Engers, Jack Smith (a first cousin of Morris Smith) ran an incredibly successful business with his brother, Eddie Smith. Jack eventually took the family to Israel to live. After Eddie's death, his son Michael took over.

Herchel Smith (1925-2001)

Born in Plymouth in 1925, the son of Nathaniel Smith and Florence Smith (née Hafercorn), Herchel Smith is arguably one of the most famous Plymothians who has yet to be fully recognised. He became one of the most groundbreaking chemists of the twentieth century. His patent enabled the American pharmaceutical industry to support further research necessary to develop the contraceptive pill and thus revolutionise the lives of women forever.

Sadie Smith with sons Cyril and Eric

---

[141] Helen Fry, *Jews in North Devon in WW2*.

Nat & Florie Smith, parents of Herchel Smith

Having been brought up in Plymouth and then Exeter, his family was members of both synagogues at one time. In 1942, Herchel study Chemistry at Emmanuel College, Cambridge and later to America. In 1953, he married a non-Jewish lady, Sheila Jones, in Exeter's White Hart Hotel, whom he had met in Switzerland whilst recovering from tuberculosis. Herchel established his career in America and successfully registered over 200 patents and became a very wealthy man. In 1982, he donated £1 million to the University of Cambridge. Yet, as he grew older, he shunned the limelight and lived a quiet life. The famous Kimberly Diamond, valued in 1970 at £500,000, was sold by Baumgold Bros in 1971 to 'an undisclosed buyer'. That buyer was Herchel Smith. It has since been sold again. Herchel built his own yacht and cruised the world.

When his father Nathaniel died at the age of 89 in 1982, his body was brought from Exeter to Plymouth for burial in the Gifford Place cemetery. An obituary, placed in the Jewish Chronicle by his nephew Eric, described him as 'a man of unique character, a grand old timer.'

Herchel Smith became, not only an internationally renown chemist, but a generous philanthropist. In the United States, Harvard University was the main focus of his benefactions. In England, he took an interest in his old college, Emmanuel at Cambridge, and Queen Mary. Of the latter, he took an active role in the activities of the Intellectual Property Research Institute and regularly attended the annual Herchel Smith lecture until prevented by ill health. He also endowed a Chair and fellowship at Queen Mary.

When he died in 2001 aged 76, his ashes were brought to Plymouth and scattered in the Sound. After his death, the extent of his bequest was made known. He bequeathed the largest legacy thus far to Cambridge University, over £45 million. He bequeathed $100 million to Harvard University. The Herchel Smith Laboratory for Medicinal Chemistry was established in his memory at Cambridge University. He established four professorships in perpetuity: the Sheila Joan Smith Chair of Immunology, the Herchel Smith Chair of Medicinal Chemistry, the Herchel Smith Chair of Organic Chemistry, and the Herchel Smith Chair of Intellectual Property Law. Herchel's wife Sheila predeceased him, and he is survived by son Marcus, and three grandchildren: Henry, Christian and Hope.

Gordon / Peck Family

The Gordon family originated from South Wales. Dr Mark Gordon (b. New Tredegar), a medical doctor, had trained in Cardiff. His wife Betty Peck was also from South Wales. They had married in Plymouth just three days after the outbreak of WW2. During the war, Dr Gordon served in the RAF in Scotland and India. Afterwards, he bought a practice in Stoke. A daughter, Valerie, was born on 8 February 1941 in Devonport. As a hobby, Dr Gordon made violins and, as such, appeared as a guest on a number of radio and television programmes. In 1955, he appeared as an amateur violin maker on the Cliff Michelmore programme on Westward Television during which he demonstrated how to make a violin. His first complete violin was later played by Hugh Maguire, then leader of the Bournemouth Symphony Orchestra. Dr Gordon entered the first National Doctors' Hobbies Exhibition in

Dr Mark Gordon on local television demonstrating how to make a violin

Michael Mellor, RAF in WW2,
COURTESY OF VALERIE MELLOR

1967 with two of his violins and was awarded First prize and a cheque for £75. He was active locally in all kinds of charitable causes, for which he was honoured with an OBE from the Queen in 1975, particularly for his work on the Plymouth Disablement Committee which he had chaired for twenty-five years. He served as president of the Plymouth Synagogue in 1967.

On 16 October 1963, Valerie Gordon married a Plymouth man, Michael Mellor (b. 1938) in the synagogue. She was an only child, although there was a sister Baby Freya Gordon who died on 6 June 1949, only a day old. In those days it was not usual to leave the grave unmarked, but her parents insisted on the erection of a headstone. Dr Mark Gordon died on 6 May 1977, his wife Betty predeceased him in 1975.

The Peck side of the family originated from Poland. Caple Peck [Pech] came from a large family of nine children. He came to England with his brother Jack and sister, Leah Pech. The surname was subsequently anglicized from Pech to Peck. Caple, Jack and Leah were the only members of the family who survived the Holocaust. Caple Peck was Valerie Gordon's grandfather. He came from London to Plymouth to retire with his wife Jennie (née Roskin). Caple died in December 1960 and Jennie in May the following year. Henry Peck, was a solicitor in Plymouth. He had served in the war, and married a second cousin, Freda Averbuck, from South Wales. Also in Plymouth was Bernard Peck, a doctor, and cousin of Valerie Gordon's mother. Bernard married Pat Fligelstone from Wales.

Aloof family

The Aloof family emigrated to England from Russia at the turn of the century. Whilst living in London and working there as a capmaker, Hyman Aloof, met Sarah Hellerman, also from Russia. They married on 16 May 1911 and had three sons: Sidney (b. 1912), Lionel and Percy, all born in London. During WW1, Hyman had served as a Private in the regiment 2nd London Field Ambulance, Royal Army Medical Corps. He was discharged on 24 November 1916 after 134 days of service 'having been irregularly enlisted'. In 1924, he moved with his family to Plymouth after Hyman saw an advertisement in the Jewish Chronicle for the post of Second Reader and Beadle for the Plymouth Hebrew Congregation. He was engaged at an annual salary of £169. Hyman died at the age of 72 on 13 July 1959, having served the community as Beadle and assistant reader

Sidney, Lionel & Percy Aloof

From left to right: The Aloof family: Sidney, Lily Aloof holding son Brian, Sarah, Percy and Hyman

Watchmaker & jeweller Sidney Aloof in his shop

Bar Mitzvah of Brian Aloof, 1952

Percy Aloof, WW2

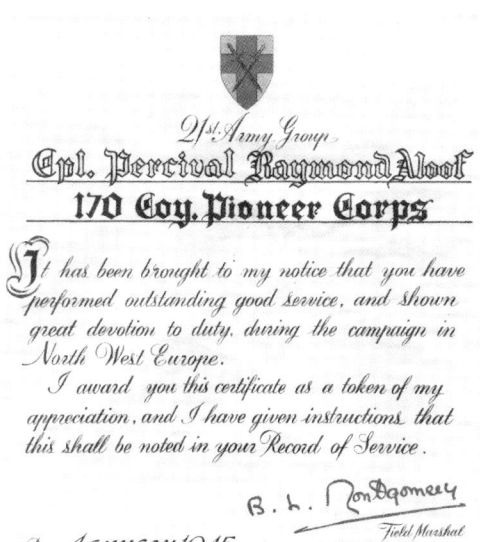
Percy Aloof's Commendation by Field Marshal Montgomery

for 35 years. An obituary described him as 'a man of much learning... besides being custodian of the synagogue, was guide and mentor to many of its members, as well as to the many honorary officials and lay leaders of the Plymouth Hebrew Congregation.' His wife Sarah died in 1963. They are both buried in the Gifford Place cemetery.

Of the sons, the eldest, Sidney married Lili Black, youngest daughter of Mr Eli Black, in Plymouth Synagogue on 2 February 1938, in a ceremony conducted by Revd. Wolfson and Revd. Goodman. The bridesmaids were Minnie and Jessie Gordon, and the bride's train was carried by Hilda Black. Sidney's brother Lionel was best man, and Percy Aloof and Israel Gordon were the groomsmen. Sidney Aloof worked in the city as a watchmaker and jeweller at 18a St Andrews Street. He and Lili had one son, Brian.

Percy Aloof, born London on 8 March 1917, was the youngest son of Hyman and Sarah. In Plymouth Synagogue on 22 January 1958, he married Bessie Fine of Llanelly, Wales. They had one son, Marcus. During WW2, Percy served with distinction with 140 Company of the Royal Pioneer Corps. The company was amongst the first wave of soldiers onto the beaches of Normandy on D-Day and landed with the Canadian Army Assault Forces. Percy served in an administrative capacity with the First Canadian Army in France, Belgium and Holland. Whilst serving with the British Liberation Army (21 Army Group) in North-West Europe in 1944-45, he was awarded the *Certificate for Outstanding Service and Great Devotion to Duty* by the Commander-in-Chief, Field Marshal Montgomery. At the end of hostilities and before his demobilization in 1948, Percy was posted to No.59 German PoW Camp as the Orderly Room Sergeant. He was described by his Commanding Officer, Lt Colonel W. M. Knatchbull, as 'very hardworking, pays great attention to detail, thoroughly reliable and very loyal. He has a keen sense of humour.'[142] He showed 'respect for his superiors, was respected by lower ranks, and had the knack of handling men.' In post-war civilian life, Percy worked as a civil servant for the Post Office. He died on 19 May 2003 at the age of 86. He, like his father, had given years of loyal service to the Plymouth Synagogue and served as its president in the 1980s and 1990s. His wife Bessie died almost two years earlier on 5 August 2001. Both are buried in the Gifford Place cemetery. Lionel Aloof, the other son of Hyman and Sarah, also married into the Fine family when he wedded Freda Fine (his sister-in-law's sister) in a ceremony in Swansea in 1955. They had four children: Martyn, Helena, Sharon and Sarah.

Brothers Percy, Sidney and Lionel Aloof were all prominent members of the Plymouth Hebrew Congregation and took services when the community no longer had a minister. Sidney acted as secretary for a number of years. His son Brian is a trustee and member of the General Purposes Committee. Brian has two children by his first marriage, Claire and Adam. Claire Aloof married Timothy Lovet from Glasgow in Plymouth Synagogue in March 2001.

Bar mitzvah of Marcus Aloof

---

[142] Papers lent to the author by Marcus Aloof.

CHAPTER 9
POST-WAR COMMUNITY TO CURRENT DAY

IN THE YEARS immediately after the Second World War, the community remained vibrant and strong. There were many key families who were pillars of the community, including the Black family, Roseman, Emdon, Aloof, Spiers, Goldberg, Fredman, Overs, Greenburgh, Cohen, Mitchell, Goodman, Hirshman, Richman, and others. For a time, the post-war community had a shochet to provide kosher meat. That changed, as Doris Black recalls: 'later, when we had no minister or shochet, we obtained our kosher food from Bournemouth, but that was fraught with difficulties. For a while we were able to get kosher chickens from a Polish non-Jewish lady in the Pannier Market in Frankfurt Place.' This was Cullifords Delicatessen who provided a range of kosher food and wines, including for Passover, until their retirement in 1983. Revd. Rockman arranged for a local baker to make kosher *chollas* [platted bread] for Shabbat which were delivered to Cullifords for collection by members of the congregation. Betty Mushin (née Goldberg, daughter of Samuel Louis Goldberg), who married William Mushin in September 1939, recalled Passover days in Plymouth:

'Whenever I see fluted white china in a shop window, I think of Pesach [Passover]. Every year at home in Plymouth, similar china was brought down from the loft, carefully washed and stored in a previously spring-cleaned cupboard. The Pesach

Bicentenary of the synagogue, greeting Dayan Grunfeld at Plymouth station

Chief Rabbi Brodie signs the Visitors Book in the Lord Mayor's Parlour, October 1958

essentials had already been ordered and would soon arrive: the matzo meal, the wine, the cinnamon and sugar, the Torma margarine, the oil and the Dutch cheese. Hundreds of eggs would be collected from a farm, and also milk… Our minister arranged to go out to the farm himself to watch the cows being milked, and the milk being poured into bottles which were then labelled "Kosher for Passover". Many members thought he had gone too far. Seder nights were full of precious memories. I had done my bit by preparing the Seder table first in my grandparents' house and later in that of my parents. I can still see my grandfather leaning back against the voluminous white pillows in his chair at the head of the table. My grandmother served us with bowls of eggs in salt water, and afterwards with delicious gefilta fish, both fried and boiled, the latter decorated with slices of carrot.'

For Shavuot, the synagogue was decorated with flowers, leaves and plants. Some of which were supplied by the Doney family, market-gardeners of Saltash, just across the Tamar Bridge. During the festival, branches were intertwined in the carved wooden screen in front of the ladies gallery. During Succot, the *succah* (which still exists today) was, and is, decorated with fruits and leaves. On the Eve of Yom Kippur, every member came to services and each lit a candle, then processed into the synagogue with their candles. 'It was a Plymouth custom,' says Hilda Marks. 'We then walked home afterwards – we would never drive on a holy day. We had another tradition which may be unique to our congregation. When a man died, his seat in the synagogue was left vacant for a year and his cushion turned over. Then the men would rotate and move along seats, each time getting a bit closer to the Ark. The most prominent seats were nearest the Ark and denoted the status of that person in the community.'

The 1950s saw the arrival of new members. Morton (Morty) Jules Davidson came from Baltimore with his wife Doreen and settled in the area after a holiday. They opened gift shops in Plymouth and Looe. Morty's real aim was to open a modern factory, producing high-grade precision engraving and light industrial engineering. He successfully opened a factory at Cattedown, staffed with skilled craftsmen and technicians. He shipped goods all over the world and to Northern Ireland. King Phillips and his wife had settled in the city; he trading as a retail and wholesale tobacconist, *Messrs. Snell & Co*. Their daughter Mollie married Colonel Roy Telfer. Telfer had a long and distinguished career in the British Army, serving in the

Essex Regiment, then in acting rank of Brigadier in India. He came to Plymouth in 1947, and later founded the Plymouth Bridge Club. Another dedicated community figure was Jack Goodman whose services were recognized by the congregation in 1983 with the title of Honorary Life President. There was Dr and Mrs Harry Cohen whose son went on to become a Professor of Medicine in London.

From the 1960s

The 200th anniversary of the synagogue was marked by a service on Wednesday 14 June 1961, attended by the Chief Rabbi Dr Israel Brodie and the Lord Mayor of Plymouth, Arthur Goldberg. The Chief Rabbi officiated with Rabbi Bernard Susser and Revd. Alec Ginsburg, supported by the president Israel (Bertie) Black, treasurer Maurice Overs and secretary Brian Pearl. At a reception afterwards, the guests dined on a lavish lunch of Honeydew Melon, followed by Mushroom Vol au Vents, then Tamar salmon with parley potatoes and green salads, followed by strawberries and Devonshire cream, and coffee and petit fours. Music was provided by the String Quartet of HM Royal Marines, Plymouth. Several toasts were proposed: first to Her Majesty the Queen, given by president Israel Black; then to the State of Israel, given by treasurer Maurice Overs, and the third to the congregation, given by Chief Rabbi Dr Brodie, with a response from Israel Black. The fourth toast for the City of Plymouth was proposed by Sir Barnett Janner, MP, President of the Board of Deputies of British Jews, with a response by Arthur Goldberg. A final toast was given for the guests by Revd. Bernard Susser with a response by the Rt. Rev. Norman H Clarke, the Bishop of Plymouth.

Another major restoration project of the synagogue was undertaken in the 1960s, overseen by the congregation's Honorary Secretary, David Maxwell. The first meeting to discuss fund-raising was held on 17 June 1963 in the Lord Mayor's Viewing Room at the top of the Civic Centre. A Restoration Committee was formed and consisted of Mr & Mrs. Hurst, Mr & Mrs R. Lewis, Mr & Mrs I. Black, Mrs Owen, J. Hirschman, Mr & Mrs. Overs, Mr & Mrs. Rutman, Mrs. Goldberg, Mr Harris, Harold Richman, Mrs R. Robins, Mrs J. Richman and Mrs Harold Richman. Secretary was Mr David Maxwell, Executive Officer was Revd. Bernard Susser. By the next meeting held on 20 August 1963, it was proposed to raise £10,000 for the necessary work. Between the first meeting in June and the second one in August, the synagogue raised £1169.93, with a promise of a further £3,000 in donations. The following year, around a thousand leaflets were printed and sent to all members of the congregation, even those who no longer lived in Plymouth. In June 1964, a successful Restoration Banquet and Ball was held at the Continental Hotel. During the renovations, services were held in Swathmore Hall, Mutley Plain. Halfway through the work, a fire broke out and the synagogue sustained some damage. The Decalogue (Ten Commandments) over the Ark was damaged. Afterwards, Revd. Ginsburg climbed a ladder and painstakingly re-painted the Ark's lettering with gold paint.

The synagogue was finally reconsecrated on 10 February 1965 in a special service led by the Chief Rabbi, aided by Rabbi Bernard Susser, Revd. Major Alec Ginsburg

Chief Rabbi Brodie with children from the religion school

Plymouth religion school, play for Purim

Children's show, 1963

and Revd. Sydney Ginsburg. During the 1960s, the young people organized shows and performances, the funds raised from which were donated to the Synagogue Building Fund. One successful show, for example, took place in 1966, a production of *My Fair Lady*, which included a cast of Isabelle Black, Melvyn Dubovie, Sonia Dubovie, Richard Goodman, Andrea Lewis, Anthony Overs, Catherine Overs, Michael Overs, Catherine Peck, Pamela Peck, Ian Philion, Sandra Richman, Joy Robins, Michael Robins, Hazel Sanger, Norman Sanger, the Solomon sisters (Bernice, Louise and Yvette) and Judi Spiers.

In 1969, the congregation welcomed new members: Pearl Ranford, Thomas Perlmutter and Edward Mark Emdon. By all accounts the congregation remained busy with religious life, charitable activities, ladies events, coffee mornings and welfare work. In August 1969, three Israeli yachts took part in the Plymouth Regatta. Their crews were entertained by members of the Jewish community led by president Arthur Goldberg and his wife Sylvia. The State of Israel has been at the heart of the community's support and, only two years earlier in 1967, the congregation raised £10,000 for appeals in Israel after the Six Days War, this at a time when the synagogue was beginning to struggle to get a numbers for Shabbat services.

The sharp decline in members began in the 1970s when there were only 350 Jewish members in the whole of the South-West. Rabbi Susser founded the monthly newsletter, the Digest, packed with community news, jokes, a monthly recipe and obituaries. A glowing obituary appeared for Jeannie Richman in the autumn of 1970, which said: 'she was endowed with a charming Yiddish wit and Jewish folk mannerism. She was devout in her religious beliefs and displayed a great love and respect for Rabbanim and Talmidei Chachamim. She sought first to adorn her homestead with paintings and pictures depicting the Hasidic giants of the past.' The ladies continued to be busy with fund-raising, monthly coffee mornings, luncheons, cheese evenings or a Bring and Buy Sherry parties, all in aid of charity. The annual Garden Party in 1970, for example, raised £130 for charity. The women conducted visits to Jewish patients in the local hospitals. The hostage-taking and mass murder of Israeli athletes at the Summer Olympics in Munich in 1972, which led to 17 deaths, was mourned at a special memorial service in Plymouth Synagogue on 11 September. In attendance was the Lord Mayor of Plymouth and other Civic dignitaries. The minister, Revd. Alec Ginsburg, received many letters of sympathy sent to the congregation by local people from all denominations.

Emdon Family

The Emdon family had a continuous presence in the community that went back to the foundation of the synagogue 250 years earlier, and traced back to founding members Abraham Emdon and Abraham Joseph I. Ernest Emdon (b.1914), Bert (Bertram, b.1916), Edward and

Children's show, 1963

Ralph were the four sons of Leon Frank Emdon and Rose Emdon, and the last of the Emdons of Plymouth. Bert took a keen interest in local history and over the years, as a historian, wrote several articles about the Plymouth Jewish community. He had in his possession a 17th century bible from Amsterdam in Yiddish printed in the Hebrew character. In his memoirs, he recalled: 'it was obviously a prized family possession because an inscription in it reveals that it was passed into the safekeeping of Solomon Hart (the artist) on the occasion of his bar mitzvah. The year was 1812, the year of Napoleon's retreat from Moscow. It was obviously preserved, and a second inscription, many years later records its presentation to my grandfather Eleazor Emdon on his bar mitzvah.' Bert served as treasurer of the synagogue from 1978 to 1980. He never married and died on 29 March 1984 at the age of 68. Ernest Emdon died on 25 May 1987. Their brother Edward died in April 1995. The brothers are all buried in Gifford Place.

The Marks Family

After the war, Manchester-born Sam Marks moved to Plymouth and, in 1946, married local Jewish girl Hilda Black, the daughter of Harry and Esther Black. He worked in the Black family's property business and went on to serve the synagogue as treasurer and president. Sam, who was born in 1917, one of nine children to Abraham and Sara Manakerman, had served in the Royal Armoured Corps during the Second World War. He landed with British forces in Singapore, and when Allied Forces surrendered to the Japanese, he was imprisoned in Changi jail and forced to work on the Burma Railway, from which many prisoners-of-war did not survive from cholera or dysentery. One of his achievements was the establishment of a synagogue in the Japanese prisoner-of-war camp where he was imprisoned. After the war, he came to Plymouth and settled. Sam and Hilda had two children: David and Rochelle. Throughout their time in Plymouth, the Marks supported many charitable causes, which continued after they moved to Bournemouth in 1957. Sam died on 8 April 2013 at the age of 95 and is buried in Bournemouth. The Marks family still feels very strong ties to the Plymouth synagogue.

Arthur Goldberg (1908-1982)

The Goldberg family were settled in Plymouth by the time when Arthur Goldberg was born in the city in 1908. He was the son of Louis [Lewis] Goldberg and Esther Goldberg (née Fredman) who had married in Plymouth Synagogue on 9 April 1902. At the time of their marriage in 1902, Lewis was a commercial traveller, registered on the marriage certificate as living at 30 Frankfort Street, the son of Abraham Goldberg.[143] Esther was the daughter of Myer Fredman. They had two children: Arthur and Betty. Betty married William Mushin, a famous anaesthetist, in Plymouth Synagogue on 27 September 1939.

Arthur Goldberg was educated at St. Boniface's College, Plymouth College and the University of London. In 1932, he qualified as a solicitor. He gained his first seat on the City Council in 1938. In the early part of the Second World War, he met his future wife, Sylvia Stone, at an engagement party in Paignton. Her family had evacuated from London to Churston, between Torquay and Plymouth, when rumours of war circulated in 1938. Sylvia was there when war finally broke out in September 1939. During the war, Arthur served in the Auxiliary Fire Service, in charge of a large company of Jewish men from the north of England. Sylvia was called up, joined the FANYS as a driver of ambulances and 10 ton lorries, and then as a driver to officers. She recalls:

> 'Arthur became head of the Fire Service in Plymouth, but continued his work as a solicitor in the day. He drove around and inspected sites. He and his team saved the synagogue after a Luftwaffe bomb fell on the Treasury next door. Before we married, he used to ask my mother where I was stationed and he would search me out. He wrote to my Commanding Officer and asked if I could be transferred to Devon, and I was. We married in 1942 in Claridges in London because our house in Brondesbury had been bombed. I believe we had

Sam Marks with his children Rochelle and David

---

[143] Louis and Esther Goldberg had three sons: Arthur, Lazarus and Henry.

Investiture of Arthur Goldberg as first Jewish Lord Mayor of Plymouth, 25 May 1961

Lord Mayor Arthur Goldberg with his wife, Lady Mayoress Sylvia Goldberg

Lord Mayor Arthur Goldberg with HRH Duke of Edinburgh, Plymouth, July 1961

the first Jewish wedding ever to take place in Claridges.'

Arthur and Sylvia had two children: Meriel and David. In 1961-2, Arthur Goldberg made local history when he was elected the first Jewish Lord Mayor of Plymouth. It plunged him and Sylvia into an incredibly busy, but interesting, schedule of civic events which he enjoyed. 'He had something nearly every day,' recalls Sylvia. 'although I didn't necessarily attend every meeting. There were lots of highlights, including meeting Royalty on key civic occasions: The Queen Mother during the opening of the Tamar Bridge in April 1962, the Duke of Edinburgh, and Princess Margaret with Lord Snowdon.' His term of office marked giant strides in the reconstruction of the blitzed city that had not yet recovered since the Second World War. His prominent public role cemented a longstanding relationship between the Jewish community and the Corporation. In May 1961, he opened a display of Jewish silver at the City Art Gallery, on loan from the Plymouth Synagogue. It is the only known public exhibiting of the synagogue's silver until the Hidden Legacy Foundation exhibition in 2000 – 2001. During Passover 1962, whilst Arthur was still in office, he and Sylvia held a civic *seder* (Passover meal) for over a hundred Jewish personnel of the American Task Force 'Bravo' who were stationed in the area on a Nato exercise. Also present at the meal were members of the Plymouth Hebrew Congregation and chaplains of the American fleet. Towards the end of his period of office in April 1962, he and Maurice Overs, the president of the synagogue, presented six goblets to the City of Plymouth

Lord Mayor Arthur Goldberg with Elizabeth, the Queen Mother, opening of the Tamar Bridge, 26 April 1962

Presentation of 6 gold goblets to the City of Plymouth by the Plymouth Hebrew Congregation, 21 April 1962

as part of the city's ceremonial artifacts.

For his services to the community, the Plymouth Hebrew Congregation honoured him as Honorary Life President. During his lifetime, he was President of the Plymouth Law Society and a plaque with his name on it was unveiled on the Law Courts. There are a number of other plaques too around the city which bear his name. He died on 19 December 1982 and is buried in Gifford Place cemetery. In paying tribute to him, the Jewish Chronicle commented that 'The Queen and Prince Philip altered the timing of their visit to Plymouth one Passover, so that he [Arthur] could attend the synagogue first, before greeting them on behalf of the city.'[144] An obituary in the synagogue magazine described him as: 'the perfect gentleman, of generous spirit, profoundly upright and filled with quiet courage which sustained all around him in time of crisis, an able lawyer who never turned away a plea for help.[145]

Meriel Goldberg

---

[144] Jewish Chronicle, 11 February 1983.
[145] Digest, February 1983.

The Spiers Family

Judi Spiers, one of Devon's best-loved and most experienced TV and radio broadcasters, grew up in the Jewish world of Plymouth in the late 1950s. She was one of four children born to Leonard and Fay Spiers. Leonard was affectionately known as 'Doc' because of his early days as a porter in a hospital. Ironically, he brought Fay from his home in Birmingham to the outskirts of Plymouth during the war to escape the bombs, little realizing that it would become one of Britain's most blitzed cities. They had four children: Michael, Rita, Stephen and Judi. Michael, who was born in Torquay, followed in his father's footsteps and began his own jewellery business. He passed away in August 1999 and is buried in the Gifford Place Jewish cemetery. Rita Spiers married Keith White, a company director from London, in Plymouth Synagogue on 31 May 1964. Keith, as captain of the Great Britain Squash Team, secured a Silver medal and a Bronze medal in the team event, at the 10th Maccabiah Games in Israel in 1977 and was recently awarded an MBE for services to sport. After Michael's death, Keith took over the running of the jewellery business mentoring Michael's son, Adam.

Damien White on his bar mitzvah with Rabbi Susser

Doc and Fay Spiers

Spiers family

Throughout his life, Doc Spiers was a senior member of the Plymouth Hebrew Congregation and a competent reader of Morning Prayers. He came from a traditional Orthodox background and had considerable knowledge of Halakhah and Rabbinic Law. His father, Wolf Spiers, came from Latvia, his original surname thought to be Shapiro. He lived, and is buried, in Birmingham. As the congregation numbers declined in Plymouth, Doc always made sure he was there when a minyan was necessary for prayers, either in the synagogue or at a funeral. In his younger days, he carried out duties for the *Chevra Kadisha*, the Jewish burial society. He died in January 1988 and is buried in the same cemetery, Gifford Place, as his wife and son.

After studying at drama school in London, Judi went on to make a name for herself on TV and radio. Today, she has her own mid-morning radio show on BBC Radio Devon, listened to by thousands. She has many memories of growing up in Plymouth:

'We walked to synagogue and back every Shabbat. My father, who came from a fairly religious background, wouldn't let us play cards or do anything on Shabbat. His motto was always "I will show you what I was taught. And when you are old enough, you can choose what to do." And that it what he did. The family lit candles and said prayers on Friday night. We didn't keep a strictly kosher home, but we didn't east pork or shellfish, and didn't eat milk after meat. We always fasted for Yom Kippur and we sent to London for matzos and special foods for the Passover. Married women always wore hats to the synagogue. I considered it to be a very normal, not particularly strict, religious upbringing. We attended Hebrew classes on Sundays, learned our prayers, and, along with my close friends Louise and Bernice Solomon, messed around… a lot! I remember with fondness the song and dance shows which Doreen Davidson directed us in once a year, the many bar mitzvahs and big parties held afterwards, usually in the Guildhall.'

Judi recalls too, how the women of the synagogue, including her own mother, were incredibly active in charitable work, coffee mornings and other social events. 'It was a very busy community in those days,' she says. 'Everyone had someone of their own age. Sadly, things have changed as many have died and many have moved away from Plymouth.'

Robert Lenkiewicz (1942-2002)

'Robert Lenkiewicz: love him or loathe him, you can't ignore him,' one of Plymouth's Lord Mayors once commented. Artist Robert Lenkiewicz became one of the most controversial and well-known characters of Plymouth

Lenkiewicz's signature in the synagogue Visitors Book

Lenkiewicz's mural on The House That Jack Built, Plymouth

from his arrival in the city in 1968 until his death in 2002. He came from an ultra-Orthodox family in Stamford Hill, which he left to study at St. Martins School of Art, then the Royal Academy, following in the footsteps of another famous Plymothian Jewish artist, Solomon Hart. He settled in Plymouth where he soon made a name for himself as an eccentric artist who constantly pushed the boundaries of contemporary art. Years later, people came to appreciate that, behind his eccentricity, lay a man of extraordinary talent. Lenkiewicz was perhaps not fully appreciated or valued in his day, but he created incredible masterpieces that included two massive murals on the Barbican. One survives next to his former studio, albeit somewhat faded, the other survives on 'The House that Jack Built' nearby. In these two enormous murals, Lenkiewicz painted local Plymothians, as the basis for his characters, including some from the Jewish community. If one studies the faces carefully, it is possible to see that he painted himself into the murals. Amongst his famous sitters were celebrities Michael Foot, Simon Callow, Jimmy Connolly, Alan Bates and Charles Dance. His style was not unlike that of Lucian Freud, but often less grotesque in their portrayal of naked women. His topics were wide and covered alchemy, witchcraft, the Last Judgment, Jewish mysticism and the Hasidic movement of 19th century Judaism. His painting of *The Last Supper* included the figures of three women at the supper table. For over 30 years, he had a long-standing friendship with Lord St. Germans who commissioned him to paint the Round Room at his home at Port Eliot. Here, Lenkiewicz created biblical scenes on an epic scale.

Lenkiewicz lived on the excesses of life in terms of heath and the numerous women in his life. He is said to have fathered several children. Keith Nichols wrote of him in his book *Robert Lenkiewicz: The Artist and the Man*: 'Robert was prone to occasional sensationalized public events that were often misinterpreted as acts of an ill-disciplined, perhaps delinquent, self-publicist.' Lenkiewicz courted media attention and controversy when he befriended a local tramp and persuaded him to leave his body to him after death. Already by 1972, he had become increasingly interested in painting vagrants and alcoholics. It was highly contentious and pushed the boundaries of known art. He courted further controversy when he faked his own death to see the reactions of the media and what people would say about him after death. Throughout his career, Lenkiewicz appeared to turn his back on his Jewish roots. Certainly he did not keep Jewish customs or a religious life, but religion, especially mysticism, continued to fascinate him. And yet, as he grew increasingly unwell, he felt a pull to his Jewish roots. On 30 March 1998, he visited the beautiful Plymouth Synagogue and signed the Visitor Book. Why he visited is uncertain. Perhaps he felt that this was his spiritual home, even though he was not a practicing Jew. Lenkiewicz died on 5 August 2002. The Plymouth Hebrew Congregation received a request for him to be buried in the Jewish cemetery at Gifford Place. Under the influence of Cedric Tarsky, sadly the request was denied on grounds that the community did not want to draw attention to itself, or make the burial ground a site for pilgrimage.

From The 1980s

Since the 1980s, the Plymouth Jewish community witnessed a sharp decline and rarely managed to raise a minyan of ten men for a service. Yet on Sunday 1st November 1987, it was able to celebrate its 225th anniversary with a special service conducted by Rabbi Alan Plancey, Chairman of the Rabbinical Council of the United Synagogue. President Percy Aloof paid tribute to the founding fathers as: 'men of piety, uprightness and learning. Their spiritual guidance was of the essence which left its mark in the annals of the Congregation.' He then recalled the outstanding contribution made to civic life by members, including Myer Fredman and Arthur Goldberg, as well as the congregation's 'good and harmonious inter-

The synagogue Youth Group

faith relationships with all of the religious communities in the city.' In 1984, for example, the Bishop of Plymouth, Rt. Rev. Kenneth Newing, convened a joint meeting of Anglicans and Jews in the Abbey Hall, Catherine Street. It was held under the auspices of the Friends of Israel Educational Trust with director, John Levy. For once, the Jews outnumbered the Christians at the meeting. During 1998 and 1999, the author worked with Evelyn Friedlander, director of the Hidden Legacy Foundation, on an exhibition entitled *The Jews of Devon and Cornwall*. The exhibition, which toured Devon and Cornwall, told the history of the Jewish communities through particular artifacts, some of which had been loaned by descendants of families connected to these synagogues. The exhibition came to Plymouth City Museum from 16 November 2000 until 28 February 2001, opened by the Mayor of Plymouth during a special evening event.

The Community Today

Plymouth Jewish community remains a small one, yet one run by extremely dedicated members. There was once talk about 'when we close', but now the emphasis has shifted to survival. Services are held regularly on Friday night, led by Dr. Peter Lee. The Shabbat morning service is led by John Mitchell and Dr Joe Bard, with the help of visiting ministers and lay visitors. Dr Peter Lee leads the Yizkor service (service for the dead) whether or not there is a visiting rabbi or minister. He comments: 'This is partly because we have our own way of presenting it and because it contains a Memorial Prayer for the victims of the Holocaust. As the son of Holocaust survivors, this has a special significance for me. It is a prayer to which I introduced our Community its chanting melody. I also started a new practice for our Community, to incorporate this prayer into its Iscor tradition. On the High Holy Days, Yizkor is celebrated on Yom Kippur and Shemeni Atzeret. It is now also celebrated at Pesach and Shavuot.' Rather movingly, the synagogue remains open for worship even if only the Gabbai, Dr Peter Lee, turns up for prayers. He said: 'when I joined the community in the 1990s, I was told that there was no point in my joining because the synagogue would have to close soon because we were a dying community. This did not deter me. Never having

Rabbi Susser with the religion school

Members of Plymouth synagogue at a function

had an active Jewish life because of the effect of my parents' Holocaust experience, I felt that at least one or two years was better than none. The closure did not happen because there is a small core of long-established members who were active enough such that their efforts, with those of incomers, to produce an effective group of dedicated workers.'

In recent years, the community has become extremely conscious of its importance in Anglo-Jewish history. Today, there is a part-time, non-Jewish residential custodian, Jerry Sibley, who was appointed in 2007. He performs functions beyond what would normally be required of a caretaker because of his natural empathy with the community and his keenness to see it grow and thrive. The current president is John Mitchell,[146] Vice-President Mrs. Pat Goodman,[147] Hon Treasurer & Gabbai, Dr. Peter Lee, and Honorary Secretary Anna Kelly. John Hirshman is membership secretary. Stuart Goodman acts as the congregation's solicitor. The Communities General Purposes Committee (the committee of trustees) are Dr. Nadine Mitchell, Mr. Adam Jacobson, Mr. Solly Mordo, Dr Judith Beckman and Mr. Brian Aloof. The success of this committee is measured by the survival of the synagogue in circumstances which would have forced other communities to close.

In May 2012, the synagogue celebrated its 250th anniversary, officiated by Chief Rabbi, Lord Jonathan Sacks, and Revd. Elkan Levy. The main sanctuary and the ladies gallery were packed with former families, guests and visitors. It was a huge occasion and one attended by a vast array of Jewish, Civic and County senior dignitaries.

---

[146] John Mitchell is Chair of Headstone Maintenance, with John Hirshman as secretary.
[147] Pat Goodman is also Chair of Chevra Kadisha/Birkur Cholim (burials).

225th anniversary of the synagogue

Amongst the County dignitaries were the Lord Lieutenant of Devon, the Lord High Sheriff of Devon and the Lord Mayor of Plymouth. In addition, the community was honoured by the attendance of the President of the United Synagogue and the Board of Deputies of British Jews. The success of the celebrations was mirrored by £50,000 of work carried out on the interior of the synagogue, and exteriors of the synagogue building, the Vestry and the cemetery chapel. The synagogue has been painted inside and out with the specialist paint required for lime mortar rendering. Repairs to the roof and three rotten windows were also carried out in accordance with the requirements for listed buildings. The outside of the Vestry building was painted and re-rendered. The chapel in Gifford Place cemetery was painted inside and out. The work was generously financed by donations from congregation members, supplemented by large donations from the Bertie Black Foundation, the Hilda & Sam Marks Foundation and David Goldberg. Peter Lee comments: 'It has provided what we regard as a secure base for future generations to build on.'

A measure of the congregation's desire to survive is seen by the fact that it recently purchased two reconditioned scrolls from Sofer Dansky of Manchester, one of the leading scribes who operates under the auspices of Dayan Steiner. Dansky takes a special interest in ensuring that communities have 'kosher' scrolls. It is hoped that the new scrolls will last a few generations and for that aim, they were given a special coating to increase their lifespan.

The Community's Life and Vision

The community has a strong vision for the present and the future. Peter Lee comments: 'Other communities have closed, but we have not. A difference between our community and others is that we have a conviction. Our Community was founded on the faith of the original families and has survived for 250 years. If we work on a day-to-day basis to carry on by dealing with each difficulty as it arises, without getting depressed by the enormity of the whole task, then maybe something will happen to keep the synagogue alive just as it has in the past. A sudden influx of a few Orthodox families would make that difference. The real dangers currently are a flat income and numbers being so low as to risk the membership dying out. However, the income is currently steady and matches expenditure (the pressure comes from rising costs) and membership has grown over the past 18 months, albeit slowly. A considerable pressure comes from the disastrously low level of current interest rates which has resulted in having to take income by reducing capital rather than relying on earned interest.'

In 2009, perhaps controversially, the congregation felt it necessary to sell its oldest and most valuable ceremonial silver to raise necessary funds for the upkeep of the Georgian synagogue. In total, the auction raised over £175,000 at Bonhams. Four pairs of rimmonim and several silver pointers were auctioned. The rarest pair of rimmonim was from the period of George III with parcel-gilt finials

250th anniversary service led by Chief Rabbi Lord Sacks and Revd. Elkan Levy, May 2012

250th anniversary, May 2012. From left to right: Peter Lee, John Hirshman, Lord Sacks, Revd. Elkan Levy and Adam Jacobson

Caretaker, Jerry Sibley speaking to guests at the 250th anniversary

and matching pointer, made in 1783, which sold for £62,400. Another pair dating to 1913, made by Joseph Zweig (London), sold for £1,800. A full list is given in an appendix at the end of the book.

The synagogue is open for visits by religious, lay and school groups by prior arrangement. In the year 2012-13, eighty-nine groups visited the synagogue, totalling 2,500 adults and children, an increase of 1,000 over the previous year. The community takes an active role in the city's Holocaust Memorial Day events. Peter Lee is the official Jewish representative at the Lord Mayor's Mount Edgcumbe inter-faith reflection. Various members, notably Liz Berg, represent the congregation at the other events held at the Plymouth University and also schools. Anna Kelly represents the Jewish community as a Trustee of the Council-sponsored Plymouth Centre for Faiths and Cultural Diversity, and also as a member on Plymouth SACRE with John Mitchell acting as representative on the Plymouth Faith Council.

The community is forward looking and, in recent years, no longer thinks about when it will close. Now there is far more optimism that it will survive, although its numbers continue to be small. The heyday of the large community may be over, but this gem of a community has a very special feel about it. The members are committed to its heritage and serve the needs of local Jews within the boundaries of an Orthodox tradition. With the dedicated work of its current officials, Plymouth Synagogue will survive. With an awareness of its heritage, the future of the building is assured. The synagogue has seen numerous happy occasions, but also survived many difficult times. Throughout its long history, even during the destruction of the city by German bombers in 1941 as one of only three buildings left undamaged, it has remained a place of continuous Jewish worship. There is every expectation that it will survive into the next millennium and beyond. Dr Peter Lee's words poignantly sum up the uniqueness of this place:

'Everyone who visits or worships in our synagogue is affected by the building. It is a wonderful place. There must be few listed buildings of its age in the country that are still being used on a daily basis for the purpose it was originally built. Praying in our synagogue has a different feel to praying in other synagogues. I can summarise that by saying that the community was founded on faith and continues through faith.'

APPENDIX 1
RABBIS & MINISTERS

Rabbi Moses Ephraim	c. 1780s-1815
Revd. Moses Isaac (Beadle/teacher)	1760s? - 1790
Hirsch Mannheim (shochet)	1764 -
Revd. Levi Benjamin	1787 - ?
Joseph ben Joseph Meir	? – 1784
Revd. Joseph Levy	1795 - ?
Revd. Phineas ben Samuel Phineas	1800 – 1803
Hayyim Issachar (Beadle)	1810 – 1830
Michael Solomon Alexander	Circa 1815 -
Revd. H Harris	1829 – 1831
Revd. Myer Stadthagen	1829 – 1861
Rev. Leopold Stern	1864 - ?
Revd. Joshua Levy	1865 – 1867
Revd. L. Rosenbaum	1863 – 1893
Revd. Moses Lewis	1884 – 1885
Revd. Abraham N Spier	1884 – 1896
Revd. M. Berlin	1896 – 1906
Revd. Posner	circa 1893 - 1903
Revd. D. Jacobs	1903 – 1912
Revd. E Jaffe	1904 - ?
Revd. A. K Slavinsky	1909 - 1918
Revd. M. Zeffert	1918 – 1928
Revd. Simon Wykansky (Chazan/Shochet)	1920 - 1932
Revd. W. Wolfson	1928 – 1944
Revd. Emanuel Goodman	1933 - 1959
Revd. S. Susman	1944 – 1952
Revd. D. Josovic	1954 – 1956
Revd. I. Broder	1958 – 1960
Rabbi Bernard Susser	1961 – 1965
Revd. A. Ginsburg	1965 – 1975
Revd. Rockman	1975 – 1977
Rabbi Bernard Susser	1977 - 1981

Revd. Spier

Revd. M Goodman

Revd. Wolfson

APPENDIX 2
OFFICERS OF THE CONGREGATION 1778 - 2012

Presidents 1778 – 1852[148]

1778 - 1780	Joseph Jacob Sherenbeck
1781 - 1782	Simon Nathan
1783 - 1785	Lazarus Joseph
1786	Samuel Simon
1796 - 1797	Solomon Cohen Tsadak
1798 - 1811	Joseph Joseph
1812 -1813	Sander Alexander
1815 - 1818	Joseph Joseph
1819	Nathan Cohen Tsadak
1821	Abraham Levi
1822	B. Jonus
1823	Mark Mordecai
1824	Benjamin Levy
1825	Nathan Cohen Tsadak
1826	Phineas Johnson
1827 – 1828	Samuel (Hart?)
1830	Mark Mordecai
1833	Phineas Johnson
1834	Phineas Levi
1835	L. Solomons
1836 - 1840	Samuel Levi
1841 – 1843	Abraham Joseph II
1844	Joshua Levy
1845 - 1846	Josiah Solomon
1847	Abraham Joseph
1848 - 1849	Charles Marks
1850 - 1851	Phineas Levi
1852	Abraham Joseph II

Officers 1858-1892

	President	Treasurer	Burial Warden
1858 -1860	Jacob Nathan	Lewis Hyman	Barnet Mitchell
1861	Abraham Joseph II	Lewis Hyman	Wolf Emdon
1862	Edward Basch	Solomon Ullman	Solomon Ullman
1863	Abraham Joseph II	Solomon Ullman	Samuel Samuels
1864	Lewis Hyman	Wolf Emdon	Samuel Samuels
1865 - 1866	Lewis Hyman	Lewis Hyman	Samuel Samuels
1867	Lewis Hyman	Lewis Hyman	Judah S. Lyon
1868	Markes Levy	William Wolf	Abraham Morris
1869	Asher Joel	George Norman	Solomon Zeffert
1870	Asher Joel	Edward Basch	Solomon Zeffert

---

[148] Doris Black's *The Plymouth Synagogue: 1761 – 1961*, and the Plymouth Hebrew Congregation Minute Book (1796-1834)

1871	Asher Joel	Edward Basch	Henry Morris
1872	Markes Levy	Abraham Ralph	Solomon Zeffert
1873	Markes Levy	Eleazer Emdon	Louis Conitz
1874	Edward Basch	Solomon Zeffert	Samuel Samuels
1875	Asher Joel	Solomon Zeffert	Aaron Wolf
1876	Samuel Samuels	Louis Conitz	Aaron E. Lyons
1877	Solomon Zeffert	Aaron Wolf	Jacob Fredman
1878	Samuel Samuels	Aaron Wolf	Louis Conitz
1879	Eleazer Emdon	Eleazer Emdon	Asher Levy
1880	Eleazer Emdon	Louis Conitz	Levin Fredman
1881	Solomon Zeffert	Levin Fredman	Herman London
1882	Louis Conitz	Aaron Wolf	Aaron E. Lyons
1883	Alexander Jacobs	Alexander Jacobs	I. Roseman
1884	Louis Conitz	Levin Fredman	Mark Emdon
1885	Levin Fredman	Edward Basch	Edward Basch
1886	Louis Conitz	Jacob Fredman	Herman London
1887	Mark Emdon	Abraham Morris	Herman London
1888	Levin Fredman	Abraham Morris	Herman London
1889	Louis Conitz	I. Roseman	Herman London
1890	I. Roseman	I. Roseman	Eleazer Orgel
1891	Asher Levy	Eleazer Orgel	S. Simpson
1892	Asher Levy	Eleazer Orgel	Myer Fredman, sen

Officers 1917-2012

	President	Treasurer	Secretary
1917	Isidore Cohen	Myer Roseman	Michael Solomon
1918 - 1919	Myer Fredman	Myer Roseman	Herman Cohen
1920	Myer Roseman	King Field	David Fredman
1921	Elias Ellis	Michael Solomon	Philip Bloom
1922	Myer Fredman	Isidore Cohen	Percy Roseman
1923	Michael Solomon	Philip Bloom	Leslie Cohen
1924 - 1925	Myer Fredman	Joseph Sanger	Jack Sanger
1926	Myer Fredman	Joseph Sanger	Samuel Fredman
1927 - 1928	Joseph Sanger	Myer Roseman	Samuel Fredman
1929	Tobias Brand	Leslie Cohen	Joseph Reese
1930	Tobias Brand	Samuel Roseman	Joseph Reese
1931	Leslie Cohen	Samuel Fredman	Samuel Cohen
1932	Leslie Cohen	Samuel Roseman	David Roseman
1933	Samuel Roseman	Tobias Brand	David Roseman
1934 - 1935	Leslie Cohen	Ernest Robins	David Roseman
1936 - 1937	David Jordan	Isidore Joseph	David Roseman
1938 - 1939	Isidore Joseph	David Roseman	Arthur Goldberg
1940	David Roseman	Arthur Goldberg	Saul Hack
1941	Arthur Goldberg	—	Saul Hack
1942	Herman Cohen	King Field & Isaac Bromberg	Saul Hack
1943	Herman Cohen	Isaac Bromberg	Saul Hack
1944	David Roseman	Isaac Bromberg	Jack Sanger & Harry Richman
1945	Isaac Bromberg	Jack Sanger	John Goodman & Harry Richman
1946	Jack Sanger	Saul Hack	John Goodman & Harry Richman
1947	Jack Sanger	Saul Hack	John Goodman
1948	Saul Hack	John Goodman	Dr Mark Gordon
1949	John Goodman	Philip Harris	Samuel Richman
1950	Philip Harris	Samuel Richman	Israel Black
1951	Jack Sanger	Samuel Richman	Israel Black
1952	Samuel Richman	Samuel Marks	Israel Black

APPENDIX 2

1953	Samuel Marks	Hyman Sanger	Israel Black
1954	Samuel Marks	Israel Black	Maurice Overs & J Dubovie
1955	Israel Black	Maurice Overs	Jack Richman
1956	Maurice Overs	Jack Richman	Jack Smith
1957	Jack Richman	Jack Smith	Maurice Rutman
1958 -1959	Jack Smith	R J Lewis	PH Cohen & DH Richman
1960	Israel Black	DH Richman	Brian Pearl
1961	Israel Black	Maurice Overs	Brian Pearl
1962	Maurice Overs	Brian Pearl	Sydney Ginsburg
1963	Maurice Overs	Israel Roseman	David Maxwell
1964	Maurice Overs	David Maxwell	J Dubovie
1965	JB Goodman	Israel Black	G Hurst & LB Fredman
1966	JB Goodman	Dr Mark Gordon	LB Fredman
1967	Dr Mark Gordon	A. Goldberg	LB Fredman
1968	Arthur Goldberg	Israel Black	LB Fredman
1969 - 1971	Arthur Goldberg	Morris Rutman	S. Aloof
1972 - 1973	Morris Rutman	John Goodman	S. Aloof
1974	Morris Rutman	John Goodman	GA Hurst
1975	Morris Rutman (with Arthur Goldberg acting)	John Goodman	GA Hurst
1976	Arthur Goldberg	John Goodman	GA Hurst
1977	Arthur Goldberg	John Goodman	Miss Riva Joseph
1978 -1980	Arthur Goldberg	Bertram Emdon	Miss Riva Joseph
1981 - 1982	Arthur Goldberg (Life) Percy Aloof (Vice)	GA Hurst	Miss Riva Joseph
1983 – 1991	Percy Aloof	GA Hurst	Miss Riva Joseph
1992 - 1995	Percy Aloof	Benny Greenberg (Gabbai)	Miss Riva Joseph
1996 - 2001	Benny Greenberg	Cedric Tarsky	Dr Peter Lee
2002	Benny Greenburg with Jack Cohen Percy Aloof (life)	John Mitchell Miriam Aggiss (assistant)	Tony Aggiss
2003 - 2004	Benny Greenburg with Jack Cohen	John Mitchell Miriam Aggiss (assistant)	Tony Aggiss
2005	Jack Cohen Pat Goodman, Vice-President	John Mitchell Miriam Aggiss (assistant)	Tony Aggiss
2006 - 2007	John Mitchell Pat Goodman, Vice-President	Miriam Aggiss	Tony Aggiss
2008 - 2010	John Mitchell Pat Goodman, Vice-President	Dr Peter Lee Solly Mordo	Anna Kelly
2011 - 2012	John Mitchell Pat Goodman, Vice-President	Dr Peter Lee (Gabbai)	Anna Kelly

APPENDIX 3
ROLE OF HONOUR

PLYMOUTH JEWS WHO SERVED IN WW1 AND WW2

WW1

James S. Abrahams, John Abrahams, Joseph Abrahams, Aaron Bash, E. Bence, Cecil Brand, Sydney Brand, Mark Brock, M. M Cohen, E. Franks, David Fredman, I. Fredman, Louis Fredman, I. Joseph, Sim Lazarus, I. Milner, M. Morris, M. Pinkofsky, M. Sanger, Barnett D. Silk, Joseph Spark, David Weinberg, M. Woolfstein, S. Woolfstein, Victor Levy, H. Goodman, M. Nissan and Jack Silverstone. Killed in action: M. Nissan and Jack Silverstone. Local Jews who served in the Special Constabulary during WW1: A. Brand, E. Brock, A. Erlich, S. Gordon, M. Jacobs, G. Lazarus, E. Robins, Myer Roseman and M. Solomons

WW2

Pte L. Aloof, Sgt P. Aloof, Pte E. Angel, Pte M. Angel, Pte L. Angel, W. Begelman, F/Sgt H. Bence, Capt D. Bromberg, Pte H. Caplan, Sgt B. Cohen, Cpl G. Cohen, Capt H. H. Cohen, Gunner J. Cohen, Sgt L. Cohen, Lt P. Cohen, Capt W. Cohen, Cpl J. Dubovie, Sgt K. Emdon, Acting Capt M. D. Solomon, Capt D. Fredman, Ldg Tel L. B. Fredman, Wvr S. Goldberg (Fany), M. E. Gordon, B. Greenberg, S/Ldr H. Greenburgh, Lt L. Hack, Capt M. Hurwitt, Lt D. A. Jordan, H. Kaphan, P. Lee, Pte R. Lewis, L. D. Lee, Cpl S. Marks, Sigmn H. H. Melichan, H. H. Milner, Capt B. Peck, Lt H. Peck, Sgt A. Wiseman, Gunner A. Richman, Pte H. Richman, Cpl I. Richman, Pte N. Richman, Pte S. Richman, Major G. Robins, Cpl A. Roland, Dvr R. Robins, Gunner I. Roseman (RA), La.C I. Roseman, Sgt M .Rutman, H. Salsberg, Pte H. Sanger, S. Sanger, Sgt I. Silver, Pte H. Simons, Tpr L. D. Spiers, Col R. L. Telfer and Sgt S. Solomon. Killed in action: Sgt R. Simons.

APPENDIX 3

Morris Smith, Jewish Battalion, WW1, wounded in action

Frank Joseph Bloom, WW2

Morry Rutman, WW2

Capt. David Fredman

APPENDIX 4
PLYMOUTH JEWISH MARRIAGES

16 August 1837: Woolf Emdon, son of Eliezer Emdon (salesman) to Rebecca Franco, daughter of John Franco (salesman)

3 January 1838: George Brock, hawker, son of Eleazer Brock (tailor) to Sarah Levy, daughter of Lyon Levy (salesman)

20 June 1838: Myer Blankensee, jeweller of Bristol, son of Levin Blankensee (merchant) to Julia Levy, daughter of Abraham Levy (pawnbroker)

1 August 1838: William Woolf, shopkeeper, son of Isaac Woolf (salesman) to Ann Levi, daughter of John Levi (salesman), married in 46 Chapel Street

25 March 1840: Abraham Emdon, widower, son of Eleazer Emdon (salesman) to Lydia Davis, daughter of Mordecai Davis (box maker)

16 September 1840: Hyam Hyam, silversmith, son of Samuel Hyman (pawnbroker) to Zipporah Jacobs, daughter of Nathan Jacobs (silversmith)

24 November 1841: Benjamin Jonas, hawker, son of Henry Jonas (silversmith) to Eliza Levi, daughter of John Levi

29 December 1841: Asher Joel, jeweller, son of Joseph Joseph to Rosina Hyman, daughter of Samuel Hyman (pawnbroker)

23 November 1842: Isaac Lazarus, jeweller of Place, Exeter, son of Eleazar Lazarus (jeweller) to Eliza Jacobs, daughter of Levy Jacobs (jeweller)

Wedding of Joe Smith and Mary Shatles, 1925

APPENDIX 4

21 May 1844: Mark Levy, widower, general dealer, son of Moses Levy to Ann Rosenthal, widow, daughter of Isaac Mark (general dealer)

16 October 1844: Jacob Casper, shopkeeper of Manchester, son of Eleazar Casper (general dealer) to Mathilda Hyman, daughter of Samuel Hyman (general dealer)

19 February 1845: Joseph Michael, pawnbroker of Bristol, son of Joseph Michael (general dealer) to Rebecca Levy, daughter of Abraham Levy (pawnbroker)

31 December 1845: Myer Woolf, optician, son of Isaac Woolf (general dealer) to Phoebe Abrahams, daughter of Solomon Abrahams (general dealer)

11 January 1846: Abraham Abrahams, general dealer, son of Mordecai Abrahams (general dealer) to Sarah Abrahams, daughter of John Abrahams (general dealer)

4 February 1846: Adolphus Goldschmidt, tobacconist, son of Isaac Goldschmidt (general dealer) to Rose Lyon, widow, daughter of Moses Solomon (watch manufacturer)

1 July 1846: Leon Solomon, jeweller of London, son of Solomon Solomon (general dealer) to Rose Joseph, daughter of Abraham Joseph (Gentleman)

26 August 1846: Samuel Samuels, jeweller, son of Samuel Cutler (dealer) to Jenetta Moses, daughter of Philip Moses (dealer)

18 November 1846: Aron Woolf, jeweller, son of Marcus Woolf (Private) to Phoebe Levi, daughter of John Levi (dealer)

12 July 1848: Sigmond Yager, general dealer, son of Joseph Yager (dealer) to Traphina Levi, daughter of John Levi (dealer)

29 August 1849: Mosley Hyman, mercer, son of Samuel Hyman (dealer) to Sarah Johnson of 6 King Street, daughter of Moses Johnson (dealer)

24 July 1850: David Levi, general dealer, son of Phineas Levi (dealer) to Eve Hyman, daughter of Samuel Hyman (pawnbroker)

25 December 1850: Edward Pasch, jeweller, son of Michael Basch (dealer) to Julia Levi, daughter of John Levi (dealer)

15 July 1851: Samuel Harris, wholesale hardware of London, son of Henry Harris (jeweller) to Sophia Levi, daughter of Phineas Levi (dealer)

27 August 1851: Henry Nathan, wholesale jeweller of Birmingham, son of Jacob Nathan (dealer) to Caroline Levy, daughter of Abraham Levy (pawnbroker)

19 November 1851: Sam Alexander, traveller, son of Solomon Alexander (dealer) to Rachel Bowman, daughter of Mordecai Bowman (general dealer)

3 December 1851: Abraham Burstein, traveller, son of Isaac Burstein (general dealer) to Rose Woolf Solomon, daughter of Woolf Solomon (jeweller)

18 August 1852: Morris Levy, tradesman, son of Mark Levy (general dealer) to Sophia Mordecai Levy, daughter of Mark Mordecai Levy (general dealer)

12 January 1853: Solomon Ullman, shopkeeper, son of Jacob Ullman (general dealer) to Sarah Joseph, daughter of Joseph Isaac (general dealer)

23 February 1853: Abraham Lemon Woolf, commercial traveller of Jewry St, Aldgate, son of Lemon Woolf (general dealer) to Henrietta Levi, daughter of Phineas Levi (Naval Agent)

23 February 1853: Nathan Lazarus, gentleman of London, son of Eleazar Lazarus (general dealer) to Fanny Lazarus, daughter of Lyon Lazarus (general dealer)

20 July 1853: Simon Mordecai Levy, commercial traveller, son of M. M. Levy (general dealer) to Rose Levi, daughter of Phineas Levi (shopkeeper)

7 September 1854: Aaron Jacob, widower, glazer, son of Jacob Jackell (tailor) to Jenetta Wolf, daughter of Aron Wolf (dealer)

7 February 1855: Barnett Barnett, wholesale jeweller, son of Isaac Barnett (gentleman) to Selina Stadthagen, daughter of Revd. Myer Stadthagen

Marriage of Esther Roseman to Harry Black, 1923

31 November 1855: Isaac Solomon, merchant, son of Jacob Solomon (gentleman) to Rose Marks, daughter of Charles Marks (jeweller)

6 February 1856: Frederick Levy, merchant of Bristol, son of Levy Levy (gentleman) to Sarah Marks, daughter of Charles Marks (jeweller)

4 December 1856: Aaron Goldston, shoemaker, son of Henry Goldstone (tailor) to Rebecca Solomon, daughter of Solomon Solomon (shoemaker)

19 August 1857: Sol Lazarus Solomon of Torquay, son of Lazarus Solomon (jeweller) to Sarah Lyons, daughter of Joseph Lyons (general dealer)

26 August 1857: Isaac Stone, Hebrew teacher, son of Abraham Stone (Reader) to Anna Mordecai, daughter of Mark Mordecai (merchant)

16 August 1858: Abraham Isaac, pawnbroker of Newport, son of Isaac Samuels (merchant) to Phoebe Stadthagen, daughter of Revd. Myer Stadthagen

5 January 1860: Lewis Brock, hairdresser, son of George Brock (hawker) to Henrietta Nathan, daughter of Aaron Nathan (dealer)

22 August 1860: Edwin Woolf, pawnbroker, son of William Woolf (retired tradesman) to Sarah Stadthagen, daughter of Revd. Myer Stadthagen

31 October 1860: Abraham Cohen, painter & glazier, son of Nathan Cohen (shopkeeper) to Priscilla Harris, daughter of Samuel Harris (dealer)

12 December 1860: Hyman Harris, glazier, son of Harris Hyman (dealer) to Bessie Myers, daughter of Israel Myers (hawker)

27 February 1861: Samuel Silver, boot & shoemaker, son of Nathan Silver (dealer) to Rebecca Myers, daughter of Israel Myers (hawker)

22 May 1861: Woolf Jacob Ullmann, general dealer, son of Jacob Samuel Ullmann (Reader) to Deborah Morris, daughter of Hyman Morris (dealer)

24 July 1861: George Norman, tobacconist of Cambridge, son of Jacob Norman (dealer) to Rose Lyons, daughter of Jacob Lyons

12 November 1861: Alexander Clapper, clothier, son of Myer Clapper (dealer) to Amelia Rain, daughter of Abraham Rain (dealer)

10 December 1862: Jesse Lawrence, tailor of Birmingham, son of Joseph Lawrence (clothier) to Annie Joseph, daughter of Nathan Joseph (gentleman)

5 July 1865: Abraham van Nierop, clerk & accountant, son of E. van Nierop (merchant) to Phoebe Joseph, daughter of Joseph Joseph (silversmith)

17 October 1866: Moses Rosenberg, jeweller, son of Abraham Rosenberg (pawnbroker) to Esther Joseph, daughter of Joseph Joseph (jeweller)

12 December 1866: Jacob Cohen, clothier, son of Joseph Cohen (general dealer) to Ellen Abrahams Heilbron, daughter of Abraham Heilbron (general dealer)

21 August 1867: Joseph L. Jacobs, jeweller, son of Jacob Jacob (traveller) to Kate Morris, daughter of Henry Morris (jeweller)

27 November 1867: Myer Levi Isaacs, optician, son of Levin Isaacs (jeweller) to Julia Levy, daughter of Mark Levy (pawnbroker)

27 October 1869: Solomon Tucker, watchmaker, son of Charles Tucker (watchmaker) to Sophy Jordan, daughter of Charles Jordan (doctor)

27 April 1870: Raphael Harris, widower and Reader (of synagogue) of 14 Clifton Villas, Paddington, son of Levi Harris (Gentleman) to Sarah Joseph, daughter of Abraham Joseph

17 August 1870: Israel Roseman, traveller, son of Levy Roseman (traveller) to Rachel Fredman, daughter of Wolf Fredman (traveller)

31 August 1870: Mark Levy, tailor of London, son of Lazarus Levy (traveller) to Miriam Newman, daughter of Isaac Newman (traveller)

19 October 1870: Adolph Posner, merchant of London, son of Samuel Posner (Gentleman) to Amelia Lyons, daughter of Jacob Lyons (deceased)

8 March 1871: Solomon Woolf, merchant, son of George Woolf (Gentleman) to Harriett Joseph, daughter of Jacob Joseph (deceased)

2 July 1871: George Nelson, shopkeeper, son of Harris Nelson (watchmaker) to Rosalin Goldberg, daughter of Levy Goldberg (deceased)

13 December 1871: Henry Simpson, shopkeeper, son of Marcus Simpson (merchant) to Clara Emdon, daughter of Abraham Emdon (pawnbroker)

17 July 1872: Solomon Woolf, ironmonger, son of William Woolf (Gentleman) to Annie Marcoso, daughter of James Marcoso (Gentleman)

APPENDIX 4

28 August 1872: Edward Marcus Marcoso, commercial traveller of Birmingham, son of James Marcoso (Gentleman) to Hannah Samuels, daughter of Samuel Samuels (Gentleman)

11 September 1872: Isaac Lyons, merchant, son of Jacob Lyons (deceased) to Esther Levy, daughter of Mark Levy (silversmith)

11 December 1872: Edward Eugene Seligman, commercial traveller, son of Marcus Seligman (deceased) to Isabella Yager, daughter of Sigmund Yager (traveller)

6 August 1873: Alfred Leonard Ticktin, merchant, son of Woolf Ticktin (deceased) to Rosina Rosenberg, daughter of Abraham Rosenberg (shopkeeper)

28 January 1874: Robert Jordan, surgeon dentist, son of Mark Jacob Jordan (surgeon) to Bella Joel, daughter of Asher Joel (traveller)

28 January 1874: Benjamin Levin, merchant tailor of Manchester, son of Joseph Levin (Gentleman) to Matilda Joel, daughter of Asher Joel (traveller)

26 August 1874: Edward Fiedler, linen merchant of London, son of Julius Henry Fiedler (Gentleman) to Pauline Basch, daughter of Edward Basch (pawnbroker)

23 May 1875: Lewis Samuel, outfitter of Bristol, son of M. Samuels (watchmaker) to Leah Jacobs, daughter of H. Jacobs (traveller)

15 September 1875: Aaron Lyons, pawnbroker, son of Jacob Lyons (deceased) to Eliza Levy, daughter of Marks Levy (pawnbroker)

29 August 1876: Solomon Lyon, widower, jeweller of Birmingham, son of Solomon Lyon (deceased) to Caroline Levy, daughter of Marks Levy (pawnbroker)

6 September 1876: Hermann London, clothier of London, son of Nahum Levin London (deceased) to Harriett Woolf, widow, daughter of Jacob Joseph (deceased)

27 December 1876: Jacob Walper, general dealer of Birmingham, son of Marks Walper (deceased) to Julia Israel, daughter of Aaron Israel (deceased)

29 August 1877: Henry Moss, dentist of Falmouth, son of Moses Moss (general dealer) to Sophia Basch, daughter of Edward Basch (pawnbroker)

6 February 1878: Eleazar Emdon, pawnbroker, son of Abraham Emdon (deceased) to Eliza Joseph, daughter of Abraham Joseph (deceased)

Ketubah for Percy and Bessie Aloof

? March 1878: Morris Elias Rotenberg, gentleman, son of Benjamin Rotenberg (deceased) to Catherine Zeffertt, daughter of Solomon Zeffertt (pawnbroker)

21 May 1878: Solomon Morris, outfitter, son of Abraham Morris (outfitter) to Ann Morris, outfitter, daughter of Morris Morris (deceased)

11 January 1882: Barnett Cohen, hawker, son of Moses Cohen (deceased) to Sarah Freedman, daughter of Samuel Woolf Freedman (hawker)

11 October 1882: Jacob Israel Pollack, corn merchant of London, son of Moses Morris (hawker) to Leah Fredman, daughter of Jacob Fredman (shopkeeper)

12 April 1883: Eleser Orgel, picture frame maker, son of Chaim Orgel (hawker) to Esther Frims Weineberg, daughter of Calman Weineberg (shopkeeper)

24 May 1883: Lewis Abrahamson, hawker, to Fanny Baum, daughter of P. Baum (outfitter)

4 July 1883: Abraham Emanuel, hawker, son of Joseph Emanuel (shopkeeper) to Rachel Stone, daughter of Samuel Stone (shopkeeper)

3 September 1884: Max Bischofswerder, commercial traveller, son of Isaac Bischofswerder (Minister of Religion) to Catherine Jacobs, daughter of Mark Jacobs (shopkeeper)

25 February 1885: Benjamin Zusman, furniture dealer, son of Hermann Zusman (furniture dealer) to Leah Lyons, daughter of Barnett Lyons (Private)

11 March 1885: Charles Brock, watchmaker, son of Louis Brock (musician) to Caroline Alberta Leah Gregory

10 June 1885: Simon Weinberg, furniture dealer, son of Kalman Weinberg (furniture dealer) to Mathilda Rosenbaum, daughter of Levy Rosenbaum (furniture dealer)

6 April 1886: Samuel Symons, furniture dealer, son of Abraham Symons (wine dealer) to Rebecca Fredman, daughter of Jacob Fredman (outfitter)

14 April 1886: Morris Sulski, furniture dealer, son of Jacob Sulski (baker) to Golda Fredman, daughter of Woolf Fredman (traveller)

1 September 1886: Moss Simons, grocer of London, son of Isaac Simons (grocer) to Annie Fredman, daughter of Levy Fredman (deceased)

15 September 1886: Samuel Morris Lewis, general dealer, son of Jacob Lewis (deceased) to Phoebe Wineberg, daughter of Kalman Wineberg (deceased)

22 September 1886: Samuel Gittelson, general dealer of Fareham, son of Joseph Gittelson (distiller) to Charolotte Gabrielson Zeitung, daughter of Morris Gabrielson Zeitung (picture dealer)

30 November 1887: Alfred Brock, Electro-Plater, son of Lewis Brock (musician) to Hannah Jacob, daughter of Mark Jacob (shopkeeper)

8 February 1888: Samuel Simpson, commercial traveller, son of Zemach Simpson (Assistant in synagogue) to Amelia Fredman, daughter of Jacob Fredman (outfitter)

22 August 1888: Isaac Lazarus, traveller, son of Eliezer Lazarus (dealer) to Janie Greenbaum, daughter of Abraham Greenbaum (Assistant in synagogue)

1 May 1889: Philip Bernstein, jeweller, son of Moses Bernstein (dealer) to Evelina Nelson, daughter of John Nelson (shopkeeper)

26 February 1890: Myer Isaac Roseman, furniture dealer, son of Levy Roseman (traveller) to Amelia Fredman, daughter of Levin Fredman (property dealer)

26 March 1890: Nathan Rosen, draper, son of Eliezer Rosen (dealer) to Annie Fredman, daughter of Jacob Fredman (shopkeeper)

20 April 1890: Jacob Nathan Brock, watchmaker, son of Eliezer Brock (musician) to Eva Lavinia Atkins, milliner, daughter of George Atkins (dealer)

26 May 1891: Joseph Feney, commercial traveller, son of Lewis Feney (dealer) to Bertha Baum, daughter of Jo Baum (shopkeeper)

16 September 1891: Godfrey Kalischer, musician of London, son of Leopold Kalischer (musician) to Beatrice Nelson, daughter of John Nelson (shopkeeper)

Wedding of Sidney Aloof and Lily Black, 1938

16 December 1891: David Hertz Gutmacher, barber, son of Saul Gutmacher (surgeon abroad) to Annie Gelb, dressmaker, daughter of Harris Gelb (butcher abroad)

31 August 1892: Joseph Jacobs, watchmaker, son of Mark Jacobs (shopkeeper) to Rose Lyons, daughter of Joseph Lyons (dealer)

APPENDIX 4

9 November 1892: Arnold Lionel Lippmann, furniture dealer of Cardiff, to Phoebe Fredman, daughter of Jacob Fredman (furniture dealer)

7 June 1893: Elias Plaskowsky, furniture dealer, son of Lewis Plaskowsky (general dealer) to Rebecca Roseman, daughter of Israel Roseman (furniture dealer)

23 August 1893: Morris Hyman, fur dealer of London, son of Israel Hyman (rag merchant) to Rebecca Spier, daughter of Abraham Spier (gentleman)

14 March 1894: Hyman Pearl, house painter, son of Wolf Pearl (deceased) to Anna Greenbaum, daughter of Abraham Greenbaum (collector)

5 September 1894: Barnett Wilson, tailor of London, son of Isaac Wilson (deceased) to Annie Ullman, daughter of Wolf Ullman (deceased)

1 January 1896: Harris Price, tailor, son of Isaac Price (tailor) to Henrietta Ullmann, daughter of Wolf Ullman (deceased)

23 January 1897: Peter Feather, tailor, son of Eliezer Feather (deceased) to Rachel Maskowsky, daughter of Mordecai Maskowsky (clerk)

30 June 1897: Philip Bloom, tailor, son of Philip Bloom (tailor) to Gertrude Augusta Ullmann, daughter of Woolfe Ullmann

8 June 1898: Mordecai Wolfson, general dealer, son of Solomon Abraham (merchant) to Annie Sarah Wineberg, daughter of Calman Joel Wineberg (deceased)

29 November 1899: Samuel Caplan, tailor, son of Aaron Caplan (deceased) to Leah Caplan of 56 Union Street, daughter of Harris Caplan (builder)

29 November 1899: David Steinberg, tailor, son of Isaac Steinberg (tailor) to Rachel Joseph, daughter of Marks Joseph (tailor)

20 June 1900: Samuel Abraham Titleboam, photographer, son of Abraham Titleboam (picture) to Emelie Esther Kuttner, daughter of William Kuttner

7 May 1901: Barnett Simmons, commercial traveller of Cardiff, son of Levi Barnett Simmons (deceased) to Esther Fredman, daughter of Jacob Fredman (deceased)

4 August 1901: Israel Malkinson, tailor, son of Solomon Malkinson (deceased) to Annie Pearl, daughter of David Pearl (deceased)

21 August 1901: Nathan Charles, tailor, son of David Solomon (deceased) to Rebecca Silverstone, daughter of Myer Silverstone (tailor)

24 November 1901: Abraham Caplan, licensed pedlar, son of Joseph Caplan (builder) to Chila Caplan, daughter of Aaron Caplan (furrier)

5 January 1902: Sam Goldberg, tailor, son of Chaim Goldberg (retired merchant) to Sarah Greenfield, daughter of Samuel Greenfield (deceased)

8 January 1902: Joel Levy, tailor, son of Myer Levy (deceased) to Augusta Silverstone, daughter of Myer Silverstone (tailor)

5 February 1902: King Field, watchmaker, son of Scholem Israel Flichtenfeld (deceased) to Eva Stern, daughter of Isaac Stern (cement merchant), married in Oddfellows Hall, Devonport

9 April 1902: Simon Louis Goldberg, commercial traveller, son of Abraham Goldberg (house painter) to Esther Fredman, daughter of Myer Fredman (furniture dealer)

16 July 1902: Morris Feigenbaum, watchmaker, son of Gershon Feigenbaum (dealer in books) to Hannah Lichterman, daughter of Hayman Lichterman (deceased)

3 June 1903: Joseph Goldberg, widower, tailor, son of Jacob Goldberg (hairdresser) to Fanny Dobkin, daughter of Lapidos Dobkin (shoemaker)

7 June 1903: Tobias Keiynah, draper traveller, son of Barnett Keiynah (dealer) to Rachel Brozofski, daughter of Lionel Brozofski (dealer)

10 June 1903: Myer Solinski, travelling jeweller, son of Woolf Solinsky (dealer) to Tilly Feather, daughter of Hyman Feather (tailor)

29 December 1903: Philip Michael Cohen, waterproof manufacturer of Manchester, son of Caspar Cohen (cap manufacturer), to Ethel Mignon Levy, daughter of Asher Levy (jeweller)

24 July 1904: Harry Nelson, jewellery & fancy goods, son of J. S. Nelson (dealer) to Lena Titleboam Abrahams, daughter of A. T. Abrahams (dealer)

23 November 1904: Lewis Joseph, photographer, son of S. Joseph (dealer), to Rose Abrahams, daughter of A. Abrahams (photographer)

30 November 1904: Lazarus Goldberg, commercial traveller, son of A. Goldberg (dealer) to Amelia Cohen, daughter of B. Cohen (dealer)

Wedding of Percy Aloof and Bessie Fine, 1958

19 July 1905: Michael Solomon, commercial traveller, son of Jacob Solomon (tailor), to Annie Cohen, daughter of B. Cohen (merchant), married in Balfour Hall

7 March 1906: Gedaliah Lechovitchkey, furniture dealer of Exeter, son of Woolf Lechovitchkey, to Deborah Roseman, daughter of Israel Roseman (furniture dealer), married in Oddfellows Hall, Devonport

20 June 1906: Joseph Sanger, commercial traveller, son of Berl Sanger (dealer), to Hetta Jacobs, daughter of Solomon Jacobs (builder)

8 August 1906: Louis Michael Jacobs, commercial traveller, son of Mark Jacobs, to Sarah Silverstone, daughter of Myer Silverstone (tailor), married in Oddfellows Hall, Devonport

23 January 1907: Reuben Tribich, Jewish Minister of Bradford, son of Asher Tribich (deceased), to Fanny Fredman, daughter of Levene Fredman (dealer)

10 February 1907: Michael Jacobs, widower, outfitter, son of Joseph Jacobs (deceased), to Rachel Nelson, daughter of John Nelson (deceased)

28 July 1907: Abraham Abrahams, tailor, son of Isaac Abrahams (traveller), to Esther Stone, daughter of Lewis Stone (tailor)

7 August 1907: Isidore Cohen, pawnbroker, son of Abraham Cohen (pawnbroker) to Phoebe Robins, daughter of Gedaliah Robins (pawnbroker)

19 February 1908: Morris Joseph, cabinet maker of Liverpool, son of N. Joseph (merchant), to Annie Dora Fredman, daughter of Myer Fredman (furniture dealer)

4 March 1908: Arthur Brand, merchant, son of Tobias Brand (merchant), to Esther Rose Robins, daughter of Gedaliah Robins (deceased)

10 June 1908: Hershell Orgel, printer, son of Eliezer Orgel (furniture dealer), to Sarah Deborah Robins, daughter of Gedaliah Robins (deceased)

19 June 1910: Morris Aaron Sanicoff, cap-maker, son of Jacob Sanicoff (merchant), to Sarah Annie Bence, daughter of Joseph Bence (bootmaker)

17 August 1910: Julius Astley, tailor of Burton, son of Joseph Astley (tailor) to Sarah Jacobs, widow, daughter of Myer Silverstone (tailor)

22 February 1911: Louis Robins, general dealer, to Helena Lulu Youngleson, daughter of Hyman Youngleson

1 March 1911: Hyman Solomon Owen, upholster master, son of Isaac Owen (deceased), to Rose Fredman, daughter of Myer Fredman (furniture dealer)

2 July 1911: Max Nisenblat, upholsterer, son of Moses Nisenblat (deceased) to Henrietta Ethel Abrahamson, daughter of Eliezer Abrahamson (deceased)

11 December 1911: Joseph Roseman, merchant, son of I.

APPENDIX 4

Roseman, to Katie Stein, daughter of M. Stein

16 October 1912: Abraham Astley, tailor, son of Joseph Astley (tailor) to Lily Cohen, daughter of Berl Cohen (dealer)

25 June 1913: Solly Gordon, commercial traveller, son of Michael S. Gordon (dealer) to Beatrice Roseman, daughter of I. Roseman (deceased)

16 July 1913: Leon Frank Emdon, tobacconist, son of Eliezer Emdon (pawnbroker), to Rose Levi, daughter of Hyman Levy (deceased)

27 August 1913: Moses Montefiore Cohen, pawnbroker, son of Abraham Cohen Pawnbroker), to Hetty Lazarus, daughter of Isaac Lazarus (house furnisher)

26 August 1915: Kasrel Angel, cap-maker, son of Aaron Angel (dealer), to Freda Lempert, daughter of Saul Lempert (watchmaker)

9 April 1916: Hyman Jacob Conick, tea salesman, son of Abraham Conick (tobacconist), to Dorothy Gertrude Lippman, daughter of Arnold Lippman (furniture dealer)

11 March 1917: Harry Israel Woolf, 30, Private in South African infantry of Devonport, South Raglan Barracks, son of Jacob Woolf (independent), to Isabella Cohen, daughter of Joseph Cohen (tobacconist)

4 November 1917: Barnett Melichan, cap-maker, son of Joseph Melichan (merchant), to Esther Milner, daughter of Aaron Hyman Milner

30 December 1917: Henry Kauffmann, Private 38th Royal Fusiliers, son of Aaron Kauffmann (shopkeeper), to Annie Goodman, daughter of Lewis Goodman (bootmaker)

12 February 1919: Abraham Alfred Green, Bombardier No. 78127, R.G.A, son of Lewis Green (independent) to Esther Etty Bishop, daughter of Max Bishop (traveller)

18 June 1919: Joseph Reese, manufacturer of Pinner, son of Jacob Moses Reese (deceased) to Emily Brand, daughter of Tobias Brand (wholesale merchant)

24 August 1919: Barnett Davis Silk, 41, general dealer, son of David Silk (dealer) to Beeny Milner, 38, widow of 25 Marlborough Street, daughter of Hyman Levy (tailor)

10 March 1920: Louis Fredman, printer, son of Myer Fredman (house furnisher), to Esther Rose Freeman, daughter of Joseph Freeman (jeweller)

17 March 1920: Myer Levy, merchant of Glasgow, son of Pinkus Levy (wholesale merchant) to Winifred Beatrice Robins, daughter of Abraham Moses Robins (jeweller)

18 May 1920: Henry Goldberg, commercial traveller, son of Abraham Goldberg (deceased) to Rachel Cohen, daughter of Barnett Cohen (house furnisher)

18 August 1920: Israel Cohen, merchant, son of Barnett Cohen (house furnisher), to Hilda Fredman, daughter of Alderman Myer Fredman

12 July 1921: Joseph Salsberg, electrical engineer of London, son of Herschell Salsberg (deceased) to Rebecca Pearl, daughter of Solomon Pearl (tobacconist)

14 August 1922: Hyman Smith, auctioneer, son of Herschell Smith (deceased) to Polly Elberg, daughter of Emanuel Elberg (caterer)

16 August 1922: Sydney Solomon, boot & shoe traveller of Newport, son of Moses Solomon (deceased), to Rosie Joseph, daughter of Barney Joseph (outfitter)

26 December 1922: Isidore Joseph, Naval outfitter, son of Barney Joseph (outfitter) to Rose Holcenberg, daughter of Froim Holcenberg (fur merchant)

14 March 1923: Hyman Black, draper, son of Eli Black (draper), to Esther Roseman, daughter of Israel Roseman (deceased)

Marriage of Hilda Black to Sam Marks, 1946

28 March 1923: Louis Kaplan, toy & fancy goods merchant of London, son of Joseph Kaplan (builder), to Fanny Cohen, daughter of Barnett Cohen (house furnisher)

27 June 1923: Charles Bisberg, commercial traveller, son of Harris Bisberg (silversmith), to Esther Greenburgh, daughter of Jacob Greenburgh (outfitter)

14 January 1925: Joseph Smith, auctioneer, son of Harris Smith (bootmaker), to Mary Shatles, daughter of Isaac Shatles (deceased)

17 August 1927: Morton Morris, master tailor of Bromley, son of Joseph Morris (house furnisher, deceased), to Eva Brand, daughter of Tobias Brand (merchant)

19 June 1929: Isidore Gasson, optician, son of Abraham Gasson (optician) to Lena Brand, daughter of Tobias Brand (merchant)

23 April 1930: Samuel Wolfe Solomon, house agent, son of Michael Solomon (house furnisher) to Gertie Kohn, daughter of Israel Kohn (deceased)

17 September 1930: Philip Harris, travelling salesman, son of Joseph Harris (tailor), to Dora Black of Manchester, daughter of Eli Black (deceased)

4 March 1931: Juda Michael Przysucher, generally known as Juda Michael Isaacs, Jewish minister of Wolverhampton, son of Simon Przysucher (known as Simon Isaacs, Jewish Minister) to Bella Wykansky, daughter of Simon Wykansky (Jewish Minister)

15 June 1932: Herman Harry Cohen, medical practitioner, son of Barnett Joseph Cohen (deceased) to Ruby Brand, daughter of Arthur Brand (merchant)

14 September 1932: Joshua Pearl, radio dealer, son of Saul Pearl (Rabbi) to Ruth Field, daughter of King Field (jeweller)

16 August 1933: Alec Fishberg, jeweller of London, son of Adolph Fishberg (jeweller) to Malka Robins, daughter of Solomon Robins (pawnbroker)

2 February 1936: Baron Percival Jaffa, manager, son of Joseph Lennard Jaffa (merchant), to Augusta Holcenberg, daughter of Frank Holcenberg (deceased)

5 February 1936: Joseph Harris Bence, aged 70, widower, of independent means, of 84 Pasely Street, son of Morris Bence (deceased), to Sarah Bootie, widow, daughter of Isaac Levinson (deceased)

17 November 1936: Myer Raymond Woolf, costumier, son of Gabriel Woolf (deceased), to Valerie Belle Robins, daughter of Ernest Robins (credit trader)

23 June 1937: Philip Levy, accounts manager, son of Alexander Levy (deceased), to Ethel Greenburgh, daughter of Harry Greenburgh (Naval outfitter)

25 July 1937: Montague Jack Le Vine, manager furnishing store, son of Abraham Le Vine (deceased), to Eileen Rachel Conick, daughter of Hyman Jacob Conick (house furnisher)

2 February 1938: Sidney Aloof, master watchmaker, son of Hyman Aloof (sexton) to Leah (Lily) Black, daughter of Eli Black (tailor)

4 January 1939: Samuel Reuben Saunders, medical practitioner, of Southampton, son of Louis Saunders (deceased) to Doris Brand, daughter of Arthur Brand (merchant)

11 January 1939: Morris Rutman, commercial traveller of Spitalfields, son of Solomon Rutman (deceased) to Annie Leila Greenburgh, daughter of Joseph Greenburgh (outfitter)

Wedding of Mark Gordon and Betty Peck, 1939

6 September 1939: Mordici Eleazer Gordon, physician and surgeon, son of Isaac Jacob Gordon (deceased) to Betty Peck, daughter of Akivah Peck (draper)

27 September 1939: William Woolf Mushin, medical practitioner of Greenwich, son of Moses Mushin (headmaster) to Betty Hannah Goldberg, daughter of Samuel Louis Goldberg (gentleman)

27 March 1940: Ephraim Abraham Milner, outfitter, son of Chaim Aaron Milner (deceased) to Polly Caplan, daughter of Mordecai Caplan (deceased)

26 May 1940: Elias Rathsprecher, domestic servant Salcombe, son of Berish Rathsprecher (manufacturer) to Anetta Hochstein, daughter of Herman Hochstein (deceased)

18 August 1940: William Rubinstein, journalist, son of Louis Rubinstein (musician) to Majorie Ernestine Robins, nurse, daughter of Ernest Robins (jeweller)

11 December 1940: Benjamin Lionel Garfield, civil engineering draughtsman of Bristol, son of Isaac Garfield (ladies tailor) to Freda Annie Goodcovitch, daughter of Coppel Garfield (gents tailor)

1 January 1941: Joseph Dubovie, Private RASC (Commercial Traveller), son of Hyman Dubuvie (furrier) to Ann Lazarus, estate agent clerk, daughter of George Lazarus (house agent)

27 April 1941: Harry Richman, furrier (master), son of Morris Richman (furrier) to Jessie Gordon, daughter of Solomon Gordon (fruit merchant)

27 April 1941: Mitchell Jackson, Flight Lieutenant, RAF (VR) of Torquay, son of Morris Jackson (tailor) to Monica Hetty Mistlin, daughter of David Mistlin (dentist), married in the Torquay Synagogue

8 June 1941: Wilfred Emanuel Friedman, RAF of Torquay (cinema manager), son of Sydney Friedman (cinema company director) to Rosa Lees, daughter of Woolf Lees (clothier, deceased), married in Torquay

18 June 1941: Hyman Roseman, house agent, son of Myer Isaac Roseman (deceased) to Aimee Joseph, daughter of Isaac Joseph (deceased)

14 September 1941: Herman Turner, 2nd Lieutenant HM Army (jeweller), Dartmouth, son of Maurice Turner (tailor) to Sophia Gradel, daughter of Leon Gradel (hotel proprietor)

22 March 1942: David Leonard Roseman, solicitor of Looe, son of Samuel Roseman (hotel proprietor) to Marjorie Enid Friedman, daughter of Sydney Friedman (cinema proprietor)

24 June 1942: Bernard Bells, Private HM Army (jeweller), son of Solomon Bells (jeweller) to Esther Ladden, daughter of Lewis Ladden (tailor)

18 August 1943: Leslie Jackson, Lieutenant RNVR (accountant), son of Marcus Jackson (photographic dealer) to Henrietta Peggy Cohen, daughter of Isidore Cohen (merchant)

23 September 1943: Leonard Pearl, Squadron Leader RAF (barrister at law) of London, son of David Pearl (deceased) to Rivka Betty Cohen, daughter of Leslie Israel Cohen (estate agent)

2 July 1946: Samuel Manackerman (otherwise Marks), general draper, son of Abram Manackerman (general merchant) to Hilda Black, daughter of Hyman Black (property owner)

26 March 1947: Israel Gordon, fruit merchant, son of Solomon Gordon (fruit merchant) to Rose Lily Abrahams, gown shop proprietress, daughter of Abraham Abrahams (tutor)

11 June 1947: Barnett Kelion, medical practitioner of Finchley, London, son of Morris Kelion (master tailor) to Doreen Cohen, daughter of Leslie Israel Cohen (estate agent)

21 March 1948: Jacob Richman, company director (fur dealers), son of Morris Richman (furrier) to Shirley Bertha Klieff of Paignton, married in Torquay Synagogue

21 July 1948: Maurice Overs, accountant, son of Isaac Overs (wholesale fishmonger) to Ruth Georgina Bloom, daughter of Wolfe Bloom (tailor)

29 December 1948: Benjamin Greenberg, fruiterer, son of Joseph Greenberg (master plasterer) to Minnie Gordon, fruiterer's assistant, daughter of Solomon Gordon (deceasded)

Marriage of Valerie Gordon to Michael Mellor, 1963

6 June 1951: Harold Richman, business proprietor (children's wear), son of Morris Richman (furrier) to Betty Shurmkovsky, daughter of Isaac Shurmkovsky (master tailor)

15 July 1951: David Lubell, widower, commercial traveller (gowns) of Cardiff, son of Aaron Lubell (deceased) to Millie Flitterman, widow of Cardiff, gown dealer, daughter of Isaac Ettinger (gent's clothier)

6 April 1952: Jacob Nathan Brock, widower, retired property, son of Lewis Brock (musician) to Miriam Frances Bash, spinster, 57, daughter of Samuel Bash (diamond polisher)

6 August 1952: Cecil Silverstone, analytical chemist, son of Leo Silverstone (master tailor) to Edna Abrahams, costumier, daughter of Abraham Abrahams (master tailor)

Marriage of Henry Peck to Freda Averbuck

20 October 1953: Israel Bertie Black, company director (property investment), son of Harry Black (gentleman) to Doris Lewis, daughter of Sidney Lewis (mantle manufacturer, deceased)

23 July 1956: Leon Dominitz (from Poland), property owner of London (NW10), son of Chaim Jacob Dominitz (property owner) to Carmel Judith Goodman (formerly Guttman), daughter of Melchior Goodman (Minister of Religion)

22 January 1958: Percy Aloof, telephone operator GPO, son of Hyman Aloof (synagogue Beadle) to Bessie Fine, daughter of Maurice Benjamin Fine (deceased)

25 June 1961: Zvulon Kaniuk, kibbutz, of Torquay, son of Jakov Kaniuk (Kibbutz) to Thelma Salter, daughter of Morris Salter (deceased), married in Torquay

16 October 1963: Michael Edward Mellor, chartered accountant, son of Abraham Mellor (retired) to Valerie Gordon, daughter of Mordici Eleazer Gordon (doctor)

4 April 1964: Bernard Henry Harris, company director, son of Philip Harris (retailer) to Susan Margaret Hirshman, daughter of Harry Hirshman (jeweller)

31 May 1964: Keith Anthony White, company director of London, son of Joseph White (food manufacturer) to Rita Ann Spiers, display designer of London, daughter of Leonard Spiers (jeweller)

11 July 1965: Geoffrey Andrew Hurst, Pharmacist, son of Sidney Hurst (jeweller) to Rona Erlich, ladies outfitter, daughter of Philip Erlich (ladies outfitter)

28 January 1968: Sydney Samuel Ginsburg, wholesale jeweller, son of Benjamin Ginsburg (deceased) to Anna Rotenberg, born Bzialoszyn, widow, daughter of Kalman Krymalowski (gentleman, deceased)

9 June 1968: Stephen Maurice Simmonds, company director of London (SW1), son of Jack Simmonds (company director) to Jacqueline Valerie Richman, daughter of Samuel Richman (company director)

2 January 1969: Anthony Golding, research student, son of Louis Golding (retired) to Gillian Harris, daughter of Julius Leo Harris (Civil Engineer)

3 August 1969: Andrew Stephen Bronn, teacher of Stanmore (London), son of Philip Bronn (deceased) to Barbara Segal, daughter of Ralph Segal (manufactuer)

31 August 1969: Leonard Maurice Miller, taxi-cab driver, son of Jack Miller (butcher) to Yvette Erica Solomon, daughter of Solly Solomon (textile merchant)

12 September 1971: Adrian Joseph Cohen, hotelier, son of Jack Cohen (merchant) to Ruth Ilani (Baum), daughter of Kalman Ilani (Baum)

Marriages after 1971 are recorded in the current marriage Register of the Plymouth Synagogue, held by John Hirshman.

Wedding of Claire Aloof to Timothy Lovat, 2001

APPENDIX 5
LIST OF BURIALS, OLD BURIAL GROUND, THE HOE

The original sections identified and noted down by Revd. Dr Berlin and Rabbi Dr Susser are followed here. The first inscriptions relate to the survey carried out by Bernard Susser in the 1960s with some biographical information in italics.

SECTION A

A1. Reichla bat Menahem, wife of the late Gabbai Zedakah Mordecai died 23 Av 5566 [= 7 August 1806]

A2. Broken and illegible

A4. Broken and illegible

A5. The worthy Isaac Eisak ben Jacob from Totnes, died 15 Kislev [= 24 November 1809] aged 73. *Isaac Jacobs, silversmith, who married Betsy Levy of Barnstaple*

A6. Missing or illegible

A12. Missing or illegible

A13. Here is buried his honour Judah ben his honour Joseph, a prince and honoured amongst philanthropists, who executed good deeds, died in his house in the City of Bath, Tuesday, and was buried here on Sunday, 19 Sivan in the year 5585 [= 5 June 1825]. In memory of Lyon Joseph Esq (merchant of Falmouth, Cornwall) who died at Bath June AM 5585/VE 1825. Beloved and respected.

Lyon Joseph (1774/5 - 1825) made a fortune shipping goods to the ports of the peninsula unoccupied by Napoleon. The above inscription is taken from the replacement headstone of 1903. An earlier headstone was photographed by Bernard Susser and survives in his archive. In translation, the original tombstone read:

[*Right hand side*]: From doing good he never stopped till he expired.

[*Left hand side*]: There he will reap the blessing he sowed here.

Here is buried an upright man who feared God, delighted in His Beloved commandments, his ways of pleasantness, his deeds were delightful. Harkening to the voice of Torah and prayer from waking to lying down,

Lyon Joseph, 1825

Lyon Joseph, 1825

bread he gave to the poor from his overflowing cup to the hungry. He sought the good of his people when the responsibility of leadership was on his shoulders. Many years he led his flock. For most of them listened to his advice, Chaver Abraham son of Chaver Joseph. He is remembered for a blessing as a righteous person. Gathered to his people, to the sorrow of his family. Wednesday 25th Iyar and buried with honour on Thursday, 69 years old, in the year 5585. Returned to heaven. [Quoted Genesis 18:33] Abraham returned to his place. May his soul be bound up in the bond of eternity.

A14. See Berlin 13/10, below.

A15. A perfect man and upright, a God fearing man, Menasseh ben Zvi. He was buried and died on Friday 16 Heshvan 5589 [= 24 October 1828]. *Emanuel Hart from Biala, watchmaker and silversmith in Southside Street, Plymouth and later premises in Clements Lane, Plymouth*

A16. Illegible

A17. Illegible

A18. Here lies a faithful man the Parnas and Manhig Alexander ben Samuel. Died and buried Thursday 10 Av 5593 [= 1 August 1832]. *Alexander Samuel who lived in Truro circa 1815.*

A19. Abraham ben Aaron, buried 11 Shevat 5593 [= 31 January 1833]. *Abraham Aaron married Phoebe, daughter of Abraham Joseph. They had eight children.*

A20. [In a semi circle at the top] 'Thou didst make his name Abraham, and Thou didst find his heart perfect before Thee' [Neh. 9;7]. Here dwells a faithful man, fearful of sin [4 lines of poetry follow]. The Parnas and Manhig, his name well known, Abraham ben Issachar Jacob. Died on Monday 17 Iyar and buried on the 18th in the year 'in order that you may be righteous'. May he rest and rise for his lot with all who are buried here. [Reverse] To the memory of Abraham Levi died 25 May 5594 [= 1834] aged 55 years. *Abraham Levy. He married Zipporah bat Aaron Moses ben Abraham, c.1810.*

A21. A God fearing man, the Parnas and Manhig Eliezer ben Solomon zts"l, died Wednesday 25 Heshvan and buried Thursday after it, 5596 [= 18 November 1835]. He lies here but shall arise at the end of days. *Lazarus Solomon from Lublin, a scholar, referred to as Torani, in Plymouth before 1802. He married Esther bat Abraham, who died 1831, and then Mathilda.*

A22. Aryeh Judah ben Zvi. [Reverse] Lyon Levi departed this life 11 August 5596 [= 1836]. *Son-in-law of Judah Moses. Plymouth Dock merchant, bankrupt April 1811.*

A23. Isaac ben Avigdor he lived 41 years, died Friday 26

APPENDIX 5

Av 5598 [= 17 August 1838]. [Reverse] To the memory of Solomon Lyon. [It had a long and barely legible piece of poetry]. *A pen and quill manufacturer in Plymouth before 1822, then goldsmith.*

A24. Illegible.

A25. [Reverse] Henry Phillips, aged 6 years, son of Charles and Anne Phillips. *Also near this spot lie Flora and Rachel their infant children.*

A26. My only son Isaac whom I loved, the son of Meir, Cantor here, 56. *Isaac, the son of Revd Myer Stadthagen.*

A27. .... in his house in the city of ... Tuesday 14 Sivan and buried here on Sunday 19 Sivan 5585 [= 1825].

A28. A child of delights Avigdor ben Samuel died Adar Rishon 5562 [= February 1802]. *Avigdor Hart aged 5.*

A29. Missing.

A30. The bachelor Abraham ben ?

A31. Missing or illegible

A42. Missing or illegible

A43. Joel ben Issachar Jacob, died on Sabbath, 22 Shevat 5591 [= 5 February 1831] and his soul shall dwell with the righteous who dwell here until He maketh death to vanish in life eternal. [Reverse] Joel Levy beloved husband of Rachel Levy, aged ?55 years. *Joel Levy, husband of Rachel bat Joseph.*

A44. See Berlin O8, below.

A45. Friedcha bat P"M Abraham Isaac, wife of Abraham ben Aaron, buried Sunday, 11 Heshvan 5593 [= 4 November 1832]. *She was Phoebe, daughter of Abraham Joseph I and wife of Abraham Aaron.*

A46. Miss Bila bat Solomon aged 51 years, died Monday 18 Kislev 5594 [= 30 November 1833]. [Reverse] Bile Nathan.

A47. Esther, wife of Mordecai ben Samuel SGL. [Reverse] Esther Mordecai died 19 August 5593 [= 1834].

A48. Tella wife of Jonah from the State of Silesia who died with a hoary head aged 72, on 12 Nisan 5594 [= 21 April 1834]. *Revd Dr Berlin read, 'Gella died 12th Nisan 5595 {= 11 April 1835}*

A49. Breincha bat Abraham, wife of Samuel ben Hayim. [Reverse] Elizabeth Hyman died 19 Kislev 5596 [= 10 December 1835] aged 52 years.

A50. Betsy Jacobs, wife of Isaac Jacobs of Totnes... 5596 [= 1836]. *Betsy Jacobs (1759 1836) née Levy of Barnstaple, married Isaac Jacobs of Totnes in 1784.*

A51. Samuel ben Hayim. [Reverse] Samuel Hyman, died 23 November 5599 [= 1838] aged 73 years. *Samuel Hyman (1771 1838), born Bohemia, came to England via Dover 1788. Married Betsy daughter of Abraham Moses, and had 11 children.*

A52. Missing or illegible

A55. Missing or illegible

A56. Here lies the modest and worthy woman Reichla bat Abraham, wife of the late Naphtali Benjamin. She died on Friday 26 Adar 5577 [= 14 March 1817] with a good name. A woman who fears the Lord, she shall be praised. She went to her rest 17 years after her husband, and there they shall rest in honour with all the righteous men and righteous women in the Garden of Eden, and they shall rise at their portion at the end of days.
Wife of Naphtali Benjamin and one of the respected women of the community. Her husband was a box maker, born in 1725 at Ilbersheim near Mannheim. The headstone has been removed from its place and lies next to B126.

A57. Missing or illegible

A59. Missing or illegible

A60. Hannah bat David KZ, wife of Issachar Ber, Santapel, SGL. Died Monday ?25 Adar 5581 [= March 1821].

A61. Missing

A62. Reichle bat Joseph wife of the late Joel Levy, died 23 Shevat 5582 [= 14 February 1822]. *Rachel Levy*

A63. Missing

A66. Missing

A67. The scholar Matathias ben Rabbi Shabbetai the Priest, from Poland, died 9 Av 5573 [= 5 August 1813] at half his days. *Mattis Cohen.*

A68. 17 Elul 5593 [= 1 September 1833].

A69. Moses ben Aryeh Lobell from the State of Germany who pitched his tent in the City of Birmingham, and who conducted there the needs of the Congregation. He was buried 5 Av 5594 [= Sunday, 10 August 1834]. *Moses Lobell of Birmingham, died 5594 aged 64 years.*

A70. Missing.

A71. Gabriel ben Judah died 28 Iyar 5598. [Reverse] Gabriel Rosenthal died 27 May [= 1835] aged 33 (?55) years. *Came from Poland. In 1844, his widow Ann married Mark Levy of Guernsey.*

A72. An old man Avigdor ben Moses Isaac, died with hoary head ... [Reverse] Francis Lyon died 23 Shevat 5597 [= 28 January 1837] aged 85 years. *Francis Lyon, watchmaker in Pike Street 1822. Children: Solomon, Judah and Mathilda.*

A73. Here lies Martha bat the Haver Judah the cantor, wife of Abraham Emdon, who died on Thursday 15 Iyar, and was buried on Thursday 18 Iyar 5598 [= 10 May 1838].

A74. Here lies the body of Elizabeth Abrahams who died Friday night and was buried on Sunday 22 Adar Sheni 5590, aged 42 years. May her soul rest in peace.

A75. Missing.

A76. The bachelor ?Zvi ?Hirsh ben Asher died Tamuz 55(?70) [= July ?1810] or 55(?90) [= July ?1830].

A77 – A82. Missing or illegible

A83. A broken slate stone, only the name barely legible. See Berlin Q19, below.

A84. Missing

A85. In 1963 barely legible. See Berlin Q16 below.

A86 - A91. Missing

A92. Moses ben Jacob from the City of London which was the city of his birth died Thursday night and buried Friday 3 Elul 5598 [= 24 August 1838]. [Reverse] Moses Solomon formerly of Scotland .... London.

A93. Judah ben Isaac, died Sunday and buried Tuesday 8 Sivan 5540 [= 9 June 1840]. [Reverse] Levin Jacobs aged 49 years.

A94. [Reverse] Betsy ... Jacobs, ?daughter of the late Lewis Jacobs.

A95. Missing or illegible

A99. Missing or illegible

A100. Merela [Berlin reads Merka] bat Joseph, wife of Judah Zvi ben Solomon died and buried 5 Elul 5572 [= 16 August 1812].

A101 - A103. Missing or illegible

A104. David ben Solomon. *Son of the late Revd Solomon Lyons who died at Brixham on his voyage to Naples, 8 February 1819 aged 20 years.*

A105 - A108. Missing or illegible

A109. 5525 [= 1835]

A122 - A124. Missing or illegible

A125. An upright and honoured man, the elderly bachelor, one hundred years old at his death, ... Isaac ben Rabbi Joseph, died on the Holy Sabbath the 11th of [month omitted on stone] and was buried on the 12th of [month omitted on stone] 5574 [= 1813/1814] with a good name.

A126. Ze'ev Wolf ben Naphtali, died and buried 13 Tishri 5574 [= 7 October 1813].

A127. Joseph ... died Sunday 27 Sivan 5582 [= 16 June 1822].

A128 - A129. Missing

A130. An upright and faithful man ... ben Naphtali. Died 5559 [= 1799].

A131 - A132. Illegible

A133. Samuel ben Judah, died 1 Adar Sheni 5627. [Reverse] Samuel Ralph died 17 March 1867 aged 64 years. *Samuel Ralph, grandson of Abraham Ralph of Barnstaple (d.1805). Samuel was son of Judah (or Lewis Ralph).*

SECTION B

B1. Here lies Avigdor ben Judah who died the eve of Tuesday 10 Heshvan and was buried on Wednesday its morrow in the year 5610. In memory of Frederik Ralph, who departed this life 15 October 5611 [= 1850], aged ?46 years. *A brother of Samuel Ralph.*

B2. Here lies the wise bachelor Abraham ben Baruch SGL, died Friday 26 Shevat and was buried Sunday, 28 Shevat 5548 [= 4 February 1788 but the day and date do not coincide]. May he remain in his grave and rise in his turn at the end of days. *A member of the Plymouth Congregation before 1759. Described on his tombstone as HaBachur HaYashish = The Wise Bachelor.*

B3. This man, perfect and upright in his works/ Whose deeds were righteous/ His death bemoaned by his friends and aquaintances/ At fifty eight years of age he was gathered to his people [Ze'ev] ben Solomon. In the year HaBrith, according to the major order of counting [= 5612]. W. Solomon, died ?2 ?March 5612 [= 1852].

B4. Our lives are in Thy hands O God, and our days are as nought before Thee. Here lies David ben Abraham for 50 years a member of the congregation of this town, died and buried with a good name on Friday ?27 Tamuz 5600 [= 28

July 1840] aged 76 years. *David Abraham, silversmith, born 1762, married Rose, daughter of Isaac and Betsy Jacobs of Totnes.*

B5. Illegible

B6. Jacob ben Judah, died ? Thursday ?8 Sivan 5553 [= May 1793] or possibly 5653 [= May 1893]

B7. B8. Illegible double stone.

B9. Eliezer ben Abraham Emden died on 16 Shevat and buried on 17 Shevat 5604 [= 6 February 1844]. The days of his years which he lived were eighty three. *Eliezer Emden born 1764 Amsterdam, died aged 80*

B10. The Parnas and Manhig Samuel ben Solomon Phineas, died Tuesday 17 Tamuz and buried Wednesday in the year 5605 [= 22 July 1845]. *Samuel Levy, son of Phineas Levy of Devonport.*

B11. Here lies the aged, full of years, Alexander ben Abraham who died Nisan 5610 [= March 1850]. *Sender Alexander, born in Devon, a tailor in Cambridge Street in 1841, Parnas of the Congregation in 1815 and 1816.*

B12. Sacred to the memory of Mark Mordecai, who departed this life 2 May 5609 [= 1849] in his 70th year. *Mordecai ben Samuel whose wife Esther died 10 August 1833. Children: Samuel, Jacob, Zvi, Simha, daughter Anna who married Isaac Stone (a brother-in-law of Phineas Levy).*

B13. Judah, thy brothers bless thee [Gen. 49:8]/ Your name is praised as generous hearted/ The poor and orphans ... at thy table/ With a perfect heart thou didst serve the Lord thy God/ In the bond of life shall thy soul rest/ Judah ben Moses, died 20 Av 5609. Lyon Lazarus died 8 August 5609 [= 1849] aged 59 years. *Lyon or Lippa Lazarus, husband of Mathilda.*

B14. The bachelor Hayim ben ... Hyman Solomon died ? August 5609 [= 1849]. *Hyman Solomon = Hayim ben Isaiah (1838-1849), son of Josiah and Rosa Solomon.*

B15. Nathan ben Joseph KZ, died Friday ?26 Tishri and was buried on the Monday after it, 5610 [12th October 1851]. *Nathan Joseph alias Altmann, born 1766 Ransporke, Bohemia, married Brina daughter of Abraham Joseph I.*

B16. An elder, honoured amongst men, his heart did not hold back from bestowing loving kindness, Phineas ben Abraham Emdin, died with a good name Thursday 15 Av 5610 [= 24 July 1850]. *Solomon (Selig) Emden, born 1771 Amsterdam, husband of Freda bat Judah (B35).*

B17. Hayim ben Mordecai. Hyman Levy died 14 Kislev 5611 [= 19 November 1850]. *Hyman Levy came from Plock, Prussia.*

Jacob Cohen from Lontschotz, died of the plague, 1832

B18. Jacob was a perfect man, upright in his flock/ He turned from wickedness, faithfulness was his love/ He departed from evil, his way was good/ The portion of Jacob is his inheritance/ A lion, with clean hands. J. P. Lyon died 23 Yiar [sic] 5612 [= 12 May 1852]. *Judah P. Lyon (1794-1852), b. Bideford, married Fanny (b.1803, Swansea). Watchmaker and jeweller of 7 Union Street.*

B19. Jacob ben Judah. John Levi died 10 Adar 5615 [= 28 February 1855]. *John Levi (b. 1793, Portsmouth), general dealer, wife probably Elizabeth. His daughters: Eliza married Benjamin Jonas in 1841, Phoebe married Aaron Wolf in 1846, Julia married Edward Basch, Traphina married Sigmond Yager.*

B20. A perfect and upright man, he walked in perfection and executed righteousness, a God fearing man all his days, Jacob ben the late Judah, he was 63 years old when he died on Tuesday 28 Nisan and was buried with a good name on Wednesday the 29th thereof in the year 5615. To the memory of Jacob Moses died 28 days in Nisan 5615 [= 16 April 1855] aged 63 years. *The Hebrew has three errors. This Jacob Moses was probably the husband of Agnes, haberdasher, and father of Esther (milliner).*

B21. By decree of the plague, Haya, wife of Jacob ben Ze'ev, died Av 5592 [= August 1832]. *Hannah Woolfson, wife of Jacob Woolfson of London, died in cholera epidemic of 1832.*

B22. Here lies an upright man amongst the princes. All his deeds was (sic) altruistic. And he clave to the living

God. David ben Jacob from Bialin in Poland, died 12 Shevas (sic) 5565 [= 12 January 1805]. *David Jacob Coppel, (b. 1748, arrived via Gravesend in 1799. Resided in Comer Lane, Plymouth in 1803. Brother: Menahem { = Emanuel Cohen}.*

B23. A God fearing man Ze'ev ben Judah from Shotwinitz in the State of Poland, died by decree of the plague on Thursday and was buried on 6 Av 5592 [= 2 August 1832.)

B24. Here is buried Aaron ben Yehiel who went the way of all the earth in the sixty eighth year of his life. Aaron Nathan died 21 February 5618 [= 1858] aged 69 years. *Aaron Nathan.*

B25. Jacob [ben] Uri Shraga ben Moses, who lived eight and sixty years, died Thursday and buried Friday, 19 Shevat 5593 [= 7 February 1833]. Philip Moses. Near this spot lies the remains of Eleazer

B26. The bachelor, a Godfearing man, Jacob ben Uri Shraga, the priest from Lontschotz, died Av 5592 [= August 1832]. *Jacob Philip Cohen, member of the Congregation in 1819.*

B27. Gitla bat Zvi, who died in her old age on the Holy Sabbath Iyar 5613. In memory of Hannah Ralph who departed this life May 5613 [=1853] aged 87 years. *Hannah Ralph wife of Judah (Lewis) Ralph (son of Abraham Ralph I of Barnstaple).*

B28. [Reverse] Sydney Solomon.

B29. Solomon Samuel ben Solomon who went to Heaven aged 1 year and two months, on Friday 22 Adar 5629 [= 5 March 1869]. [Reverse] Charles Samuel Solomon.

B30. A child of delights ...

B31. Sarah bat Benjamin Aryeh. [Reverse] Sarah Levi died 2 February 5601 [= 1851] aged 78 years.

B32 - B34. Missing

B35. Here lies a woman who feared the Lord in her heart/ To help with loving kindness the living/ and the dead, Mrs/ Friedcha bat Judah, wife of Phineas ben Abraham Emden, died Monday 6 Adar Rishon 5603 [= 6 February 1843].

B36. [Reverse] Esther Simons.

B37. [Reverse] Rosie ... Sander Alexander, aged ?66 years.

B38. Yetta bat Mordecai the Levite, wife of Eliezer ben the late Abraham, died in her old age on the Holy Sabbath, 10 Tamuz 5606 [= 4 July 1846]. *The wife of Eliezer Aaron, son of Abraham Aaron, who in turn was son-in-law of Abraham Joseph I.*

David Jacob Coppel, 1805

B39. [Reverse] [?] Harris.

B40. Esther bat ?Judah, wife of Alexander.

B41. Rachel Yettela bat Abraham, wife of Avigdor Isaac, died Nisan 5609 [= March 1849]. *Sara Lyon.*

B41a. Abraham ben ... died and buried 22 Adar 5566 [= 12 March 1806]. *Miniaturist Abraham Daniel.*

B42. Here lies the aged woman/ Who kept the commandments of the Lord/ And was gathered up in good hoary age/ Mrs Miriam bat Abraham Zvi KZ. Died 4 Iyar 5609. Meriam Abrahams died 25 April 5609 [= 1849] aged 96 years.

B42a. The child of delights Jacob ben Elijah Moss, born on Friday, 12th Tishri 5573 [= 18 September 1812], died and buried Friday 4 Nisan 5575 [= 14 April 1815]. *Son of Elias Moss of George Street, Plymouth Dock. Navy Agent in 1816. Elias was brother to Barrow Moss.*

B43. 5577 [=1817].

B43a. Sacred to the memory of Mordecai Levi son of Lyon and Leah Levi, died 3 Av 5577 [= 16 July 1817] aged 5 years and 2 months.

B44. Blima bat Eliezer wife of Isaac from Portsmouth. [Reverse] Blumey, wife of Isaac Marks of Portsmouth died December 5610 [= 1849] aged 77 years.

B45. Leah bat Issachar Baer, wife of Zvi ben Judah. *Wife of Zvi ben Judah Lyons from Warsaw, lived in Devonport.*

APPENDIX 5

B46. Miss Pessla bat Simeon the Levite, died Tuesday ?25 Tevet 5610 [= ?9 January 1850]. [Reverse] In memory of Eliza Levi ....

B46a. Joseph ben Isaac, died first day of Rosh Hodesh Shevat 5591 [= 15 January 1831]. *Joseph Isaac of Devonport.*

B47. Telza wife of Abraham Joseph. [Reverse] Eliza Joseph, died 4 Shevat 5610 [= 17 January 1850], aged 42 years. *She was the daughter of Lemon Wolf, granddaughter of Moses Jacob of Redruth, and great granddaughter of Zender Falmouth. Wife of Abraham Joseph II.*

B48. Miriam bat Abraham wife of Nathan from Dartmouth. [Reverse] Miriam Jacobs, wife of Nathan Jacobs, formerly of Dartmouth, 5610 [= 1850]. *Miriam Jacobs born in Devon (1771- 1850), silversmith in 1841 in Bedford Street. Her nephews are said to have founded Crockfords.*

B49. Ginandel bat Judah, wife of Judah, 5611 [= 1851]. *Nandell Moses, probably the wife of Judah Moses I. Born in Devon in 1766*

B50. [Reverse] Leah (?) Levi.
(Front: Illegible)

B51. Hannah bat Isaac, wife of Judah, died on the Holy Sabbath, ?20 Tevet 5612 [= 12 January 1852]. [Reverse] Ann wife of Mark Levy aged ?43 years. *Ann, widow of Gabriel Rosenthal who died 27 May 1835, daughter of Isaac Mark. Married Mark Levy II in 1844.*

B52. Rachel bat Abraham, wife of Aaron. Rachel Bellem. *Rachel Bellam or Bellem (b. 1783, Plymouth), died 1863. Married Aaron Bellam of Dartmouth. Children: Harriet, a deaf and dumb seamstress, Jacob (general dealer) and Abraham (a dyer)*

B53. Illegible.

B53a. Aaron ben Mordecai, died Monday 11 Av 5555 [= 27 July 1795]. *Born 26 March 1786, and fifth child circumcised by Joseph Joseph.*
B54. Missing.

B55. Frumat bat Moses, wife of Abraham. *First wife of Abraham Emden, died 13 May 1838.*

B56. A child's stone, illegible.

B57. [Reverse] Kitty, wife of Phineas Levi, also her daughter Traphina. *Kitty Levi born Portsea 1788, died 15 July 1851.*

B58. Leah bat Mordecai, wife of Abraham Emdin, died Av 5611 [= August 1851]. [Reverse] Leah wife of Abraham Emdon. *Lydia Emden (b. Devonport, 1811), daughter of Mordecai Davis of Market Street, second wife of Abraham Emden.*

B58a. Zvi ben Moses, died Sunday and buried Monday 9 Iyar 5536 [= May 1776].

B59. [Reverse] Rebecca .... Lemon Wolf. *Wife of Lemon Wolf (the son of Hyman Woolf of Penzance). Rebecca was a daughter of Moses Jacob and Sarah Moses, and a granddaughter of Alexander Moses of Falmouth.*

B60. [Reverse] Rosetta Solomon, wife of Isaac Solomon. *Rosa bat Asher ben Hayim, a daughter of Hyman Woolf of Penzance. Born Cornwall, circa 1810/1811. Children: Solomon, Sarah, Henry, Julia, Ellen E, Simon W, David. Husband was the son of Jacob Solomon of Exeter, had a fancy goods warehouse at 22 Whimple Street. Moved to New York by 1872. Rosetta's older sister Eliza was the first wife of Abraham Joseph II.*

B61. Fanny, beloved wife of Joseph Joseph, died ?Av ?5615. *Fanny, b. Poland 1815, the daughter of Lazarus Solomon of Plymouth. Married Joseph Joseph of Redruth.*

B62. Miriam bat Moses, wife of Aaron Nathan. May her pains and affliction which she bore in her life be an atonement for her sins. Died Friday, 5 Heshvan 5618. Mary Nathan died 23 October 5618 [= 1858] aged 61 years.

B63. Miss Sarah bat Aaron, aged 38 years, died Tuesday Rosh Hodesh Kislev 5632. [Reverse] In loving memory of Sarah, daughter of Aaron and Mary Nathan, died 14 November 1871, aged 38.

B64. Bila bat Eliakim, died ?2 Kislev 5619 [= December 1859]. [Reverse] Elizabeth ... John Levi.

B65. Sarah bat Mordecai to the grief of her parents. [Reverse] Sarah Levy died 2 Tevet 5619 [= 9 December 1858], aged 15 years.

B66. Miss Gitla bat Isaac, died 5619 [= 1859]. [Reverse] Julia Marks, sister of Charles Marks. *Julia Marks, a strawbonnet maker in Cornwall Street in 1836.*

B66a. The bachelor Moses ?Menahem ben Solomon, died [?] Heshvan ?5564 [= October ?1804].

B67. Bila bat Moses Isaac. She was 60 years old at her death. [Reverse] Arabella, wife of Myer Stadthagen, died 26 Nisan 5622 [= 26 April 1862]. *Daughter of Judith Jacob and Moses Isaac Joseph of Redruth, granddaughter of Alexander Moses of Falmouth.*

B68. The Parnas and Manhig to his congregation, Abraham ben Joseph. [Reverse] Abraham Joseph died 28 Eyar 5628 [= 20 May 1868]. *Abraham Joseph II (1799-1868) married first Eliza Wolf, daughter of Asher Wolf of Penzance. Second wife: Rose who died 1896.*

B69. A woman of valour and of upright heart, Sheincha, wife of cantor Lima [?Lita], died Wednesday, the eve of

Rosh Hodesh Nisan 5553 [= 13th March 1793]. *Cantor Lima, appointed Reader in 1786.* **B70.** Mordecai ben Israel, an old man and honoured, who served in the fear of the Lord. Died with hoary head on Tuesday, 14 Shevat and buried on Wednesday in the year ?5618 [?= Friday 29 January 1858].

B71. Samuel ben Menahem the Priest, an honourable and faithful man from the stock of martyrs, eager to do loving kindness to the poor and hastening to his prayers, evening, morning and noon. Died 5 Iyar 5620 [= 27 April 1860]. *Samuel Cohen from Chelmsford. He left £5 to the Synagogue when he died in 1860.*

B72. [Reverse] Marcus Wolf. *Ze'ev ben Mordecai (b.1781-died c.1860). Born Poland, married to Kitty (b. Poland), left £1 to Synagogue at his death.*

B73. Aaron.

B74. Judah Lyon. *Judah ben Avigdor. Probably son of Francis Lyons, died 1837. Brother of Solomon Lyons and Mathilda Lazarus. Watchmaker in Bedford Street, Plymouth 1836.*

B75. Illegible, but a ewer and basin at the head of the stone.

B76. Here lies a man who walked in uprightness and righteousness, he feared the Lord God all the days of his life. 32 years he was cantor here in the Holy Congregation of Plymouth. Meir ben Rabbi Isaac, he died on Monday, the 7th day of Passover, aged 58 years and was buried with great honour on the last day of the Passover, 5622. Myer Stadthagen died 21 Nisan 5622 [= 21 April 1862] aged 58. *Myer Stadthagen, born Prussia 1804, married Arabella Joseph. Children: Selina, Phoebe, Sarah, Ellen and Isaac.*

B77. Abraham ben Yekutiel. ... buried with honour ... [Reverse] Abraham Kaufman, died 16 January 1863, aged 54 years. May his soul rest in peace. *Abraham Kaufman, hawker (b. Prussia, bachelor). Watchmaker, brother of Bernard Kaufman.*

B78. Miss Harriet Nathan. *Harriet Nathan (b. Plymouth 1773), an aunt of Abraham Ralph II, probably the sister of Hannah Ralph. Listed in the Plymouth Directory 1850 under 'gentry' and of Bedford Street.*

B78a. Joseph ben Judah Jacob. *Joseph Jacob Sherrenbeck, leader of the Plymouth Congregation in 1745. Generous benefactor to the synagogue. Died between 1779 and 1782.*

B79. Miss Rachel ben Jacob Judah, died 22 Tamuz 5629 [= 1 July 1869]. Reverse: R. Benjamin aged 88 years. *Rachel Benjamin (b. Plymouth), feather maker, daughter of Levi Benjamin (cantor in Plymouth, 1813). She and Miss E. Benjamin gave £7. 5s. for the Gifford Place Cemetery in 1858.*

B80. Hannah bat Menahem the Levite, died Adar Sheni ?5635 [? = March 1875]. *Hannah Jonas.*

B81. Illegible.

B81a. Shraga ben Abraham KZ, died 13 Shevat 5551 [= 17 January 1791]. *Hands of priest on the stone.*

B82. Leah bat Shemaiah, wife of Menahem ben Jacob the priest, aged 81 years. *Her husband was Emanuel Cohen (b. Carlsberg, near Mannheim 1775), came to Plymouth in 1802. Left Plymouth in 1820 for Falmouth and Redruth.*

B83. An upright and pure man, the late Gershon ben Judah Jacob, died Kislev 5542 [= December 1781]. *Gershon Sherrenbeck, brother of Joseph Jacob Sherrenbeck.*

B84. The woman elder Mrs ... wife of .... died Tishri 5543 [= September 1783].

B85. Illegible.

B86. Jacob Zvi ben Joseph. Reverse: Jacob Lyons. *Jacob Lyons (b. 1795, Poland) of 19 Barrack Street, general dealer. Children: Rosa, Rebecca, Moses, Isaac, Amelia and Aaron. Rosa married George Norman, a secretary of the Synagogue in 1861.*

B87. Here lies a man who feared God, his body lies in the ground, but his soul is in the Garden of Eden. Ze'ev Hayim ben Eleazer who lived 58 years and died with a good name on Friday the 8th of Adar Sheni and was buried with great honour on the 11th thereof in the year 5627. In memory of Woolf Emden died 15 March 1867, aged 58 years. *Woolf Emden (b. 21 April 1810), the son of Eliezer Emden. He married Rebecca Franco, daughter of John Franco.*

B88. Jacob Joseph ben Aryeh, died 21 Kislev 5624 [= 2 December 1863]. Aged 58 years. Reverse: Jacob Joseph. *On an 1858 inscription in the Plymouth synagogue his Hebrew name is Isaac Joseph ben Aryeh.*

B89. Abraham ben Aaron Bellem, the reaper passed over him and he died 27 Tishri 5627. Abraham Bellem died 6

October 5627 [= 1866] aged 44 years. *Son of Aaron ben Hayim of Dartmouth.*

B90. Here lies the worthy bachelor it is a duty to remember him in honour/ because he dealt in faithfulness,/ charity to the poor he gave,/ his righteousness will remain forever,/ may he reap the reward of the righteous./ He left his wealth as an everlasting memorial/ to see the pleasantness of the fruit of his work./ Jacob ben Solomon died with a good name Tuesday 16 Iyar and was buried on Wednesday the 17th thereof in the year 'You shall be remembered', in his 83rd year. Beneath are deposited the remains of one of the worthies of his native town Plymouth. Jacob Nathan who departed this life the 21 May 5627 [= 1867]. Reader ponder on the momento of a good man. His path during life was upright, just and righteous. The name of Jacob Nathan was proverbial for deeds of kindness and acts of charity to the needy and unfortunate.

Jacob Nathan, the largest single benefactor to the Plymouth Congregation leaving the bulk of his estate of £14,000.

B91. Nathan ben Solomon, died Sunday 5 Elul 5625. Nathaniel Nathan died 27 August 5625 [= 1865] aged 87 years. *Brother of Jacob and Henry Nathan.*

B92. Missing.

B93. Zvi ben Solomon, died on the Holy Sabbath 23 Tevet 5624 [= 2 January 1864]. Henry Nathan. *Brother of Jacob and Nathaniel Nathan.*

B94. Illegible.

B95. ..... in the year 5522 [= 1762].

B96. Illegible.

B97. The upright and worthy Joseph ben Joseph Meir, died Sunday, Rosh Hodesh Heshvan ?5545 [?= 15 October 1784]. *Beadle of the Congregation in 1779 and a member as early as 1759.*

B98. Illegible.

Jacob ben ???, February 1763, one of the oldest extant stones

B99. The worthy bachelor Jacob ben .... died 23 Shevat 5523 [= February 1763].

B100. Abraham ben .... died Iyar 5540 [= 1780].

B101. Illegible.

B102. Menahem ben Judah, died Friday, 2 Kislev 5557 [= 2 December 1796]. *He and his wife Esther bat Solomon left £2. 2s. to the Synagogue.*

B103 - B104. Illegible.

B105. Date only - 1804.

B106. Feigala bat Samuel, died 19 Shevat 5628. Reverse: Frances, daughter of Samuel and Phoebe Levy, 12 February 1868.

B107. Brina bat Gershon. Brina, wife of Henry Morris died 28 August 1867, aged 56 years. *Brina Morris (née Joseph, b. Exeter) married in 1830. He was born Prussia, a jeweller, of 35 Cambridge Street in 1851. Children: Cordelia, George, Deborah, Kate, Jacob and Judah.*

B108. Brina bat Abraham, died 2 Elul 5625 [= 24 August 1865]. Reverse: Brina Joseph. *Brina Joseph (b. 1781 Plymouth), daughter of Abraham Joseph I, married Nathan Joseph (Altmann), had twelve children.*

B109 - B111. Missing.

B112. Here lies a man who went in the path of uprightness, feared God, generous of heart, pursued righteousness and loving kindness and gave to the needy. Abraham ben Eliezer who reached days and years of hoary head and who died on Monday 12th of the month of Ziv [= Iyar], his body lies in the earth but his soul is accepted in the Garden of Eden. He was gathered with great honour to the place of his fathers on Tuesday, the 13th of said month in the year 5632. In memory of Abraham Emdon T.C. Devonport, died 20 May 1872/5632, aged 73 years. *Abraham Emden (b. 1799, Plymouth), son of Eliezer Emden I. First wife: Martha Frumat. Second wife: Lydia, daughter of Mordecai Davis.*

B113. The outstanding Torah scholar, righteous, and upright. Isaac ben Abraham. When he was 73 years old he was called to the Yeshiva on High. 10 Shevat 5732. Isaac Isaacs died 19 January 1872 aged 72(!) years. *Isaac Isaacs (b. Bavaria, 1803) married Fanny (b. Exeter, 1812). Children, all born in Plymouth: Amelia, Isabella, Nancy, Julia, Jeanette.*

B114 - B115. Missing.

B116. At the age of ?13 years he ascended to Heaven. The bachelor Ze'ev ben Abraham, in the year ?5610 [= ?1850]. Reverse: Wolf Rosenberg.

B117. Alexander ben Meir, died 19 Av 5629 [= 27 July 1869]. *Alexander Klapper (b. 1834), a clothier, married on 12 November 1862 to Amelia, daughter of Abraham Rain.*

B118. Missing.

B119. The righteous man Mordecai ben Jacob, died Friday and was buried on Sunday ... 5567 [= 1806/7). *Mordecai Jacobs (b. 1727, Prague), umbrella maker. Died 4 October 1806.*

B119a. Joseph ben Baruch, died 27 Heshvan 5627 [= 5 November 1866] aged 72 years.

B119b. Hannah Moses. *A broken stone. According to Revd. Berlin, she was the wife of Phillip Moses II, died Friday, 23 December 1864 aged 83.*

B119c. Rose Philip [Berlin read: Rosie Phillips], died 5 January (1803) aged 55 years. *Reizcha bat Samuel SGL, a clothes broker of 15 Market Street, Plymouth Dock in 1823. From 1825-1826, she was one of the few women members of the Plymouth Meshivat Nefesh Society.*

B120. Illegible or Missing.

B125. Illegible or Missing. Tombstone number A56 (Mrs Reichla Benjamin) lies next to B126.

B126. ... ben Abraham KZ, [died] 55[??]. *Priestly hands have been carved at the top.*

Joseph ben Joseph Meir, 1784

SECTION C

C1. Abraham Isaac ben Joseph, died 22 Kislev ... *Abraham Joseph I (1731- 24 November 1794), aged 63. Prominent member of the community.*

C2. Upon the mountains I will raise my cry and upon the heavens my lamentation [Jer. 9:9] for the young maiden, the daughter of our people Gella bat Abraham known as Arbilai. She died on the Holy Sabbath, 11 Kislev 5574 [= 4 December 1813]. May her soul be bound up in the bond of life. *Daughter of Abraham Joseph I.*

C3 - C4. Illegible.

C5. Joseph ben Abraham Isaac. *Joseph Joseph (1766 - 1846), son of Abraham Joseph I. Silversmith and slop merchant, generous benefactor of the synagogue.*

C6. Here lies a modest women, precious in her actions, her glory was at home and she was praised without, ninety were the days of the years of her life when she was gathered to her people and to her fathers. She was the benefactress, a woman of worth, Edal bat Abraham Zvi, who died with a good name on Thursday, 11th Adar and was buried here in honour on Friday, the 12th thereof 5621 [= 21 February 1861]. *Wife of Joseph Joseph, born Liskeard in 1771.*

C7. Zvi ben [?] Nahum, died ... ?5552 [= 1792].

C8. Missing.

C9 - C10. Illegible.

APPENDIX 5

TRANSCRIPTIONS BY REVD DR M. BERLIN

Original numbering and locations as noted by Dr Berlin have been retained:

8/6. With bitter cry we bemoan the child Abraham ben Samuel, died on the 2nd day of Shavuot 5564 [= 7 May 1804] aged 5 years.

8/7. The child Isaac ben ?Avigdor/?Abimelech. 5564 [= 1804].

9/10. May he be with the congregation of the upright, there with the sweet voiced may he dwell, the perfect man Moses ben Isaac, Shammash and Trustee of the Holy Congregation of Plymouth. Died and buried on Thursday, 18 Sivan in the year 'and ye shall circumcise the foreskin of your heart' [1790]
Moses Isaac (b. 1728, Mezeritz, Poland). Husband of Dikah bat Jacob.

10/2. A woman of worth Golda bat Judah, died and buried Sunday, 19 Adar Rishon 5559 [= 24 February 1799].

10/3. With bitter cries we mourn the child Elijah ben Abraham, died and buried on Sunday, 9 Adar Sheni 5527 [= 10 March 1767].

10/4. The generous Israel ben Jacob, died 29 Adar Rishon 5559 [= 5 April 1799].
Israel Jacobs (b. 1743, Oberhausen), silversmith in Southside Street. Member of the Congregation in 1767, subscribed one guinea in 1779 for the Plymouth Congregation's War Levy, and one guinea in 1782 for a new Scroll of the Law. Probably a brother of Nathan Jacobs of Dartmouth.

10/5. Naphtali Hirtz ben Benjamin, died on Friday, 4 Iyar and was buried on Sunday 5561 [= 17 April 1801] aged 75. *Naphtali Benjamin (b. Ilbersheim, near Mannheim, 1725), settled in Plymouth by 1759. Beadle in 1778, and a boxmaker shortly before his death.*

10/6. An upright man, a righteous priest, who helped the poor, to services he went morning and night, Federale ben Abraham KZ. Died and buried with a good name on Wednesday, 13th Adar Sheni 5562 [= 17 March 1802].

11/2. My heart weeps for the praised woman, wife of Lapidot [Judges 4:4] Gittla bat Michael, wife of the late Zalman Mannheimer, who died on 4 Iyar 5565 [= 3 May 1805]. *Wife of Solomon Zalman ben Abraham KZ Mannheimer, a member before 1782.*

13/7. Nathan ben Jacob from Dartmouth, died Friday 14 Heshvan 5592 [= 24 October 1831]. Reverse: Nathan Jacobs, late of Dartmouth, 6 November 5592 [sic]. *Nathan Jacobs, member of the synagogue before 1779, jeweller in Dartmouth. Wife: Miriam, children: Alexander, Angel, Betsy, Martha and Zipporah. On his death, his estate amounted to thousands of pounds.*

13/7b. Yehiel ben Naphtali, died and buried Wednesday, 3 Nisan 5581 [= 5 April 1821]. *Possibly Henry Hart, the father of Moses Hart. In Plymouth before 1805.*

13/10. Judah ben Moses Jacob, died [or was buried] the eve of Rosh Hodesh Shevat 5586 [= 8 January 1826] aged 87 years. *Judah Moses I (b. 1741, Hartheim in Wurzburg), played an important part in the affairs of the Congregation in the early 19th century. Subscribed to the Plymouth Congregation's War Levy of 1779. Insured as a watchmaker, silversmith and slopseller at 62 Southside Street in 1805. His daughter Esther married Alexander ben Samuel of Truro.*

13/12. Ezekiel Judah ben the late Abraham, died 15 Tevet 5583 [= 29 December 1822.]

13/13. Simha ben Isaac the Levite who was called Bunam Segal died Monday 25 Tevet 5579 [= 25 January 1819.) The Parnas and Manhig of the Holy Congregation of Plymouth, aged 53 years.
Benjamin Levy (b. 1776, Germany), came to Plymouth 1786, insured as a silversmith, haberdasher and optician at 47 Market Street from 1800. Then an optician in Southside Street until his death in 1819. An ewer and basin are carved at the top of the stone.

13/14. Baruch ben Isaac Moses, died on the eve of Rosh Hodesh Shevat 5577 [= 17 January 1871] aged 35 years. *Barrow Moss of Devonport. Berlin says that there was poetry on the reverse, but did not record it. Wife: Sally, whose father Solomon Isaac came to Plymouth in 1776 and left her a fortune of about £1,500. She donated a silver besomim box to the Plymouth Synagoue after the closure of the Dock Minyan.*

13/15. Mordecai ben Abraham, died Friday, 21 Heshvan 5572 [= 8 November 1811]. *Mordecai Abraham (b. 1743, Gelheim), in 1803 a silversmith at 37 St Andrews Street. Died at North Corner Street, Plymouth Dock. In his will he is described as a shopkeeper and licenced hawker. Wife: Rachel, children: Abraham, Judah, Rebecca and Phoebe.*

13/16. Jacob ben Mordecai, and was gathered to his forefathers on Wednesday, 2nd day of Rosh Hodesh Elul and was buried on Friday ?10 Elul. *Jacob Jacob, son of Mordecai Jacob, insured as a silversmith and toyman of Market Place from February 1796. His will left £100 to the synagogue, 'to be invested in 5% annuities, the interest to be given to the poor Jews of Plymouth every year in Elul..., a mourning ring to each of my nephews and the residue to my dearly beloved wife Hannah Jacobs, daughter of Hayim Barnett of the City of Gloucester.'*

13/17. The old man Solomon ben Nathan, died on the Holy Sabbath 15 Shevat 5571 [= 9 February 1811]. *Solomon Nathan (b. 1740, Merionthal, Germany), Plymouth in 1756. Children: Jacob, Henry, Nathaniel and Bila Nathan. His wife was Rachel (sister of Abraham Daniel, a noted miniaturist). He was a goldsmith, and apparently the only registered Jewish master who took registered apprentices in the South West. Judah Lyons was apprenticed to him in 1772 for £42.*

O8. My wife Feigela bat Mordecai, wife of Isaac ben Avigdor, died on account of the plague, Tuesday, 2nd day of Rosh Hodesh Elul 5592 [= 28 August 1832]. Reverse: Fanny, wife of S. Lyon. *First wife of Solomon Lyon. She was a straw hat maker in Pyke Street in 1822.*

O10. Esther bat Abraham from the State of Poland, the Holy Congregation of Lublin, died 25 Tevet 5591 [= 7 January 1831]. *Wife of Lazarus Solomon.*

O11. (Jose) Cohen, she died 2 April 5589 [= 1829] aged 3 months.

O12. Sarah bat David the Priest, died 15 Heshvan 5581 [= 23 October 1820].

O13. An elder, honoured and respected, who attained 80 years like a mighty man. He ran like a hare and was as swift as an eagle to do that which was right and upright, the scholar Sampson ben Nathan, who died on Tuesday, 27 Iyar 5577 [= 13th May 1817] the 42nd day of the Omer according to the counting of the children of Israel. May he arise in his turn at the time appointed which is sealed in the Book. *Simon Nathan (b. 1747 near Marienbad, Bohemia), came to Plymouth 1773, a dealer and chapman at 85 Market Place by 1803.*

O16. Nencha bat Yehie[l], wife of the late Zvi ben Nathan, died 15 Heshvan 5574 [= 8 November 1813].

O17. Brina bat Solomon known as Zalman KZ, wife of Reuben known as Zelig, died Tuesday 21 Kislev 5574 [= 14 December 1813]. *Mrs Brina Isaacs, the wife of Solomon Isaacs.*

O18. The elder, Reuben Zelig ben Isaac, died the Holy Sabbath 21 Kislev 5576 [= 23 December 1815]. *Solomon Isaac (b. 1751 in Mannheim) arrived in Plymouth 1776, a silversmith, a tenant of one of Joseph Joseph's houses in Southside Street. Wife: Brina or Briney. Executors of his estate which was sworn at £3,000: Leviah (wife of Levy Zachariah), Sally (wife of Barrow Moss), Isaac Isaacs and three of his children.*

O21. Minnela bat Menahem, wife of the Parnas and Manhig Zvi ben Samuel who went to her rest on Sunday, 25 Heshvan and was buried on the 28th thereof 5572 [= 12 November 1811]. *Wife of Henry Hart, a Trustee of the synagogue in 1797.*

O22. The bachelor Abraham ben Nathan, Dartmouth, died on the Holy Sabbath, the eve of Shavuot, and was buried on Isru Hag 5572 [= 16 May 1812] aged 20 years. *A son of Nathan Jacobs of Dartmouth.*

O23. The child Miriam bat Yehiel, died on Friday, 6 Elul 5572 [= 14 August 1812].

P7. Moses Isaac ben Judah, died Friday and buried Sunday 14 Elul 5593 [= 2 September 1833]. *Isaac Moses, known as Ike Moses, probably a son of Judah Moses I who came to Plymouth in 1763.*

P16. The Parnas and Manhig Yehiel Michael ben Zvi, died Thursday, 20 Adar 5579 [= 17 March 1819]. *Michael Hart (b. 1739 near Mannheim) came to England via Harwich 1763. A silversmith in Howes Lane in 1803.*

P17. Alexander Aryeh ben Menahem, died 14 Heshvan 5579 [= 16 November 1818], with hoary head and full of days.

P18. Edal bat Samuel, wife of Alexander Aryeh ben Menahem, died Sunday, 9 Heshvan 5579 [= 8 November 1818], aged 65 years. *His surname was Emanuel. Children: Samuel, Ezekiel and Menahem.*

P20. Genella bat Baruch, wife of the late Joseph ben Zvi, from the Holy Congregation of Falmouth, died Friday, 9 Kislev 5577 [= 29 November 1816].

Q5. The child Miriam bat Jacob, Betsy Miriam Jacob, daughter of the late Lewis Jacobs.

Q6. Judah ben Isaac, died 8 Sivan 5600 [= 7 June 1840]. Reverse: Lewis Jacobs; 7 June 1840, aged 49 years. *Lewis Jacobs I, goldsmith in 1823 in Totnes.*

Q16. The bachelor Issachar ben Joel, died 25 Shevat 5582 [= 16 February 1822].

Q19. The bachelor Aaron ben Simeon the Levite, died 13 Tishri 5579 [= 13 October 1818]. *The stone has an ewer and basin at the top.*

Q24. Joshua Falk ben the late Isaac from Breslau. He was slain in the place of Fowey by the uncircumcised and impure man Wyatt and drowned in the waters, 14 Kislev 5572 and buried on the 17th thereof [= 30 November 1811], aged 26 years. *Isaac Valentine who was enticed to bring £260 to Fowey by innkeeper Wyatt and murdered. Wyatt was hanged for his crime at Bodmin.*

Q25. Zadok ben Asher, died 5 Tamuz 5570 [= 7 July 1810].

R8. Joseph ben Zvi, died 16 Adar Rishon 5603 [= 16 February 1843]

R15. Abraham ben Isaac, died Monday, 5 Tishri 5585 [=

27 September 1824].

Abraham Isaac (b. 1741 Furth), old clothes dealer, Southside Street in 1803. Congregational records describe him as Abraham ben Isaac Schnapfuchs.

R22. The Torani Aaron ben Michael, died 10 Av [followed by the chronogram] 'According to the counting of the children of Israel' [= ?1753 or ?1813].

R24. The bachelor Issachar Behrman ben Joshua Levy the righteous Priest from the Holy Congregation of London, died ?Yom Kippur 5565 [= 15 September 1804] in the Island of Madeira, and was buried here in Plymouth on Friday, the eve of Sabbath, Iyar 5565 [= May 1805].

The Plymouth Congregation has a silver bowl and jug for the use of the Priests given by his family in gratitude for 'the loving kindness done to the bones of our son'.

S1. A most exalted man Menahem ben Isaac from London who laboured .... he died on Monday and was buried on Tuesday..... Av 5580 [= ? July 1820]. *Emanuel Levy.*

S3. Joseph ben Naphtali, died and buried on Wednesday 13 Tamuz 5559 [= 16 July 1799].

Joseph Henry (AL48), born 1735, Sandfelt, came to England in 1766, a clothes dealer in Lower Lane.

S6. Joseph ben Jacob Mannheim called Yosepha Mannheimer, died Sunday, 24 Sivan 5582 [= 11 June 1822]. *Joseph Hart (b. 1756, Mannheim) came to Plymouth via Harwich in 1770.*

S9. David ben Moses from Norwich, died and was buried 23 Heshvan 5573 [= 29 October 1812]. *David Moses (b. 1737 near Saarbruck), moved to Plymouth 1793. In 1803 he lived in Southside Street.*

T1. My husband Isaac Eliezer ben Sampson, died the first Intermediate Day of Succot 5611 [= 23 September 1850].

Burials in Jewish Cemetery, Gifford Place

A burial register does not appear to exist for the site. Information has been taken from a burial map and the cemetery itself. Survey carried out by the author in 2012.

ROW A
1. MYER ISAAC ROSEMAN, 15 February 1935, aged 68, husband of Amelia
2. MYER FREDMAN, 5 August 1927, aged 57
3. LEVIN FREDMAN, 18 October 1912, aged 68
4. WILLIAM WOLFE, 1 February 1873, aged 63
5. S. WOLFE, 2 April 1874, aged 26
6. SON OF JUDAH WOLFE, 1874
7. A. NELSON, 10 February 1874, aged 45
8. RALPH CORREA, 26 April 1875
9. HENRY MORRIS, 19 December 1875

Gifford Place Jewish cemetery

10. Unknown
11. RICHARD KAUFMAN, June 1879, aged 66
12. ASHER JOEL, 1 September 1880, aged 70
13. SIGMUND YAGER, 2 April 1882, aged 65
14. 10 May 1883, English inscription illegible
15. ABRAHAM JACOBS, 5 March 1886
16. EZRA NATHAN, 1 January 1894, aged 74
17. PHILIP BLOOM, 14 February 1934, aged 59
18. FRANK HOLDENBERG, 23 May 1934, aged 54
19. MYER ROSEMAN, 5 February 1936, aged 56, husband of Lena
20. TOBIAS BRAND, 16 February 1936, aged 71
21. MR STONE, 11 July 1936
22. ISAAC FORMAN, 27 July 1936, aged 59
23. ALEXANDER GOLDSTEIN, 6 February 1937, aged 25
24. HARRY BROCK, 15 March 1937, aged 76
25. CHARLES BASS, 22 April 1937, aged 48
26. MR H. PRICE, 21 December 1937
27. MORRIS SMITH, 11 may 1946, aged 61, husband of Sadie (Sarah)
28. ALFRED BROCK, 10 July 1946, aged 81
29. SAMUEL W SELWOOD, 2 April 1947, aged 39
30. ERNEST HYMAN CAPLAN, 19 November 1949, aged 49, eldest son of Leah & late Abraham Caplan

ROW B
1. FANNY KAPLAN, 29 July 1929, aged 25
2. RACHEL ROSEMAN, 3 March 1928, aged 80, widow of Israel Roseman
3. REBECCA FREDMAN, 3 July 1919, aged 43, wife of Myer Fredman
4. HETTY FREDMAN, 22 February 1910, aged 77, widow of Aryeh Eliezer Fredman
5. Unknown
6. FANNY LYONS, 1873, aged 78
7. Unknown
8. AMELIA RALPH, 26 November 1874, aged 62
9. JULIA LEVY, 31 December 1874, aged 54
10. GELA LEVI, 10 April 1875, aged 54
11. Unknown
12. BELLA LEVI, 16 April 1878

Double grave of Mary & Esther Smith killed in the blitz

13. MARIA MITCHELL, 25 April 1879, aged 74
14. HANNAH JOSEPH, 25 May 1879, aged 74
15. HARRIET JACOBS, 28 August 1879, aged 69, wife of Alexander Jacobs
16. ESTER ISRAEL, 18 April 1880
17. CHAYA SARAH COHEN, 20 March 1891, aged 80
18. BERNARD BAUN, 12 June 1938, aged 71
19. LOUIS GOLDSTEIN, 10 February 1939
20. HARRIS BENCE, 9 March 1939, aged 76
21. AARON ERNEST ROSEMAN, 17 March 1939, aged 66
22. HYMAN LIPMAN, 10 October 1939, aged 40
23. ABRAHAM ISAAC ERLICH, 6 January 1940, aged 59
24. SAMUEL ERLICH, 28 January 1940
25. ALEXANDER VERNON JONAS, 5 June 1940
26. DAVID JONAS, 6 July 1941, husband of Bertha Jonas
27. ISAAC LAZARUS, 30 July 1946, aged 80
28. CHARLES SOLOMON BROCK, 13 March 1947, aged 83
29. LOUIS ROBINS, 22 January 1948, aged 73
30. MR BOLTON, 6 December 1949
31. SOLOMON PEARL, 26 January 1950, aged 83

ROW C
1. BERT ROSEMAN, 2 January 1911, aged 26, son of Rachel & Israel Roseman
2. ISRAEL ROSEMAN, 16 October 1910, husband of Rachel Roseman
3. SAMUEL JACOBS, 12 June 1884, aged 84
4. HENRY WOLFE, 14 April 1881
5. LOUIS ZEITUNG (GABRIELSON), 16 August 1886, aged 19, eldest son of Morris & Henrietta Gabrielson
6. LEON ISAAC, 7 May 1887, aged 48
7. LEWIS HYMAN, 16 June 1888
8. ISAAC NEWMAN, 27 May 1889
9. Unknown
10. ABRAHAM RALPH, 4 October 1890, aged 76
11. ABRAHAM JACOBS, 29 October 1890, aged 62, formerly of Exeter
12. ALEXANDER JACOBS, 13 August 1893, aged 86, of Paignton & Torquay
13. AARON WOLFE, 17 February 1890, husband of Phoebe Wolf
14. BARNETT LYONS, 2 April 1888, aged 70
15. LEVI FREDMAN, 17 January 1886, aged 54
16. CALMEN WINEBERG, 1 September 1884
17. JACOB FREDMAN, 2 December 1898, aged 64
18. MARY SMITH, 10 July 1940, aged 72, killed by enemy action
19. ESTER SMITH, 10 July 1940, aged 38 – double stone with C18
20. SALLIE STOLLER, 23 October 1940, aged 39
21. MRS MATHILDA PHILLIPS, 18 November 1940, aged 53
22. BERTHA SPERLING, 30 September 1941, aged 82, widow of Samuel Sperling

APPENDIX 5

23. ANNIE ERLICH, 6 August 1946, aged 63
24. MRS ROSE
25. MISS PAULINE SILVERSTONE, 20 March 1943, aged 31
26. JANE WEINBERG, 7 March 1943, aged 76
27. FLORA PEARL, 1 September 1943, aged 67
28. RAY WOLFSON, 18 November 1943
29. CAROLINE ALBERTA LEAH BROCK, 25 January 1944, aged 79
30. PAMELA ROBINS, 3 March 1944, aged 22, only daughter of Louis & Lulu Robins

31. LULU ROBINS, 7 December 1954, aged 62

ROW D

1. LIBBY ROBINS, 4 September 1919, aged 69
2. ABIGAIL NATHAN, 20 December 1894
3. MRS P LEVI, 17 November 1880, aged 71
4. SARAH NEWMAN, 5 February 1881
5. RACHEL BAUM, 30 October 1882, wife of Philip Baum
6. SARAH BROCK, 5 January 1884
7. PHOEBE SHEPPERD, 28 April 1884, aged 35
8. HENRIETTA SUSMAN, 15 November 1884, aged 40
9. Unknown
10. ESTHER LEVI, 31 December 1895, aged 74
11. MISS BETSY ALEXANDER, 1 December 1886, aged 86
12. JANETTE SAMUELS, 3 march 1888, aged 67
13. JULIA BASCH, 8 April 1888, aged 58
14. MISS BLOOMEY ALEXANDER, 1 September 1889, aged 81
15. FANNY ISAACS, 8 December 1889, aged 77
16. JANE ELIZABETH LYONS, 25 February 1890, aged 65
17. JANE LYONS, 25 February 1890
18. RACHEL FREDMAN, 28 January 1922, aged 84, widow of Jacob
19. HARRIS NATHAN, 8 November 1940, aged 70
20. ELIJAH BARKE, 4 December 1940, aged 62
21. MAURICE SANGER, 14 July 1941, aged 53
22. MORRIS, 20 October 1941
22. BARNETT COHEN, 17 May 1942, aged 83
23. MORRIS SOLOMON, 21 July 1942 (402679, Sgt of Royal Australian Air Force)
24. MORTON MORRIS, 23 October 1942, aged 46
25. JACOB GREENBURGH, 23 November 1942, aged 86
26. MICHAEL SOLOMON, 7 January 1943, aged 62
27. JOSEPH GREENBURGH, 30 September 1943, aged 56
28. JOSEPH MILNER, 5 April 1944, aged 61
29. NATHAN CHARLES, 15 October 1944, aged 65
30. JOSEPH (JACK) GORDON, 17 December 1944, aged 61, of St Austell
31. ABRAHAM LEVY, 17 February 1945

ROW E

1. GEDALIA MORDECAI ROBINS, 7 December 1907, aged 59
2. S. FREDMAN, 25 March 1899, aged 78
3. Unknown
4. HERMAN LONDON, 4 January 1894, aged 48
5. ELIJAH MYER SONNENBERG, January 1894, aged 47
6. WOLFE JACOB ULLMAN, 26 January 1894, aged 59
7. MOSELY JOEL, 9 April 1895, 39 (born 12 August 1855)
8. LOUIS CONITZ [stone down], 24 July 1895
9. VICTOR LIEPA ROTH, 1 February 1896, aged 13, son of Benjamin & Bertha Roth
10. ROSALIA SIMPSON, 13 July 1890, aged 6 months
11 - 12. Unknown
13. DORA SARA DEBORAH SIMPSON, 1 January 1896, aged 1 year 10 months
14. Unknown
15. LEAH ROSEMAN, 5 January 1897, aged 16 months, infant of Israel & Rachel Roseman
16. HANNAH SARAH ROSEMAN, 10 June 1897, aged 2 months, daughter of Myer Isaac & Amelia Roseman
17. AMELIA MANDELSTAM, 30 April 1892, relict of Emil Mandelstam
18. FRANCIS NATHAN, 29 October 1896
19. Unknown
20. RALPH BENJAMIN EMDON, 10 February 1944, aged 25, ex-Sgt of Queens Royal Regiment
21. SAMUEL ISAAC OWEN, 10 September 1945, aged

WW1 grave

68, husband of Rebecca Sarah Owen
22. ABRAHAM (BOBBY) ROBINS, 12 October 1945, aged 77, husband of Rose
23. LEWIS LADDEN, 31 May 1946, aged 71
24. SOLOMON GORDON, 3 October 1947, aged 62
25. BARNETT MELICHAN, 21 June 1948, aged 55
26. ELY MYER AZERMAN, 7 February 1950, husband of Winifred
27 - 28. Void
29. ABRAHAM SILVERSTONE, 6 May 1952, aged 78
30. HYMAN JOHN NELSON, 24 January 1952
31. ISIDORE COHEN, 29 December 1950, aged 70, husband of Phoebe Cohen
32. JOSEPH SPARK, 2 October 1950, aged 73, husband of Augusta
33. ERNEST BROCK, 11 February 1950, aged 77, husband of Lilian Ada Brock

ROW F

1. LIEBA FREDMAN, 15 May 1919, aged 100, widow of Samuel Wolf Fredman
2. REBECCA EMDEN, 9 March 1895, aged 79, widow of Wolf Emden
3. Unknown
4. ESTHER NELSON, 17 March 1891, aged 39, wife of J.S Nelson
5. HARRIET BELLEM, 28 October 1890, aged 80
6. HANNAH ISAACS, 26 October 1890, aged 72
7. MATILDA HANNAH WINEBERG, 27 March 1890, aged 28
8. ROSE JOEL, 6 March 1890, aged 77, relict of Asher Joel
9. PHOEBE WOLF, 23 June 1894, aged 73, wife of Aron Wolf
10. EDITH ROSE EMDEN, 2 July 1886
11 - 16. Unknown
17. BARNET GOODMAN, 18 May 1890
18. FRANCES NATHAN, 29 October 1896, aged 73, daughter of Lionel Nathan
19. Unknown
20. EDITH BLANCHE LANGNER, 1 November 1945
21. FANNY HARRIS, 26 December 1946, aged 63, wife of Saul Harris
22. ESTHER SCHULMAN, 5 April 1946, aged 85
23. FRUMA LEMPERT, 17 January 1947, aged 81
24. HETTY BARKE, 19 May 1947, aged 72
25. HANNAH BROCK, 15 August 1947, aged 82
26. ANNIE ROBBINS, 5 November 1947, aged 49
27. LENA ROSEMAN, 9 November 1947, aged 66, widow of Myer Roseman
28. MRS STONE, 3 June 1948
29. RACHEL LESKIN, 5 June 1948, aged 57
30. CHARLOTTE ESTHER LAURENCE, 12 January 1949, aged 76
31. REBECCA SILVERSTONE, 17 December 1949, aged 76

32. GERTRUDE AUGUSTA BLOOM, 6 April 1949, aged 72
33. LILIAN ADA (CISSIE) BROCK, 20 May 1978, aged 92, widow of Ernest Brock

ROW G

1 – 9. Twelve unknown children
10. SAMUEL LAZARUS, 18 September 1890, aged 11 months, son of Isaac & Jane Lazarus
11 - 12. Unknown
13. ABRAHAM ORGEL, 16 December 1893
14 - 16. Unknown
17. BARNETT GOODMAN, 18 May 1890, aged 9 months
18. Baby SILVERSTONE, 1946
19. Baby LEWIS, 1946
21- 26. Unknown
27. JANEY LAZARUS, 3 February 1951, aged 85, widow of Isaac Lazarus

ROW H

1 - 5. Unknown
6. ESTHER FREDMAN, 1883
7-12. Unknown
13. Baby FREYA GORDON, 6 June 1949
14 - 15. Unknown
16. RAYNOR TUCHMAN, 13 June 1954, aged 86
17. ROSE LEWIS, 31 March 1954, aged 78
18. CATHERINE BISHOP, 3 February 1954, aged 90
19. MIRIAM FRANCES BROCK, 27 December 1953, aged 58, wife of John
20. CISSIE PHYLLIS GOODMAN, 27 April 1952, aged 44, wife of Jack Goodman
21. HETTIE SANGER, 21 March 1952, aged 67
22. CLARA ABRAHAMS, 4 June 1951, aged 65
23. AMELIA ROSEMAN, 10 January 1951, aged 51, widow of Myer Isaac Roseman
28. MIRIAM HANNAH BRAND, 22 June 1950, aged 87
29. FANNY FREDMAN, 31 March 1950, aged 96, widow of Myer Fredman
30. REBECCA CHARLES, 8 March 1950, aged 74
31. ESTHER ABRAHAMS, 8 December 1949

ROW J

1. LOUIS ROSEMAN, 2 May 1902, aged 7½, son of Myer Isaac & Amelia Roseman
2. Unknown
3. REBECCA MINDEL PEARL, 18 December 1904
4. NATHAN JOSEPH, 20 December 1904, aged 11
5. Unknown
6. SAMUEL BENJAMIN PEARL, 11 January 1905, aged 8 years & 1 month
7. BERTHA ROBINS, 20 February 1906, aged 9, eldest daughter of Abraham & Rose Robins

APPENDIX 5

8. EVA JACOBS, 17 July 1906, aged 3½, daughter of Revd D & Mrs Jacobs
9. Unknown
10. Unknown
11. ROSY COHEN, 4 December 1898, aged 10½ months, daughter of Barnett & Sarah Cohen
12 -18. Ten unknown children, amongst which appears to be buried HERMIONE CONICK, 13 May 1938
19. LOUIS GRAHAM ROBINS, 24 February 1953, aged 2 & 9 months, son of Gerald & Rita Robins
20. Baby STEIN, 19 September 1953
21. REVD. EMMANUEL GOODMAN, 17 March 1959, aged 62
22. JOSHUA HURWITT, 3 September 1959, aged 62
23. JOHN (JACOB NATHAN) BROCK, 13 March 1959, aged 91
24. HYMAN ALOOF, 13 July 1959, aged 72
25. ABRAHAM EPHRAIM MILNER, 30 December 1958, aged 77
26. KING FIELD, 20 October 1958
27. ABRAHAM ABRAHAMS, 7 October 1957, aged 75
28. MORRIS SALTER, 7 November 1956, aged 43, husband of Annie
29. HARRY BLACK, 25 January 1956, aged 56
30. SAMUEL LOUIS GOLDBERG, 31 January 1956, aged 84
31. HYMAN SOLOMON (SOLLY) OWEN, 4 November 1955, aged 78, wife of Rose

ROW K
1. DAPHNE IRIS JORDAN, 25 October 1914, aged 4½, daughter of David & Elizabeth Jordan
2 - 3. Unknown
4. (Baby) KALISHER, 7 April 1940
5. Unknown
6. RACHAEL GNOBBOK,
7. MILLY SLAVINSKY, 1 November 1912, aged 3, daughter of Rev & Mrs Slavinsky
8. FANNY GREENBURGH, 24 January 1911, aged 11 years & 9 months, daughter of Jacob & Betsy Greenburgh
9. HARRY CRONENBURG, 17 November 1909, child, English illegible
10. MYER FREDMAN, 6 January 1927, aged 71, husband of Fanny Fredman
11. ABRAHAM COHEN, 23 August 1927, aged 82
12. LAWRENCE LEVY, 4 July 1930, aged 43
13. SAUL PHINEAS LEMPERT, 12 August 1932, aged 69, husband of Fruma Lempert
14. HENRY COHEN, 3 November 1932, aged 22, son of Isidore and Phoebe Cohen
15. ELIEZAR GREENBURGH, 29 December 1932, aged 60
16. HARRY ROGERS, 12 July 1932
17. MAX BISHOP, 7 October 1928, aged 69
18. MAURICE BURNS, 29 September 1928, aged 40
19. HENRY ISAACS, 6 May 1927
20. Unknown

Narrow gap
23. BELLA GOLDSTEIN, 8 December 1958, aged 74
24. Reserved MRS BLACK
25. JEANNIE RICHMAN, 24 September 1970, aged 77
26. Reserved MRS SALTER
27. ELLEN GOODMAN, 15 June 1957, aged 83
28. KING FIELD, 19 October 1958, aged 77
29. RACHEL GOLD, 5 April 1956, aged 64
30. JANET LADDEN, 5 October 1955, aged 79
31. MINNIE (AMELIA) LAZARUS, 1 July 1955, aged 70
32. NELLIE BROCK, 26 April 1955, aged 60
33. FREYDA ROSEMAN, 22 April 1955, aged 60
34. ETHEL LILIAN (LEAH) CAPLAN, 26 February 1955, aged 73

ROW L
1 - 2. Unknown
3. BERTHA ROTH, 20 December 1931, wife of Benjamin Roth
4. ELLEN AUGUSTA BROCK, 8 January 1932
5. JULIA ISAACS, 23 July 1932, aged 84
6. BECK
7. LEAH PERLA MILNER, 31 August 1933, aged 46
8. SARAH MILNER, 17 November 1933, aged 75
9. REBECCA BENCE, 27 July 1934, aged 76
10. BESSIE GOLDSTEIN, 26 November 1934, aged 44
11. HESTER ROBINS, 5 January 1936
12. BESSIE GREENBURGH, 24 September 1936, aged 74
13. SARAH COHEN, 24 January 1932, aged 70, wife of Barnett Cohen
14. HINDA ROSEMAN, 22 May 1937
15. ROSE ALEXANDER, 15 June 1937
16. RACHEL DINA COPLANS, 1 December 1937, aged 78
17. BEENY SILK, 31 May 1938, aged 64
18. ABIGAIL JACOBS, 10 June 1938, aged 59, daughter of late Mark & Henrietta Jacobs
19. ANNIE RACHEL YOUNGLESON, 23 July 1938, aged 73
20. LEAH DEBORAH WOOLFSON, 11 August 1939, aged 66
21. ESTHER GOLDBERG, 11 December 1939, aged 59
22. Unknown BABY, 25 March 1957
Gap
27. ESTHER BLACK, 7 September 1967, aged 72
28.
29. EVA HOLCENBERG, 12 December 1956, aged 75

ROW M
1. DAVID DANIEL HIRSCH, 25 April 1927, aged, 43, son of late Leah & Woolf Hirsch
2. ABRAM LEVIN, 20 April 1927
3. LEWIS FORMAN, 4 April 1927
4. MAURICE SIMON
5. SILK, 7 January 1926

6. ABRAHAM SAMUEL CAPLAN, 17 October 1925, aged 51
7. MICHAEL JACOBS, 17 September 1925, aged 65, husband of Rachel Jacobs
8. JOSEPH FREEMAN, October 1924
9. SAMUEL SPERLING, 2 September 1924, aged 76
10. HARRIS GOODMAN, 30 August 1924
11. ALFRED NELSON, 19 December 1923, aged 44
12. MYER SILVERSTONE, 9 July 1923, aged 78
13. SAMUEL BASH, 5 July 1923, aged 58, husband of Rachel, father of Esther, Miriam, Leah, Eva
14. ABRAHAM COSTA, 8 June 1923
15. ARTHUR PEARL, 13 March 1923, aged 27
16. ABRAHAM CONICK, 29 November 1922, aged 61
17. JOSEPH LYONS, 11 August 1921, aged 78
18. ISAAC ABRAHAMS, 13 October 1920, aged 33
19. JACOB SAMUEL JACOBS, 16 March 1920
20. GUS BASCH, 11 November 1919, aged 67
21. LEWIS LAZARUS, 7 August 1919 (born 9 August 1844)
22. JOSEPH LEWIS, 6 April 1955 (???), aged 80
23. JOSEPH SANGER, 30 December 1954, aged 69
24. ASHER TUCHMAN, 8 December 1954, aged 87
25. DAVID JORDAN, 1 October 1954, aged 78
26. MORRIS RICHMAN, 9 September 1954, aged 63, husband of Jeannie
27. HENRY LAURENCE, 28 August 1954, aged 83
28. JOSEPH ABRAHAMS, 9 June 1954, aged 66
29. LEO SILVERSTONE, 22 February 1954, aged 70
30. LEWIS GEORGE BROCK, 3 February 1954, aged 62, son of late Alfred & Hannah Brock
31. ELEAZAR BARKE, 28 January 1954, aged 73
32. CECIL ISRAEL BRAND, 2 September 1953, aged 55
33. ERNEST AARON ROBINS, 22 May 1953, aged 80

ROW N
1. CORDELIA MORRIS, 23 February 1910
2. Unknown
3. ANNIE PRICE, 12 February 1918, wife of Isaac Price
4. YETTA JANKOWSKY (KAY), 23 September 1918, aged 69
5. EDITH CHARLES, 4 February 1920
6. JEANETTE ISAACS, 10 May 1920
7. LAWRENCE
8. FANNY ABRAHAMS, 6 October 1920, wife of late Lewis Abrahamson
9. ABRAHAM STEIN
10. ESTHER SILVERSTONE, 1 February 1922, aged 73, wife of Myer Silverstone
11. FANNY SAMUELS, 27 September 1922, aged 72
12. MARIA JACOBS, 7 October 1922, aged 84, relict of John Jacobs
13. PHOEBE BARKE, 26 June 1922, aged 77
14. RACHEL BASH, 17 January 1924, aged 60, wife of the late Samuel Bash
15. ELIZA EMDON, 22 June 1924, age 75
16. SARAH SILVERSTONE, 29 January 1925, aged 75

17. SARAH LILIAN SIMMONS, 9 March 1926, aged 15
18. FANNY ABRAHAMS, 27 December 1925
19. MINNIE ISAACS, 3 April 1926
20. LEAH BURNS, 12 November 1929, aged 69
21. REBECCA CONICK, 27 April 1930, aged 63
22. ELIZABETH JACOBS, 1 June 1930, aged 73
23. BELLA EDELMAN, 3 June 1931, aged 63
Gap
30. ETTIE ASH, March 1964, aged 55 (née da Costa)
31. MISS DORIS BAUN, 12 December 1963, aged 62
32. ANNE LEVY, 4 April 1962, aged 47, wife of Herman Levy
33. BRONIA FELDMESSER-REISS, 25 January 1960, aged 61, born 30 April 1898
34. MRS AZERMAN
35. MAUD BRADLAW, 8 April 1957, aged 81, widow of Henry Jack Bradlaw [N35]
36. MRS PRICE, 19 March 1956
37. LEAH KERSCHENBAUM, 13 March 1955, aged 64, widow of Barnett Kerschenbaum

ROW O
1. ABRAHAM TITLEBAUM, 20 January 1927, aged 75
2. BENJIMAN JOSEPH, 28 January 1926, aged 61
3. AARON JOEL WEINBERG, 16 November 1912, aged 46
4. MARK JACOBS, 28 October 1913, aged 74, husband of Henrietta Jacobs
5. HUGH EMDON, 31 May 1914
6. JOSEPH LEAPMAN JACOBS, 29 June 1914, aged 76
7. AFROIM DAVID, 6 December 1914, aged 70
8. Unknown
9. HARRIS BROMBERG, 23 March 1916, aged 78
10. JOSEPH DAVIS, 3 March 1917
11. MOSES DAVID MEANDL, 27 April 1917
12. ISAAC PRICE, 21 September 1917
13. JOSEPH JACOBS, 12 November 1917, aged 60
14. HARRY NELSON, 8 January 1918, aged 39
15. BENJAMIN ROTH, 11 January 1918, aged 75, husband of Bertha Roth
16. HARRY PHILLIPS, 2 April 1918 (war grave)
17. Unknown
18. JOHN JACOBS, 7 May 1918, aged 87
19. DOUBTFUL
20. MORDECAI SLAVINSKI, 1 November 1919, aged 13, son of Aaron & Rachel Slavinski
21. JOHN LITHMAN, 8 January 1919 (war grave)
22. MYER NYMAN (Pte Michael Burns), 2 February 1919, aged 18 (war grave)
23. ABRAM BERNSTEIN, 10 March 1919, aged 58
24. ALBERT STANLEY BRADLAW, 10 December 1959
25. GEORGE DEFRIES, 21 March 1946, aged 70
26. BARNETT KIRSCHENBAUM, 17 June 1946, aged 58
27. GOLDSTONE, 17 November 1946
28. ISRAEL LEVY, 8 April 1948, aged 79, husband of Amelia Levy

APPENDIX 5

29. SUGAR, 1948
30. WOLFF, 18 December 1949
31. MR F. WALL, 9 May 1950
32. ARTHUR RALPH WALFORD, 7 June 1950
33. MASTER RONALD CARMONA, 25 January 1952
34. ALEXANDER WEMBURY, 7 September 1953, aged 63
35. MR HARRIS, 23 January 1957
36. AARON SPERLING, 4 April 1957, aged 68

ROW P

First plot left clear for drainage
2. BERTHA JOSEPH, 31 March 1952, aged 79
3. HENRIETTA JACOBS, 25 November 1909, aged 63, wife of Mark Jacobs
4. LEAH SAMUELS, 19 November 1909
5. HENRIETTA BROCK, 3 January 1909, aged 79, wife of Lewis Brock
6. KATE JACOBS, died 6 January 1899, aged 55, wife of J.L Jacobs
7. DEBORAH ULLMAN, 3 April 1899, aged 62, widow of Wolfe Jacob Ullman
8. HANNAH NATHAN, 26 January 1901, aged 74
9. FANNIE GOLDBERG, 28 June 1901, wife of Joseph Goldberg
10. ESTHER NATHAN, 23 November 1902
11. REBECCA NATHAN, 19 November 1903, aged 79
12. HARRIET MORRIS, 7 August 1904, wife of Abraham Morris
13. RAINA TITLEBOAM, 20 May 1905, aged 53
14. ESTELLE LOVEGUARD, 15 September 1905
15. HENRIETTA COHEN, 18 October 1905, aged 49, wife of Abraham Cohen

16. JANE NATHAN, 2 November 1905
17. ESTHER LEVY, 12 February 1907, aged 26, wife of Philip Cohen of Manchester
18. NANCY NATHAN, 5 January 1908
19. JULIA HARRIET PEARL, 7 December 1908, aged 59
20. RACHEL SOLOMON, 23 March 1909, aged 22
21. BESSIE OWEN, 7 April 1909, aged 66
22. RACHEL FREEMAN, 15 July 1909
23. PHOEBE LEAH FRANKS, 27 October 1909, aged 67
24. ANNIE BROMBERG, 8 September 1928, aged 81
25. MARTHA LEAH WOOLF, 3 August 1891, aged 58, wife of late Henry Woolf
26. CAROLINE SMITH, 25 April 1933, aged 83
27. MRS CURTIS, 11 November 1940
28. LEAH MICHON, 12 July 1944
29. MRS E KETNERIDGE, 1945
30. MRS SCHOLMAN, 5 March 1948
31. LILY KINGDON, 23 October 1948
32. KITTY PURCELL, 19 March 1949
33. Unknown
34. DOROTHY BARNETT, 3 June 1954, aged 53
35. M. J BOSMAN, 8 August 1954
36. JULIA BROCK, 17 December 1954, aged 80

ROW Q

1. RABBI JACOB BARUCH ELLINSON, 8 February 1924, aged 82
2. LEWIS BROCK, 24 July 1920, aged 83
3. ELIEZER DAVID LEMPERT, 26 September 1912, aged 28, son of Fruma & Saul Lempert
4. SIMON MILNER, 4 October 1911, husband of Beeny Milner
5. HUGH RALPH EMDEN, 31 May 1914, son of the late Eliezer and Telza Emden
6. GEORGE BROCK, 24 July 1897, aged 81
7. SAMUEL SAMUELS, 5 July 1899, aged 79
8. MICHAEL BASCH, 24 September 1899, aged 38, 'a dutiful son and brother'
9. ELEAZAR EMDON, 26 February 1900, aged 59
10. HAYMAN LIGHTERMAN, 23 August 1900, aged 43
11. Unknown
12. HENRY JACOBS, 16 September 1903, aged 86
13. JOHN SELIG NELSON, 6 March 1904, aged 71
14. ISAAC LEIPMAN, 10 August 1904
15. EDWARD BASCH, 6 November 1904
16. ABRAHAM MORRIS, 4 September 1905, aged 78
17. EPHRAIM BARKE, 14 May 1904, aged 58
18. JOSEPH GOLDBERG, 14 July 1907
19. NATHAN FREDMAN, drowned 8 June 1884, buried 29 June 1884
20. BORUCH JAFFE, 18 August 1907
21. LOUIS MICHAEL JACOBS, 30 November 1907, aged 29, husband of Sarah Jacobs
22. BENJAMIN S. PIK, 11 March 1908

23. Unknown
24. HENRY BLUMENTHAL, 19 January 1911, son of Abraham and Leah Blumenthal of London
25 - 27. Unknown
28. GEORGE RALPH, 7 February 1877
29. SAMUEL WHITE, 1 April 1924
30. LAZARUS LADDEN, 5 July 1933, aged 18
31. WILLINGTON, 15 March 1937
32. GEORG KOVAES (KOOD), 31 January 1938, husband of Bertha who lost his young life on Alba which sank off St Ives on 31 January
33. EMANUEL SPERLING, 18 January 194, aged 59
34. RONNIE CASMONA, 24 January 1952, aged 15, born Malta
35. MARK LOUIS MICHAELS, 15 December 1961, of Torquay
36. GOLDSTEIN, 27 May 1960
37. MR BARRS

ROW AA
1: MATHILDA (MORRIS) DICKER, 16 July 1963
2: AARON BASH, 6 August 1963, only son of Rachel Bash
3: LESLIE MORRIS, 22 December 1963
4: DANNY (GOLDSTEIN) COHEN, 8 December 1964
5: CLARA HILL, 1 April 1966
6: RETA REBECCA MATTHEWS, 28 April 1976
7: PHILLIP LEVY, 9 December 1976
8: GOLDA LEAH RICHARDSON, 6 December 1977
9: ABRAHAM WEMBURY (WEINBERG), 2 January 1978
10: ELIZABETH ARANKA MARSDEN, 30 April 1978
11. CHARLES ROSE, August 1979
12. KITTY LUBELL, 28 December 1980
13. SARAH ANNIE HORTON, 14 June 1980
Large gap
20. NICOLA MARJORIE ZELDA ROBINS, 15 February 1965
21. VIVIENNE EMDON, 3 December 1962

ROW AB
1. ESTHER SPERLING, 24 June 1959
2: HENRY GOLD, 30 December 1959
3: PERCY LESKIN, 8 January 1960
4. Empty
5: HERMAN ELIAS COHEN, 16 December 1960
6: SARAH MARCHEVITZ, 18 January 1960
7: ARTHUR BRAND, 15 June 1960
8: CAPLE PECK, 18 December 1960
9: JENNIE PECK, 31 May 1961
10: JENNIE GREENBURGH, 5 May 1961
11. HYMAN ROSEMAN, 17 October 1961
12. PERCY ROSEMAN, 25 March 1962
13. MARIE SEGAL, 21 January 1963
14. LEON FRANK EMDON, 2 February 1963
15: MOSES MONTEFIORE COHEN, 11 February 1963
16: GEORGE (LAZUR) LAZARUS, 17 February 1963
17: ISSAC EDWARD BROMBERG, 19 April 1963
18: ALICE AGNES NELSON, 10 January 1965
19: ESTHER MELICAN, 26 February 1965
20: HYMAN WISEMAN, 6 April 1965
21: ESTHER PERLMUTTER, 25 November 1965

ROW AC
1: ETHEL GRACE ROBINS, 19 April 1963
2: SARAH ALOOF, 7 May 1964
3: LEAH BENCE, 17 May 1964
4: ROSE EMDON, 7 June 1954
5. LEAH CAPLAN, 9 February 1966
6. AUGUSTA SPARK, 25 June 1966
7: BEATRICE GORDON, 11 September 1966
8: ETTY ESTHER GREEN, 5 October 1966
9: SIM LAZARUS, 4 February 1967
10: ISIDORE JOSEPH, 28 February 1967
11: EVA FIELD, 28 June 1967
12: JOE ERLICH, 5 August 1967
13: ROSE OWEN, 1 February 1969
14: WOLFE STERNE, 2 April 1969
15: PHOEBE COHEN, 30 August 1969
16: REBECCA DEGGOTS, 13 December 1969
17: PHILIP ERLICH, 21 August 1970
18: MORRIS LESKIN, 11 March 1972
19: ESTHER ROSE BRAND, 8 December 1970
20: ANNIE DORA JOSEPH, 31 May 1971

ROW AD
1: DOROTHY EMDON, 1 February 1966
2: EMMANUEL KLIEFF, 4 February 1969
3: ISRAEL ROSEMAN, 15 May 1969

APPENDIX 5

4: BELLE ERLICH, 8 July 1970
5. SIMON ROSEMAN, 23 August 1970
6: JEANNIE FREDMAN, 4 January 1886, aged 54
7: SAMUEL W. FREDMAN, 2 February 1971
8: LILY COHEN, 19 July 1972
9: MINNIE GREENBURGH, 28 March 1973
10: JULIAN (LEO) HARRIS, 16 July 1973
11: ROSE CAPLAN, May 1974
12: ADA SILVERSTONE, 28 December 1974
13: MORRIS RUTMAN, 14 April 1975
14: PAULINE JUNE JOSEPH, 10 July 1975
15: BETTIE GORDON, 27 August 1975
16. JOSEPH SALISBURY, 28 September 1975
17. ISRAEL ELIAS SHAW, 24 June 1976
18: BERT DEGGOTTS, 22 February 1977
19: DR MORDICAI ELEAZER (MARK) GORDON, 6 May 1977
20. Unused

ROW AE
1. DORA HARRIS, 9 November 1972
2. ANNIE SARAH (ENA) ROSEMAN, 8 March 1975
3: PEGGY ROSE JOSEPH, 8 April 1977
4: JOSEPH GERALD JOSEPH, 21 September 1977
5: MORTON JULES DAVISON, 11 October 1977
6: RUBY FURGUSON, 23 February 1978
7: PERCY LIONEL COHEN, 29 April 1978
8: HETTIE MARIE NELSON, 1 August 1978
9: THELMA SOLOMON, 1 August 1978
10: EPHRAIM BENCE, 7 October 1978
11 RUTH ELSIE DOROTHY BROCK, 28 February 1979
12: GOLDA FACTOR, February 1980
13: FORTUNÉE MORDO, March 1980
14: HETTY COHEN, 20 May 1980
15. REBECCA SALISBURY, June 1980
16. JOSEPH DUBOVIE, December 1980
17. RALPH SEGAL, 5 July 1981
18. GERALD ROBINS, 19 July 1981
19. BERTHA HURST, 7 December 1981, aged 77
20. SIDNEY HURST, 10 November 1987, aged 85

ROW AF
1. BARNET PERLMUTTER, 20 July 1981, aged 90
2. EDNA SILVERSTONE, 24 January 1982
3. HARRY GREENBURGH, 6 March 1982, aged 92
4. LILY PEARL, 15 July 1982, aged 82
5. ARTHUR GOLDBERG, 29 December 1982
6. COLONEL ROY TELFER, 10 January 1983, aged 84
7. GERALD BUSTELL, 26 January 1983, aged 48
8. LOUISE SOLOMON, 17 May 1952 – 20 July 1993
9. SARAH LEWIS, 8 August 1983, aged 88
10. AIMEE ROSEMAN, 1896-1983
11. IRENE ROSEMAN, 16 March 1984, daughter of Aaron & Hinda Roseman
12. BERTRAM HARRIS EMDON, 17 January 1916 – 29 March 1984, aged 68
13. LAURA HARRIS, 15 July 1984
14. HERMAN HENRY COHEN, physician, 6 September 1984, aged 81
15. LILY WISEMAN, 1894-1984
16. JOHN BERTRAM GOODMAN, 5 October 1905 – 21 January 1985
17. DR HARRY GREENBURGH, 28 June 1917 – 28 March 1985
18. Empty?
19. HENRY PECK, 26 July 1985, aged 70, husband of Freda
20. LEAH ROSEMAN, 19 September 1985, aged 73

ROW AG
1. ISIDORE PERLMUTER, 18 October 1985, aged 69
2. RUBY HANNAH BEGLEMAN, 29 September 1986, wife of Jock
3. WOLFE (BILL) BLOOM, 16 May 1987, aged 85
4. ETTA BAS AARON HETTY ROSEMAN, 1897 – 1987, widow of late Simon Roseman
5. FRANCES SARAH LEWIS, 28 January 1925 – 25 May 1987
6. MARK BROCK, 20 April 1900 – 13 December 1987
7. ERNEST EMDON, 27 April 1914 – 25 May 1987
8. DOC SPIERS, 26 January 1988
9. ROSE BAUN, 15 February 1988, aged 91
10. ROSA HAZAN, 16 May 1989
11. BEATRICE COHEN, 6 March 1990, aged 93
12. HARRY HIRSHMAN, 6 July 1990, aged 81
13. ANN SOWDEN, 22 December 1933 – 28 December 1990
14. FREDA SARAH ROSEMAN, 4 February 1991, aged 86, daughter of Myer Isaac & Amelia Fredman
15. BERTHA SHAW, 26 April 1991
16. RUBY COHEN, 24 December 1991, aged 82, widow of Harry Cohen
17. MYER LADDEN, 30 December 1991, aged 86, son of Lewis & Janet Ladden
18. VIVIAN ABRAHAM ROBINS, 22 January 1992
19. BERTHA ROSEMAN, 31 January 1992, aged 80
20. LEAH (LILY) ALOOF, 12 December 1986

ROW AH
1. JACK COHEN, 1 August 2006, aged 94
2 - 3. Empty
4. ISRAEL GORDON, 24 October 2001
5. ROSE GORDON, 25 June 1997
6. BENJAMIN GREENBERG, 22 April 2005
7. MINNIE GREENBERG, 16 March 1997
8. PATRICIA LIPSON, 6 February 1997
9. LIONEL JOHN ALOOF, 5 August 1996
10. LEONARD MILLER, 1937 - 1995
11. EDWARD MARK EMDON, 26 April 1995
12. WLADIMIR BLEIER, 29 March 1995
13. LEILA ANNIE RUTMAN, 2 October 1994

14. HENRY ROY CAPLAN, 18 August 1994
15. LOUIS ROSEMAN, 13 April 1994
16. ETTY CANT, 31 August 1993
17. SIDNEY ALOOF, 9 April 1993
18. REVA ERLICH, 27 December 1992
19. EVE LOMAN (SOLOMON), 27 October 1992
20. EILEEN BEATRICE ROSEMAN, 22 March 1992

ROW AI

1 - 2. Empty
3. FAY SPIERS, 26 November 2007
4. DAVID JOSEPH RUTMAN, 20 August 2007
5. BETTY ROSS, 1 December 2006
6. BERNARD HENRY LEVAN-HARRIS
7. SOLLY SOLOMON, 12 November 2006
8. SHEILA LEAH BRISK, 5 August 2005
9. PERCY ALOOF, 19 May 2003
10. CECIL LUI (SONNY) SILVERSTONE, 19 January 2002
11. HETTY SAMUEL, 1901 - 2002
12. MAX BRISK, 8 October 2001
13. BESSIE ALOOF, 5 August 2001
14. PHYLLIS THOMAS (MORRIS), 27 November 2000
15. LESLIE D. LIPSON, 16 June 2000
16. ANN DUBOVIE, 4 October 1999
17. MICHAEL ANTHONY SPIERS, 25 August 1999
18. WILLIAM (JACK) BEGLEMAN, 25 February 1999
19. VIOLET EVELYN, 24 December 1998
20. ROY SILVERSTONE, 23 June 1997

ROW AJ

1 -14. Empty
15. REVA JOSEPH, 29 December 2011
16. RITA ROBINS, 10 July 2010
17. HANNAH (ANNE) ESTHER BENTLEY, 1919 - 2009
18. ALBERT JOSEPH PERLMUTTER, 17 March 2009
19. MILTON JACOBSON, 8 April 2008
20. MITZIE WINSTON, 8 December 2007
Rows AK & AL: no burials up to January 2014

ROW BA

1: Hebrew only
2: RACHEL JACOBS, 27 December 1966
3: ISAAC TSINOWAY, 9 March 1967
4: ROSE FINE, 12 November 1967
5: BERNARD HYMAN GOODMAN, 7 January 1969
6: HARRY LEWIS, 18 May 1969
7. DIANA STADDON, 29 April 1974
8. Empty

ROW BB

1. Empty
2. HENRY CONYBEARE WOOLFSTEIN, 15 June 1969
3. ALF LAZARUS, 28 October 1985, aged 77
4. TOBY, mother of Jack, Jill, Elan, Daphne & Ari
5. SIDNEY COLLINS, 18 June 1990, aged 72
6 - 8. Empty

ROW BC

1- 4. Empty
5. VALENTINE GHZALA BATE, née Sillam
6. JOSEPH VARLEY (VASHAFSKI), 23 November 1912 – 24 August 1995
7. ISRAEL MARKS, 23 September 1995, aged 69
8. Empty

ROW BD

1. LEAH LEVY, 13 December 1995, aged 70
2. Empty
3. SAUL BERGER, 11 January 1998, aged 83
4. RACHEL HOUSE, 11 April 1936 – 1 March 2000
5 - 6. Empty
7. RACHEL COLLINS, 8 June 2008, aged 91, née Halperin
8. Empty

APPENDIX 6
SYNAGOGUE CEREMONIAL SILVER: SOLD BY BONHAMS, 2009

1. Pair of rare George III silver rimmonim with parcel-gilt finials and matching pointer, made 1783. Sold: £62,400.

2. Pair of silver rimmonim: dating to 1913, made by Joseph Zweig (London). Topped with eagle finial on ball mount. These were made "in memory of her late husband and son Jacob and Abraham Cohen 13 September 1914.' Sold: £1,800.

3. Pair of silver rimmonim made by Jacob Rosenzweig, London 1923. Sold: £1,320.

4. Pair of silver rimmonim by Aaron Taitelbaum, London 1931, presented by Mrs Myer Isaac Roseman. Sold: £3,600.

5. Late 18th century, early 19th century silver Torah shield and pointer, circa 1800, possibly Italian. Estimated: £1,000 - £1,000. Sold: £10,200.

6. A silver pointer, Berlin circa 1782, inscription: 'Given by in memory of Judah Ralph, son of Abraham Ralph of Barnstaple in the year 5442.' Sold: £15,600.

7. A silver Torah pointer, body unmarked, circa 1745, the ring mount by Simon Levy of Exeter, hallmarked 1803, sold for £7,800. The Hebrew inscription: 'Here in Plymouth 5505, in memory of Yehuda Jacob son of CaHarar, this pointer belongs to Joseph Harar.' Sold: £7,800.

8. A George III silver and silver gilt pointer by Simon Harris of Plymouth Dock, hallmarked Exeter 1813. Hebrew inscription: 'Shabbat portion Lech Lecha, Shmuel son of Zvi Hart 5774 [1813].' Estimated: £3,000 - £5,000. Sold: £19,200.

9. A later 18th century / early 19th century silver Torah pointer, unmarked, slender form, Hebrew inscription: 'Belongs to Abraham son of Joseph 5525 [1764]. Sold: £3,360.

10. A silver Torah pointer, maker's mark M.S, London 1924. Inscription: 'Presented together with Breast Plate by Mrs Hilda Cohen and Mr David Fredman 25 Jan 1925, 5685.' Sold: £1,920.

11. A 19th century continental silver Torah pointer. Hebrew inscription 'Vosfa son of Abraham, Yaacov son of Mordecai, Yehuda son of Samson, Asher son of Abraham Zvi, Yecheil son of Samson, Asher son of Zvi.' Sold: £3,120.

12. A 19th century continental silver spice box, engraved 'A gift from Mrs B Moss to the Plymouth Dock Room June 21st ???. In consequence of the discontinuance thereof

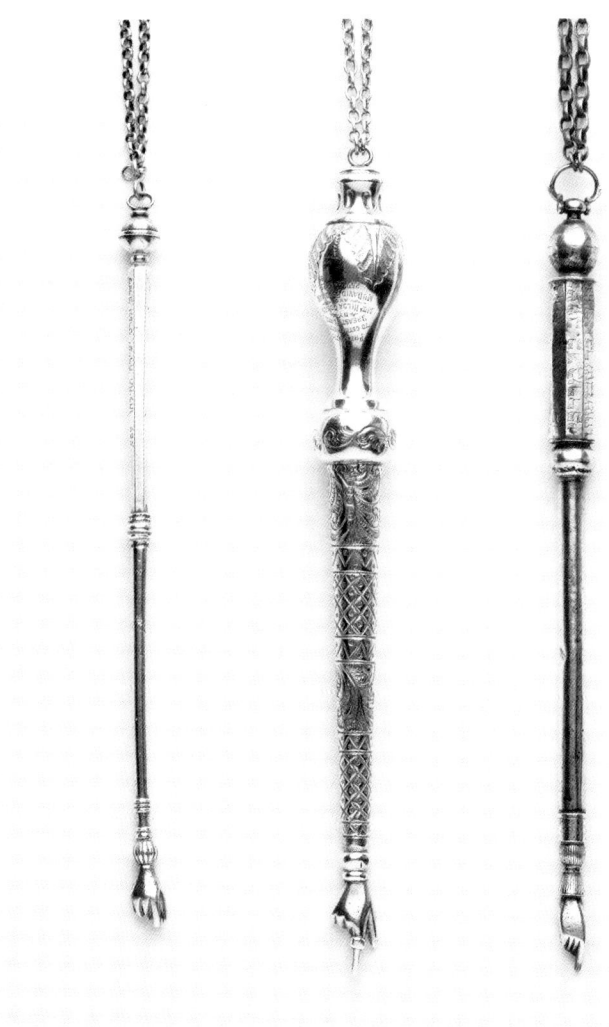

Three silver pointers. From left to right: 18th/19th century pointer, silver pointer 1924, and 19th century silver pointer engraved with 7 names, COURTESY OF BONHAMS

A rare 18th century silver Torah shield & chain, circa 1765, COURTESY OF BONHAMS

APPENDIX 6

Silver Torah shield to mark the Jubilee of Queen Victoria 1887 (left), and (right) A silver Torah shield, 1924, given by Lady Lila, daughter of Reb Abraham Avines, COURTESY OF BONHAMS

(left) Pair of silver rimmonim, 1931 presented by Myer Isaac Roseman, and (right) a silver Torah shield and chain, circa 1800, COURTESY OF BONHAMS

presented to Plymouth, Sept 1844.' Estimated: £500 - £700. Sold: £4,320.

13. A 19th century Polish silver-gilt Torah shield, possibly Warsaw, circa 1820. Inscription: 'To the Plymouth Hebrew Congregation in celebration of the Jubilee of her most Gracious Majesty Queen Victoria June 21st 1887. Presented by Alexander Jacobs formerly of Paignton, late president of the congregation.' Estimated: £1,500 - £2,000. Sold: £14,400.

14. A silver Torah shield by Jacob Rosenzweig, London 1918. Inscription: 'A gift from the lady Lila (?) daughter of the Reb Avraham Avines (Evans?) in memory of her husband Gedalya Mordechai R'Shabsi- For putting on the scrolls destined to be read on Rosh HaShanah.' Sold: £2,400.

15. A very rare 18th century silver and silver-gilt Torah shield with chain, stamped IH, probably Jason Holt of Exeter and WP, probably William Pearse of Plymouth, circa 1765. Estimated: £4,000 - £6,000. Sold: £25,200.

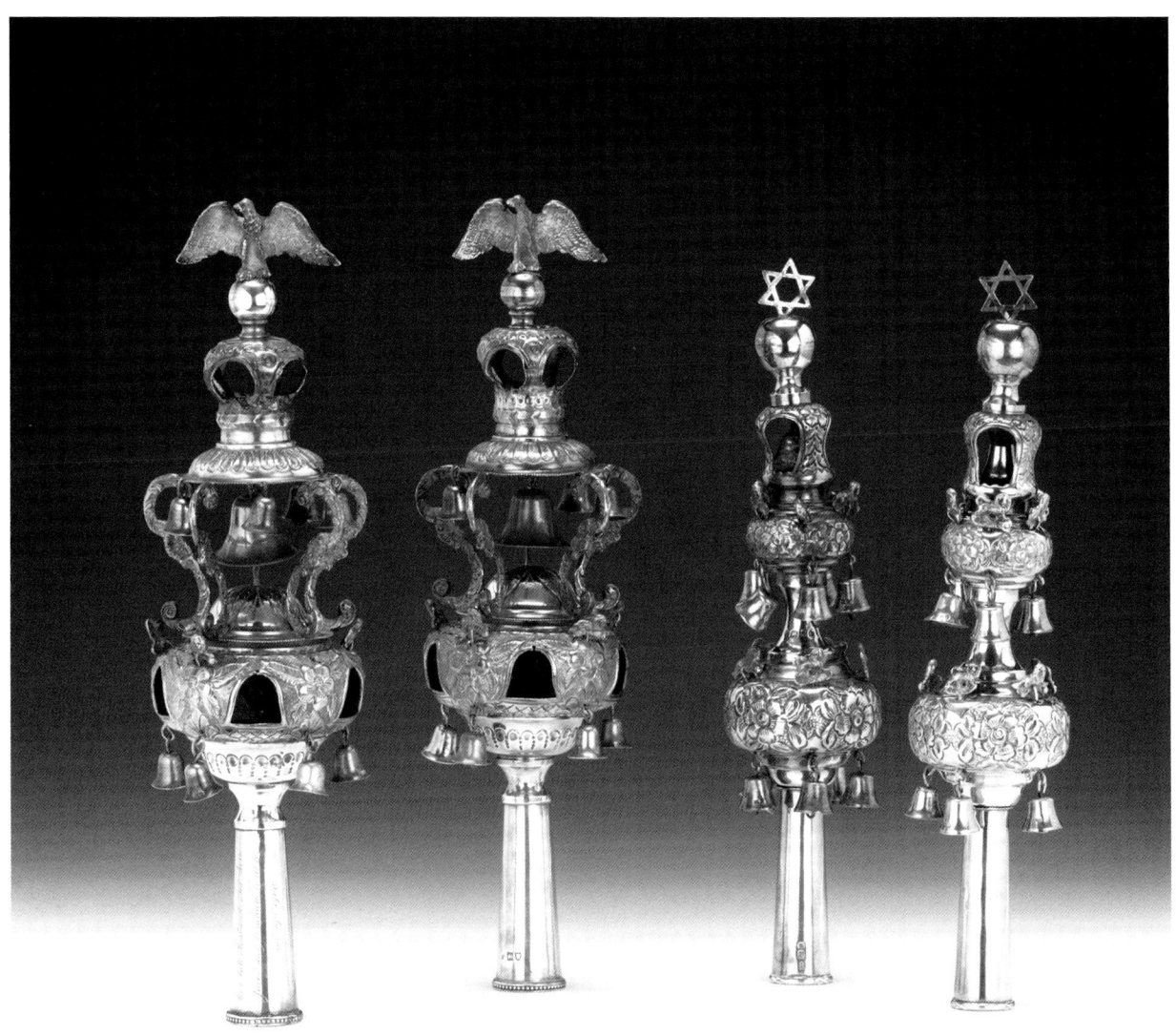

(left) A pair of rimmonim, Joseph Zweig, 1913, and (right) a pair of silver rimmonim, Jacob Rosenzweig, 1923.
COURTESY OF BONHAMS

BIBLIOGRAPHY

Short Bibliography
Archives consulted at: The Plymouth and West Devon Record Office, Jewish Military Museum, The Jewish Museum and Plymouth Synagogue. Minute Book 1963-1996: courtesy of Pat Goodman.

Published and Unpublished Works
Berger, Doreen. *The Jewish Victorian: Genealogical Information from the Jewish Newspapers 1871-1880*, Robert Boyd: 1999
Doris Black, *The Plymouth Synagogue 1761-1961*.
Emdon, Bert. *Ancestral Tapestry*, unpublished reminiscences about the Emdon Family.
Fry, Helen. *The Jews Exeter*, Halsgrove: 2013
Fry, Helen. *Jewish Cemeteries of Devon*, Amazon: 2012
Fry, Helen. *Jews in North Devon during the Second World War*, Halsgrove: 2005
Green, Geoffrey. *The Royal Navy and Anglo-Jewry 1740-1820*, Naval & Maritime Bookshop: 1989
Hidden Legacy Foundation. *The Jews of Devon and Cornwall*, Redcliffe Press: 2000
Jackson, Leslie. *Pawn on a Chessboard*, The Book Guild: 2001
Jamilly, Edward. *The Georgian Synagogue: an architectural history*, Jewish Memorial Council: 1999
Kadish, Sharman. *The Synagogues of Britain and Ireland*, Yale University Press: 2011
Kadish, Sharman. *Jewish Heritage in England: An architectural Guide*, English Heritage: 2006
Nichols, Keith. *Robert Lenkiewicz: the Artist and the Man*, Halsgrove: 2005
Nicholson, Martin. *Some Relatives of Carroll and Nancy Nicholson*, privately published: 1986
Pearce, Keith. *The Jews of Cornwall: A History*, Halsgrove: 2014
Pearce, Keith & Helen Fry (ed). *The Lost Jews of Cornwall*, Redcliffe: 2000
Roth, Cecil. *The Rise of Provincial Jewry*, The Jewish Monthly: 1950
Schonfield, Major William. *The Josephs of Cornwall*, a paper read to the Jewish Historical Society of England in 1938
Susser, Bernard. *The Jews of South-West England*, University of Exeter Press: 1993

INDEX

Aaron, Abraham 13, 133
Abraham, David 22
Abrahams, Alexander 10
Abrahams, Joseph 10
Abrahams, Solomon 11
Alexander, Rev. Michael Solomon 43-44
Alexander, Sender 11, 22, 36, 37, 115, 135
Aloof family 27, 32, 88-89, 97-99, 100, 118, 123, 124, 130, 151
Aloof, Hyman 40, 89, 97, 99, 147
Aloof, Percy 99, 109, 117, 126, 130, 152
Aloof, Sidney 72, 97, 98, 124, 128, 152
Americans, servicemen (WW2) 77, 91-93, 107
Basch, Edward 26, 32, 33, 115, 116
Bellem family 18, 137, 138, 146
Benjamin, Rev. Levi 42, 55
Berlin, Rev. M 33, 46, 53, 64, 70, 114, 131
Black, Doris (née Lewis) 78, 79, 80, 100
Black, Esther 55, 77, 79, 93, 147
Black family 77-80, 100, 105, 127, 128
Black, Harry 77, 79, 121
Black, Israel (Bertie) 33, 35, 77, 78, 79-80, 102, 112, 116, 117, 130
Blanckensee, Solomon 16
Bloom, Frank Joseph 119
Brand, Arthur 26, 81, 82, 87, 126, 150
Brand, Tobias 24, 25, 71, 81, 116, 126
Brock, Charles 26, 74, 124, 144
Brock, Ernest 74
Brock, Jacob Nathan 33, 74, 124, 129, 147
Broder, Rev. I 49, 117
Burial grounds *see old cemetery & new cemetery*

cholera epidemic (1832) 12, 27, 55, 69, 72, 135, 136
civic life (Jews in Plymouth) 58, 60, 64, 72, 73, 74, 75, 79, 82, 106-7
Cohen, Abraham 26, 29, 122, 147
Cohen, Emanuel 11, 138
Cohen, Eve 27

Cohen, Dr Herman Harry 81, 87, 102, 128
Cohen, Isidore 71, 82, 90, 116, 126
Cohen, Joseph 10, 11
Cohen, Percy 55
Coppel, David Jacob 11, 136
Conick, Abraham 24, 25, 71, 72, 127, 148

Daniel, Abraham (miniaturist) 17-18, 42, 55, 136
Dartmoor Prison 45, 47, 48, 50
Dartmouth 15, 18, 27, 142
Devonport 9, 12, 15, 19, 20, 24, 27, 33, 35, 37, 38, 39, 41, 58-9, 60, 64, 68, 71, 72, 73, 74, 75, 76, 80, 82, 83, 85, 89, 91
Devonport Synagogue (Dock Minyan) 29, 32, 25-41, 52, 63, 65, 67, 71, 75, 76, 81, 82, 84, 88, 153
Drake, Sir Francis 7

Ellis, Elias 25, 72, 85
Emanuel, Abraham 23, 29 36, 37, 52, 59
Emden, Wolf 31, 64, 115
Emdin, Gompert Michael 10, 22
Emdon, Abraham (1799-1872) 64, 104, 137, 139
Emdon family (Emdin/Emden) 10, 11, 59, 73, 104-5, 118, 120, 127, 134, 135, 138, 145, 146, 150, 151
Emdon, Bert 14, 38, 40, 41, 51, 64, 85, 87, 104-5, 117, 151
Emdon, Eleazar 16, 23, 31, 33, 40, 61, 64, 116, 138
Emdon, Eleazar II 64-5, 105
Emdon, Hugh Ralph 38, 39, 40, 65, 149
Emdon, Phineas 31
Ephraim, Rabbi Moses 13, 18, 42, 114
Exeter 7, 12, 18, 31, 51, 60, 63, 69, 71, 79, 83, 85, 95, 96, 153, 156
Ezekiel, Philip 59

Falk, Rev l 86
Falmouth 7, 12, 18, 44, 55, 60, 71, 91, 137, 138, 142
Feather, Hyren (Feodor) 38
Feather, M 71
Feather, Pol 25
Field, King 27, 72, 80-1, 116,

125, 128, 147
Fredman family 74-76, 80, 90, 100, 125, 127, 145, 146, 152
Fredman, David 27, 75, 76, 118, 119, 153
Fredman, Israel 25, 33, 41, 75, 85, 118
Fredman, Levin 39, 75, 76, 116, 143
Fredman, Myer (d. 6 Jan 1927, husband of Fanny) 80, 147
Fredman, Myer JP (d. 5 Aug 1927, husband of Rebecca) 20, 24, 29, 33, 71, 72, 75-6, 109, 116, 143
Fredman, Rebecca 29, 75, 76, 144

Ginsburg, Rev. Alec 26, 30, 49-50, 79, 80, 102, 104, 114
Goldberg, Arthur & family 33, 49, 80, 91, 100, 102, 104, 105-7, 109, 112, 116, 117, 125, 147
Goldberg, Joseph 40
Goldston, Joseph 24, 34, 39
Goodman, Rev. Emanuel 47-8, 55, 91, 92, 93, 94, 99, 114, 147
Goodman, Pat 111, 113, 117
Gordon, Dr Mark 58, 89, 96-7, 116, 128, 151
Greenburgh family 40, 83-4, 87, 100, 145, 147
Greenburgh, Dr Harry 38, 41, 84, 89, 118, 151
Greenburgh, Jacob 38, 39, 41, 83, 87, 145
Greenburgh, Joseph 40, 84, 145

Harris, Rev. H 43, 44, 114
Hart, Asher 10
Hart, Emanuel 59, 67, 132
Hart, Hayil 10, 11
Hart, Henry 22, 142
Hart, Lemon 14, 60
Hart, Samuel 10, 11, 17, 18, 22, 27, 36, 59, 60
Hart, Solomon RA 17, 33, 60-1, 105
Hirshman, John 111, 113
Holcenberg family 33, 72, 144, 147
Homberg, Lyon 22
Hore-Belisha, Leslie (MP) 73, 82, 83, 87
Hyman, Hyman 23, 31, 32, 58, 59, 120

Isaac, Rev. Moses 42, 55, 114

Issachar, Hayyim (Beadle) 36, 42-3, 114

Jackson, Leslie 91, 129
Jacob Nathan School 24-5, 32, 33, 64, 73
Jacobs, Rev. D 24, 47, 71, 75, 81, 114, 147
Jacobs, Mordecai (1727-1806) 12, 140
Jacobs, Nathan (of Dartmouth) 11, 18, 27, 137, 141, 142
Jacobs, Sarah 11
Jaffe, Rev. E 24, 47, 114
Jewish Battalion (WW1) 86-7, 94
Johnson, Phineas 59, 115
Jonas, Benjamin 12, 18, 37, 120
Joseph, Abraham I (1731-1794) 10, 12-13, 14, 26, 27, 29, 59, 104, 133, 139, 140
Joseph, Abraham II (1799-1868) 16-17, 22, 45, 55, 61, 64, 115, 137
Joseph, Brina 15, 16, 139
Joseph, Henry 13, 16-17, 22
Joseph, Isidore 72, 116, 127, 150
Joseph, Joseph (1766-1846) 11, 13, 14-15, 16, 18, 22, 23, 26, 28, 31, 33, 36, 37, 42, 52, 53, 65, 115, 137, 140
Joseph, Lyon 131-2
Joseph, Nathan (Altmann) 11, 15-16, 36, 59, 135, 139
Joseph, Rose 14, 16, 61
Joseph, Samuel (b.1759) 13
Josovic, Rev. D 49, 114

Kelly, Anna 111, 113, 117

Lazarus, Hyam 22
Lazarus, I 25
Lazarus, Lyon (Lippa) 63, 68, 135
Lee, Dr Peter 110-111, 112, 113, 117
Lempert, Saul 40, 41, 147
Lenkiewicz, Robert 108-9
Levi, Lion 22, 74, 132
Levi, Nathan 22
Levi, Phineas 12, 22, 37, 60, 135, 137
Levi, Samuel Mordecai 22
Levy, Abraham 22, 59, 132
Levy, Asher 23, 24, 25, 26, 33, 61, 64, 70, 116
Levy, Benjamin 52, 115, 141
Levy, Elkan 51, 57, 111, 113

159

Levy, Joel 11, 125, 133
Levy, Joseph 11, 37
Levy, Rev. Joseph 42-3
Levy, Rev. Joshua 46
Levy, Mordecai 11
Levy, Samuel 115, 135
Lewis, Rev. Moses 114
Lima, Cantor 36, 43, 138
Lubell, David 87, 129
Lyon, Francis 68-9, 134
Lyon, Judah 11, 68, 69, 115, 138
Lyons, Alexander 16
Lyons, Solomon 22, 142

Mandovsky, Jonas 22, 58
Mannheim, Hirsch (shochet) 42, 114
Marks, Charles 22, 58, 59, 115, 137
Marks, Hilda (née Black) 55, 77, 78, 91, 93, 99, 101, 105, 111, 127
Marks, Sam 78, 79, 105, 111, 116, 117, 127
Meir, Joseph ben Joseph 42, 114, 139
Mitchell, John 110, 111, 113, 117
Mordecai, Moses 18, 37
Morris, Deborah 67, 68
Moss, Barrow 12, 32, 59, 141
Moss, Sarah 11

Nap, Benjamin 10
Nathan, Aaron 74, 136, 137
Nathan, Henry 17, 36, 59, 139
Nathan, Jacob 12, 25, 32, 33, 55, 61, 63-4, 67, 115, 139
Nathan, Simon 11, 115, 142
Naval connections (*see also Navy Agents & slopmen*) 7, 9, 10, 37, 50, 59-60, 81, 83, 85, 88-9
Navy agents & slopmen 10, 11, 13, 14, 15, 37, 59, 60, 65, 67, 81, 82, 83, 85-6, 89
Nelson family 62, 73, 122, 125, 143, 146, 148, 150
Nelson, John Selig 62, 73, 125

New cemetery (Gifford Place) 18, 39, 41, 55-57, 64, 75, 77, 79, 80, 82, 83, 84, 95, 99, 108, 112, 143-152

Old cemetery (The Hoe) 10, 12, 14, 21, 36, 42, 43, 45, 52-5, 63, 64, 67, 131-143
Orgel, Eleazar 23, 24, 37, 38, 62-3, 81, 116
Orgel, Hershell 24, 26, 63, 71, 81, 126
Orgel, Huish 25
Orgel, Shiel 25, 63
Orgel, Solly 25, 59
Orgel, Tilly 25, 63
Overs, Maurice 102, 107, 117, 129
Owen, Rose 80, 86, 90, 150

Pearl, Ruth 81
Peck, Caple 27, 86, 97, 150
Peck, Henry 27, 85, 97, 118, 130, 151
Penzance 7, 12, 14, 16, 18, 44, 60, 65, 71, 85, 137
Plymouth Dock *see Devonport*
Portsmouth 12, 14, 31, 62, 63, 83
Posner, Rev J 24, 33, 38, 46, 64, 114
Prisoners 45, 47, 49

Ralph, Abraham 25, 27, 29, 31, 37, 65, 134, 153
Ralph, Abraham II 55, 64, 65, 67, 144
Ralph, Henry 37, 59, 65
Ralph, Judah (Lewis) 22, 27, 29, 36, 59 65, 66, 134, 136, 153
Richman family 100, 102, 104, 116, 117, 118, 129
Richman, Morris 27
ritual silver 9, 13, 26-30, 39-40, 66, 112, 153-6
Robins, Abraham 26, 73
Robins family 27, 71, 81-2, 85, 104, 118, 126, 145, 146, 152
Robins, Gedalia(h) 40, 63, 81, 82, 145
Robins, Hester (OBE) 82-3, 147
Robins, Solomon 38, 39, 40, 76, 82
Roborough, Lord 29, 40, 58
Rockman, Rev. 51, 100, 114
Roseman family 76-7, 118, 121, 122, 125, 126, 129, 151
Roseman, Israel 20, 58, 75, 77, 116, 117, 122, 144
Roseman, Jacob 75, 75
Roseman, Myer Isaac 25, 27, 40, 75, 76, 124, 144, 155
Roseman, Rachel 20, 77
Roseman, Simon 40
Rosenbaum, Rev. L 114
Rutman, Morry 119, 128, 151

Samuels, Charles 68, 69
Sanger, Joseph 27, 71, 76, 116, 126
Schomberg, Sir Alexander 8
Schreiber, V 8
Sherrenbeck, Gershon 10, 55
Sherrenbeck, Jacob Myer 11
Sherrenbeck, Joseph Jacob 9, 11, 22, 29, 30, 52, 55, 115, 138
Sherrenbeck, Sarah 9, 52
Silverstone, Jack 8
Silverstone, Myer 39
Simpson, Wallis 16, 61
Slavinsky, Rev. A. K 24, 40, 43, 47, 71, 75, 114, 147
Smith Esta (Esther) 57, 58, 89, 95, 144
Smith family 94-6, 119, 120, 128
Smith, Herchel (1925-2001) 95-6
Smith, Jack 55, 95, 117
Smith, Mary 57, 88, 95, 144
Smith, Morris 119
Solomon, Lazarus 11, 42, 58, 132
Solomon, Leon 16, 21, 23-4, 61-2, 121
Solomon, Moses 9, 58, 59
Spier, Rev. Abraham 29-30, 46-7, 114
Spiers family 100, 104, 108, 118, 151, 152
Stadthagen, Rev. Myer 32, 44-5, 55, 114, 132, 137, 138
Stern, Rev. Leopold 45, 114
Stone, Issac 45, 122
Stonehouse 9, 19, 33, 35, 58, 60, 64, 77, 81
Susman, Rev. S 48-9, 93, 114
Susser, Rabbi Dr Bernard 29, 30, 33, 37, 49, 51, 52, 53, 55, 102, 104, 110, 114, 131
Synagogue House (Vestry) 19, 24-5, 111

Telfer, Colonel Roy 101, 118
Titleboam, Abraham 25, 33, 38, 60, 73, 125, 148

Ullman family 67-8, 115, 121, 122, 149
Ullman, Wolfram 60, 67, 68

Valentine, Isaac Falk 36, 55, 142

Weinberg, Mordecai 25
Weisman, Rev Malcolm 51
West Indies (link to) 7, 9, 58
White, Keith 108, 130
Wolfson, Samuel (of Devonport) 39
Wolfson, Rev. W 20, 40, 81, 89, 91, 99, 114
Woolf, William (Councillor) 55, 58, 115
WW1 8, 34, 40, 46, 47, 55, 57, 76, 83, 85-7, 97, 118, 145
WWII 20, 32, 41, 47, 57, 68, 72, 75, 76, 77, 82, 84, 85, 88-93, 99, 105, 107, 118
Wykansky, Rev. Simon 20, 40, 41, 47, 81, 114

Yonge, Charles 13

Zeffert, Rev. M 25, 40, 75, 76, 114